AF522525

Rural Financial Sector

RURAL FINANCIAL SECTOR

ALTERNATE MODEL

Edited by

Tamal Datta Chaudhuri

2010

Icfai Books

The Icfai University Press

RURAL FINANCIAL SECTOR: ALTERNATE MODEL

Editor: Tamal Datta Chaudhuri

First Edition: 2010
Printed in India

Published by

The Icfai University Press
52, Nagarjuna Hills, Punjagutta
Hyderabad, India – 500 082
Phone: (+91) (040) 23430–368, 369, 370, 372, 373, 374
Fax: (+91) (040) 23352521, 23435386
E-mail: info@icfaibooks.com, icfaibooks@icfai.org, ssd@icfai.org

ISBN: 9788131408742

Editorial Team: Nabanita Choudhury and Tanuja Ranjan
Quality Support: R Kalyani and Ramesh Ch

Contents

SECTION II

STRATEGIES FOR IMPROVED PERFORMANCE

Overview

Rural development has always been a focus area for policy-makers in India as a large part of the population in India is engaged in the rural sector. A significant part of the Indian poor in India live in its villages. Thus, rural development measures and poverty alleviation measures have been perceived to be synonymous.

With the liberalisation of the Indian economy and growing competition, there has been a shift in the perception of the rural sector, particularly from the point of view of financial intermediaries. This sector is now perceived to be a continuous source of savings and an opportunity for profitable deployment of funds. Commercial Banks, NABARD, Co-operative Banks and Regional Rural Banks have geared themselves up to cater to this segment of the economy through innovative schemes, focused approach, dedicated manpower and training and educational programs. Microfinance Institutions and Self Help Groups are contributing significantly to this process. Phrases like "Opportunities at the Bottom of the Pyramid" and "Financial Inclusion" are now understood by financial sector players and the understanding has shifted from "Helping the Rural Sector for Uplift of the Poor" to "Exploiting Profitable Opportunities for Revenue and Profit Generation". The required financial architecture is being discussed and design of appropriate institutions being debated.

The purpose of this book is to update the reader on the performance of various players involved in rural financial sector development and to take stock of the policies that have been adopted in this regard. Accordingly the book is divided into two parts. The first part deals with various institutions involved in rural financial sector development and their performance. The second part explains strategies that can be adopted for improved credit delivery.

Section I: Institutions for Rural Financial Sector in India and their Current Status

The first article is "**Rural Financial Sector Development in India – An Introduction**" by *Tamal Datta Chaudhuri*. This first paper of the book introduces the reader to the need for emphasis on rural financing. It discusses various institutions involved in rural financing in India and the credit delivery channels. Performance measurement is done in terms of flow of institutional credit to agriculture from Co-operative Banks, Regional Rural Banks (RRBs) and Commercial Banks. Data on sanctions and disbursements from the Rural Infrastructure Development Fund (RIDF) is provided and so is total number of Kisan Credit Cards issued. The reader is provided with the latest available data on the SHG-Bank linkage programme and also on the linkage position, model-wise. The paper concludes with a brief review of various measures initiated by the Reserve Bank of India for improved performance of the institutions involved in rural financing.

The second article "**Rural Banking: Review and Prospects**" Speech by *Y V Reddy*, is in line with the first paper. This paper also provides an overview of the progress in rural banking and the problems that need to be sorted out. The paper highlights the fact that a piecemeal approach to rural finance will not work and a comprehensive approach to various issues has to be taken.

The paper provides the brief historic background that the RBI Act had vested the responsibility of rural credit to RBI. Subsequently, RBI hived-off its role as provider of agricultural credit to NABARD which received line of credit from the World Bank. Given that co-operative banks were not servicing the rural poor efficiently, RRBs were formed, RIDF was set up, Kisan Credit Cards were introduced and Bank-SHG linkages were encouraged. Since 2004, vigorous efforts have been made to increase credit flow to agriculture through General Credit Cards, no frills accounts, microfinance programmes, Special Area Plans etc.

The author, however, maintains that non-institutional credit still continues, the credit deposit ratio is low in the rural areas, the performance of many public sector banks has been inadequate and the co-operative credit sector has not delivered. These inadequacies have to be addressed in view of the 11th Five Year Plan Approach paper which has emphasized on the need for increase in agricultural growth, a second green revolution, corrective policies for small and marginal farmers and also middle-level and large farmers. The author concludes by stating that any plan for growth in agricultural credit has to address the four deficits, namely public investment and credit deficit, infrastructure deficit, market economy deficit and knowledge deficit.

The third article is **"NABARD's Innovations in Rural Development"** by *A K Bandyopadhyay*. The paper is on NABARD's (National Bank of Agriculture and Rural Development) initiatives for rural development. These include exploring innovative investment opportunities, creating infrastructure base, creating leadership and entrepreneurship, educating the rural masses, building sound network of rural financial institutions and building research and development activities. There are also facilities for investment credit for a variety of purposes like water management, sprinkler irrigation, farm mechanization etc. NABARD has also initiated direct lending through co-financing with financial institutions. The paper deals with specific schemes of NABARD, the details of the schemes and their intended impact.

The fourth article "**Microfinance in India: Coming of Age**" by *V Vipin Sharma*, starts with a brief background of the SHG movement in India and the value chain in SHG-Bank linkage program is elaborated upon. The relationship among SHGs, NGOs and Self-Help Promoting Institutions and various sources of funds are discussed. The paper also discusses the scale which the sector has been able to attain, and the pace at which it has grown consistently over the last few years. Interesting data is provided as to how this sector has been attracting a host of foreign investment funds, venture capital funds, and even private-equity investors like Grameen Capital, USA, Lok Capital, UNITUS and Bellweather Fund. The paper then provides an account of the functioning of microfinance institutions in India and the policy shifts. The paper claims that microfinance has improved the access of women to finance, increased the mobility of women and improved their economic returns and also their confidence. An impact assessment of CARE's microfinance program demonstrates that the program has resulted in better health and nutrition, greater role of women in household decision-making and their empowerment them to contributing to the communities' decision-making process.

The fifth article "**Microfinance in India: Empirical Evidence, Alternative Models and Policy Imperatives**" by *Rajaram Dasgupta*, starts with analyzing the reasons for the bad performance of public and private sector banks in extending credit to the weaker sections of the Indian population. It identifies the high proportion of the Non-performing Assets as the prime reason for this. This conclusion has been arrived at by mapping credit to the weaker sections with NPA percentage, bank-wise. It prescribes the necessity of a paradigm shift from 'financial sector reform' to 'microfinance reform'.

The paper then defines microfinance and its requirement, the role of SHG credit and the varied pace of development of SHGs in different states. It presents performance of SHGs through indicators like SHG credit per poor, penetration among poor through SHGs and coverage. In India, the growth of SHGs has not been even and data indicates that in the SHG developed states, the commercial banks depend on NGOs for development of SHGs. The performance of various models of SHGs are discussed. The paper prescribes other models, besides the SHG model, for extending micro credit to the poor and the weaker sections.

The sixth article is **"Access, Use and Contribution of Microfinance in India: Findings from a National Study"** by *Frances Sinha*. This paper observes that significant contribution has been made by microfinance initiatives to both savings and borrowings of the poor. It then discusses three models of microfinance – SHGs, Grameen and Individual Banking. Based on these three models, twenty MFIs are studied and their performance analysed. The sample covers 83 clusters reflecting varying market contexts and accessibility and an index of involvement has been defined.

The paper observes that the main use of micro credit is for direct investment. It then goes on to discuss microfinance services like micro savings, insurance and non-financial services. Informal credit sources are also looked at. The paper, however, points out that although presence of microfinance has increased the borrowing options for poor clients, it seems to have not significantly affected the terms and conditions of different informal credit providers. Accessibility, capability, willingness to lend without security and flexible repayment schedules are some of the reasons why microfinance clients also seek finance from informal sources.

The seventh article, **"Impact of Self-Help Groups on Formal Banking Habits"** by *Mahendra Varman P*, a study by National Bank for Agriculture and Rural Development (NABARD), which covered

560 SHG-member households from 223 SHGs across 11 states, indicates positive results on the impact of participation of the rural poor in the SHGs. It shows that there have been perceptible and wholesome changes in the living standards of SHG members in terms of ownership of assets, borrowing capacities, income-generating activities, income levels and increase in savings. It traces that almost all members developed saving habits in the post-SHG situation.

In the same vein, this paper examines whether there is any association between growth of SHGs and the increase in female bank deposit accounts and whether SHGs have a tendency to influence account holding in formal banks. The paper tries to establish whether banking habits are dependent on availability of right institutions or this has something to do with sex, gender, education and income levels. The paper provides data on growth in the SHG-Bank linkage and on banking habits across various states of India.

The paper concludes that microfinance SHGs have improved the number of accounts in formal banks by inculcating the habit of banking, especially among women. Further, banking habit is a positive function of the years of experience of microfinance programmes through SHGs in that area. That is, track record is important to establish credibility.

The eighth article **"The Changing Role of Financial Sector in the Provision of Credit for Agricultural Growth: A Study with Reference to West Bengal"** by *Subrata Kumar Roy*. The paper is an empirical investigation of the extent of institutional credit delivery in rural West Bengal. It assumes that agricultural development bears a close relationship with credit and looks at the multi-agency approach to the provision of agriculture credit. It then tries to evaluate its impact on agricultural growth by sample states. Then a district-wise study is made on West Bengal.

The paper analyses the trend on provision of credit by commercial banks, PACS credit and co-operative credit. Credit by size of land holdings is also analysed, state-wise. The paper concludes that institutional credit has increased for agriculture and in West Bengal there has been a shift towards smaller size of land holdings. Further, it has been shown that institutional credit has made an impact on agricultural production through change in the cropping pattern. The paper provides extensive data on provision of rural credit by the co-operative banking sector.

The ninth article "**Kisan Credit Card – An Engine of Growth**" by *S D Mishra*, evaluates the Kisan Credit Card scheme which is a dominant feature of government initiatives in the rural areas. The objective of Kisan Credit Cards is to improve the asset base of the lower strata of farmers (small, marginal and tenant farmers) through access to financial services and provide them with opportunities to gainfully employ themselves. This, in turn, would enhance their contribution to the development of the overall economy.

The paper evaluates the scheme with help of a sample study. The differences in productivity of cardholders and non-card holders are highlighted. It is shown that cardholders have opted for better technology and hence their productivity has been higher. The results also indicate difference in mean percentage gross area sown. There are differences in mean average yield in wheat and paddy and output and net income is found to be higher for card holders vis-a-vis non-card holders.

Section II: Strategies for Improved Performance

The tenth article "**A Design for Efficient Financial Intermediation and Deepening of Rural Financial Markets**" is by *Tamal Datta Chaudhuri*. After a discussion on various credit delivery channels and their performance, this section dwells on strategies for improved performance. These could include novel institutions, new products, better state-market interaction etc. This paper presents the basic ingredients and arguments for an efficient design.

There are four ways of looking at rural financial sector development and accordingly the policy approach will differ. If it is poverty alleviation, the Government has a crucial role to play. If the rural financial market provides opportunities for revenue generation, banks will naturally enter without government intervention.

Constraints for availing one self of financial resources from formal sources like banks include limited information on each individual that can be observed and monitored, lack of any collateral/security for the loan, no recorded evidence of their abilities and loan repayment capabilities, small credit requirements and high monitoring costs, and lack of easy accessibility.

Given the above characteristics and constraints, the paper develops a design for efficient financial intervention through a mix of market forces and social intervention. Areas where the state should intervene and where the market forces should be given full play, are highlighted.

The eleventh article "**Paradigm Shift in Rural Banking: A Case of Microfinance Movement in India through SHG-Bank Linkage Program**" by *A Ramanathan*. This paper argues that the existing loan products in India consisting of concessional rates of interest and longer repayment period backed by physical collateral as security has not served the credit needs of the poor. For long-term growth of the economy, the poor need to be integrated with the rest of society. This is where NGOs have stepped in and gradually many of them are converted into Microfinance Institutions. The paper examines the paradigm shift that has taken place in credit delivery to the poor.

The paper argues that the principles on which microfinance works are well suited for credit delivery to the poor. Information about the rural household, a democratic framework of operation including fixing of interest rates and repayment periods, and peer pressure for repayment have differentiated microfinance initiatives from formal credit delivery channels. The paper concludes with a tabular comparison between the existing formal delivery channels and the new microfinance channel.

Value Addition: The arguments in favour of providing finance to the rural poor on commercial terms for productive deployment include income generation, freedom from the local moneylenders, empowerment of women, promotion of rural artisans and traditional art, better awareness and education. Here, the growth in SHG Bank linkages and the efforts of NABARD in this regard are highlighted.

The twelfth article "**Financing Rural Poor: Performance of Micro-Finance Sector in India**" is by *Paramita Raut.* Micro finance system in India has opened up numerous opportunities for the rural population to gain access to formal finance. The largest component of micro-finance has been the Bank-SHG linkage model. Micro financing in rural India is mainly organized by Self-Help Groups formed by the rural people through collective savings and investments in income generating activities. The model comprises mainly rural womenfolk. The paper shows that the SHG-Bank linkage model has grown in a skewed fashion in India with some states like Andhra Pradesh being ahead of others. Further, scheduled commercial banks have done a better job than co-operative banks. The paper analyses in detail the merits and demerits of the SHG-Bank linkage program and makes suggestions for further improvement.

The thirteenth article "**Revival of Regional Rural Banks through Restructuring and Mergers**" by *Janardhan G Naik,* highlights the growth of RRBs in India and their reach. It then lists the shortcomings of this institutional form of credit delivery. However, capital infusion and other reform measures like permission to reallocate loss-making branches to better business centers and conversion of loss-making branches into satellite/mobile offices without impairing their performance in the service areas, have had a positive effect on their financial performance. The paper then outlines various options in terms of design for improved performance of the RRBs for effective credit delivery.

The fourteenth article "**Indian SME Sector Financing – Some Winning Strategies with Specific Reference to Commercial Banks**" by *K Ramakrishnan*. This paper, while highlighting the need to develop SMEs, also deals with the constraints these units face like fragmented markets, use of inferior technology, lack of access to national and international markets and considerable delay in settlement of bills due to lack of bargaining power. In this context, the efforts by the government for provision of credit like venture capital funding, cluster based approach, credit rating of SMEs etc. are explained. Further, some winning strategies, including setting up of dedicated SME branches, quicker processing of cases, continuous support and conducting training programmes are suggested. The paper highlights opportunities for joint financing of SME projects with SIDBI and other financial institutions.

The fifteenth article "**Emerging Tools for Mitigation of Risks in Agro Business**" by *Prasun Kumar Das*, begins with the reasons for failure of traditional means of agro-financing in India and classifies them under various heads ranging from the risks involved, high transaction costs to lack of collateral. It then identifies various measures undertaken by the Government to mitigate these shortcomings. Various risk factors identified are credit, market and price operational, production and yield and weather. The other risks listed are dispersed clientele, seasonality of agricultural crops, distorted credit cultures and change in policies.

The paper then moves on to identifying Government initiatives for risk mitigation which include minimum support price, farm income insurance schemes, revamping agro-marketing, development of commodities markets and weather insurance. The paper concludes with a discussion on emerging tools for risk mitigation like rainfall index insurance and lending against warehouse receipts.

The sixteenth article "**Inclusive Growth: Role of Financial Education**" is a Speech by *Shyamala Gopinath*. Empirical evidence suggests that access to formal financial services leads to economic development. For this, it is necessary to have financial education, which includes knowledge regarding markets, players and instruments. Financial education makes a microfinance entity plan better and optimize on the use of financial resources. Financial education is particularly relevant for people who are resource poor and who operate at the margin and are vulnerable to persistent downward financial pressures. The paper suggests various themes for conducting educational programmes for the poor.

Section I

Institutions for Rural Financial Sector in India and their Current Status

1

Rural Financial Sector Development in India – An Introduction

Tamal Datta Chaudhuri

Rural development has always been a focus area for policy makers in India as a large part of the population in India is engaged in the rural sector. It is also a sector, which contains a significant part of the Indian poor. With liberalisation of the Indian economy and growing competition, there has been a shift in the perception of the rural sector, particularly from the point of view of financial intermediaries. This sector is now perceived as a continuous source of savings and opportunity for profitable deployment of funds. Thus, in recent years, India has seen a lot of emphasis on rural financial sector development.

Commercial Banks, National Bank for Agriculture and Rural Development (NABARD), Co-operative Banks, Regional Rural Banks (RRBs), Self-Help Groups (SHGs) and Micro Finance Institutions (MFIs) are the major institutions involved in rural financing. The purpose of this paper is to provide an introduction to the book and it covers the performance of the above financial institutions. It also gives an idea about the various policy reforms that have been undertaken in India for rural financial sector development.

1. Introduction

Rural development has always been a focus area for policy-makers in India as a large part of the population in India is engaged in the rural sector. It is also a sector, which contains a significant part of the Indian poor. Thus, rural development measures and poverty alleviation measures have been perceived to be synonymous.

With liberalisation of the Indian economy and growing competition, there has been a shift in the perception of the rural sector, particularly from the point of view of financial intermediaries. This sector is now perceived as a continuous source of savings and opportunity for profitable deployment of funds. Thus, in recent years, India has seen a lot of emphasis on rural financial sector development. Commercial Banks, National Bank for Agriculture and Rural Development (NABARD), Co-operative Banks, Regional Rural Banks (RRBs), Self-Help Groups (SHGs) and Micro Finance Institutions (MFIs), the major institutions involved in rural financing, have geared themselves up to cater to this segment of the economy through innovative schemes, focused approach, dedicated manpower and training and educational programs. Phrases like "Opportunities at the Bottom of the Pyramid" and "Financial Inclusion" are now understood by financial sector players and the understanding has shifted from "Helping the Rural Sector for Upliftment of the Poor" to "Exploiting Profitable Opportunities for Revenue and Profit Generation". The required financial architecture is being discussed and design of appropriate institutions is being debated.

The purpose of this paper is to lay out the performance of the various players involved in rural financial sector development and also to take stock of the various policies that have been adopted in this regard. This will provide a backdrop to the other essays in the book, which are much more focused. Accordingly the plan of the paper is as follows. Section 2 provides data on the performance of various financial institutions engaged in the rural sector. Section 3 gives an account of the policy measures undertaken in this sector and Section 4 concludes the paper.

2. Performance of Financial Institutions Engaged in Rural Sector Financing

The various institutions that are involved in rural sector financing are Commercial Banks, Regional Rural Banks, Co-operative Rural Credit Institutions, NABARD, SHGs and MFIs. Tables 1, 2 and 3 provide data on the extent to which they have facilitated advance of credit to this sector.

Table 1: Flow of Institutional Credit to Agriculture

(Rs. crore)

	2002-03	2003-04	2004-05	2005-06 (upto Dec 2005)
Co-operative Banks	23716	26959	30639	28947
RRBs	6070	7581	11718	11146
Commercial Banks	39774	52441	72886	77806
Total	**69560**	**86981**	**115243**	**117899**

Source: Economic Survey, 2005-06.

Table 2: Sanctions and Disbursements of Rural Infrastructure Development Fund (RIDF)

(Rs. crore)

	Sanctions	Disbursements
December 31, 2004	37,718	22,946
December 31, 2005	48,896	28,338

Source: Economic Survey, 2005-06.

Table 3: Number of Kisan Credit Cards Issued

September 30, 2004	435.61 lakh
November 30, 2005	555.85 lakh

Source: Economic Survey, 2005-06.

In the following, some data is provided on the performance of RRBs, rural co-operative banks and Self-Help Groups.

a. Regional Rural Banks (RRBs)

Tables 4 to 7 provide data on total outstanding advances of RRBs, their total assets and also their financial indicators. Table 4 is indicative of the coverage of RRBs which includes agriculture and non-agriculture. RRBs advance both short- and long-term loans in agriculture. They have also provided financial assistance for non-agricultural activities like retail trade and financial assistance to artisans.

Table 5 shows that not all RRBs are profit-making. However, their Net NPA percentage is quite low. Table 6 gives some financial indicators and the data suggest that their salary outgo as percent of total assets has not increased and their profit margin has stayed more or less the same. Table 7 shows that their income from advances have increased and so has their credit-deposit ratio.

Table 4: Outstanding Advances of RRBs Purpose – wise (As at End March)

		Purpose	2005	2006
		1	2	3
1.		Agriculture	16710	21394
	i.	Short-term Loans (Crop Loans)	10980	14690
	ii.	Term Loans for Agriculture and Allied Activities	5730	6704
2.		Non-agriculture	16161	18319
	iii.	Rural Artisans	713	702
	iv.	Other Industries	580	824
	v.	Retail Trade	4364	3925
	vi.	Other purposes	10504	12868
		Total (1 and 2)	**32871**	**39713**
		Memo Item		
	a)	Priority sector	26077	32453
	b)	Non-Priority Sector	6794	7259
		Share of the Priority Sector (percent)	79.3	81.7

Source: NABARD.

Table 5: Financial Ratios as % of Total Assets of RRBs

Items	2004-05			2005-06		
	Loss-making (30)	**Profit-making (166)**	**RRBs (196)**	**Loss-making (111)**	**Profit-making (111)**	**RRBs (133)**
1	2	3	4	5	6	7
Total Assets (Rs. Crore)	9780	68086	77866	11747	77898	88652
Operating Profits	−1.04	1.63	1.29	−0.88	1.14	0.89
Net Profits	−1.57	1.32	0.96	−1.45	0.87	0.57
Income	6.52	8.07	7.88	5.82	6.31	6.32
Interest Income	6.1	7.46	7.29	5.41	5.89	5.89
Other Income	0.42	0.62	0.59	0.41	0.42	0.43
Expenditure	8.1	6.75	6.92	7.27	5.44	5.74
Interest Expended	4.39	4.01	4.06	3.73	3.01	3.14
Operating Expended	3.18	2.43	2.53	2.98	2.15	2.29
Wage Bill	2.55	1.88	1.96	2.47	1.66	1.78
Gross NPAs			8.5			7.3
Net NPAs			5.15			3.96

Source: NABARD.

Table 6: Business and Financial Indicators of RRBs

Indicator	2000-01	2001-02	2002-03	2003-04	2004-05	2005-06
1	2	3	4	5	6	7
No. of RRBs	196	196	196	196	196	133*
Net Profits (in crore)	600.6	607.9	519.3	768.7	748.2	510.3
Per Branch Productivity	3.8	4.4	5	5.7	6.6	7.7
Per Employee Productivity	0.8	0.9	1	1.2	1.4	1.6
Accumulated Loss as Percentage to Assets	5.6	4.7	4.4	3.9	3.5	2.9
Salary as Percentage to Assets	2	2.2	2.3	2.6	2	1.8
Financial Return (percent)	9.4	10.6	9.6	8.9	8.2	6.6
Financial Cost (percent)	6	6.8	6.1	5.4	4.6	3.5
Financial Margin (percent)	3.4	3.8	3.5	3.5	3.6	3.1
Risk Operational and Other Cost (percent)	2.1	2.6	2.6	2.2	2.3	2.9
Net Margin (percent)	1.2	1.2	0.9	1.3	1.3	0.7

* Reduction in the number of RRB was due to amalgamation which began in September 2005.

Source: NABARD.

Table 7: Deployment of Funds by RRBs *(Rs. crore)*

	2000-01	2004-05	2005-06
1	2	3	4
Share of Income from:			
Advances	34.8	49.7	53.8
Investment	60.5	42.9	39.5
ID Ratio	72.2	59.2	57.6
CD Ratio	41.3	52.9	55.7

Source: NABARD.

b. Co-Operative Rural Credit Institutions

Chapter 8 of this book gives a more detailed account of the performance of co-operative credit institutions in India. Tables 8 and 9 provide an overview of their membership and the size of their balance sheet. The data suggest that, although the coverage of these institutions is far greater than those of RRBs, their total assets sizes are comparable. However, their recovery percentage is lower than that of RRBs.

Table 8: Primary Agricultural Credit Societies Membership – end March

			2004	2005
1.		No. of Societies	105735	108779
2.		Total membership (in million) of which:	135.41	
	a)	SC	30.61	30.93
	b)	ST	11.89	11.8
3.		Total No. of Borrowers (in million) of which:	51.27	45.07
	a)	SC	6.49	7.25
	b)	ST	3.44	3.46
4.		Total No. of employees	347176	388118

Source: NABARD.

Table 9: Select Indicators of Primary Agricultural Credit Societies

			Item	As at the end of March		Percentage Variations	
				2004	2005	2003-04	2004-05
			1	2	3	4	5
A.			**Liabilities**				
	1.		Total Resources	60797	68423	5.6	12.5
	2.		Owned Funds	8397	9197	2.4	9.5
		a)	Paid up Capitals of which	5166	5571	4.3	7.8
			Government Contributions	630	621	1.8	–1.4
		b)	Total Reserves	3231	3626	–0.4	12.2
	3.		Deposits	18143	18976	–5.1	4.6
	4.		Borrowings	34257	40250	13.1	17.5
	5.		Working Capital	62047	75407	1.5	21.5

Contd...

Contd...

B.			**Assets**				
	1.		Total Loans Issued	35119	39212	3.3	11.7
		a)	Short-Term	29326	31887	7.8	8.7
		b)	Medium-Term	5793	7325	–14.8	26.4
	2.		Total loans Outstanding	43873	48785	3.1	11.2
		a)	Short-Term	30808	32481	5.8	5.4
		b)	Medium-Term	13065	16304	–1.8	24.8
C.			**Overdues**				
	1.		Total Demand	44237	47785	9.7	8
	2.		Total Collection	27942	31733	11.5	13.6
	3.		Total Balance (Overdues)	16295	16052	6.6	–1.5
		a)	Short-Term	12279	11656	6.1	–5.1
		b)	Medium-Term	3918	4396	5.3	12.2
	4.		Percentage of Overdues to Total Demand	36.8	33.6		

Source: NAFSCOB.

c. Microfinance Institutions (MFIs) and Self-Help Groups (SHGs)

Conventional financial institutions find it difficult to lend to small farmers, rural artisans and rural people engaged in non-agricultural activities. The reasons are lack of credit worthiness, lack of collateral, lack of steady income, small size of the loan etc. Thus, instead of terms of credit, it is lack of access to credit, which is the main issue in the rural financial sector.

However, experience has shown that poor people, when given access to responsive and timely financial services at market rates, repay their loans and use the proceeds to increase their income and assets. Community banks, NGOs and grassroot savings and credit groups around the world have shown that these microenterprise loans can be profitable for borrowers and for the lenders, making micro finance one of the most effective poverty reducing strategies.

Formal sector financial institutions and informal sources of finance in the rural sector have their own strengths and can complement each other in providing credit to the rural poor efficiently. Formal institutions with their large infrastructure and expertise and informal sources with their first hand knowledge about the rural poor can join hands and be a formidable force in the rural sector. Each can fill up the deficiency of the other and this can lead to effective delivery of credit.

The literature on Micro Finance Institutions in India and across the globe has dealt with the role of such institutions, the linkages with the formal banking system, the various models that can be adopted and the regulatory structure. Some of the Micro Finance Institutions in India are SEWA, SADHAN, SKS, Streedhan and Association of Sarva Seva Farms. Some of the support institutions in the formal sector are NABARD, SIDBI and Rashtriya Mahila Kosh. A reference point for all micro finance institutions is Grameen Bank of Bangladesh.

There are specific chapters in the book which deal with the role of Micro Finance Institutions and the extent of their success in India. Table 10 gives some idea about the extent of linkages discussed so far.

Table 10: Progress of SHG-Bank Linkage Programme

	SHGs Financed by Banks (No.)		Bank Loan (Rs. crore)	
	During the Year	Cumulative	During the Year	Cumulative
1992-99	32995	32995	57.07	57.07
1999-00	81780	114775	135.91	192.98
2000-01	149050	263825	287.89	480.87
2001-02	197653	461478	545.47	1026.34
2002-03	255882	717360	1022.34	2048.68
2003-04	361731	1079091	1855.53	3904.21
2004-05	539365	1618456	2994.25	6898.46
2005-06 (upto Dec. 2005)	211391	1829847	1420.67	8319.13

Source: Economic Survey, 2005-06.

3. Policy Measures

In this section, the reports of various committees set up for improvement of credit flow to the agricultural sector and also for improved performance of the institutions involved in rural financing are discussed.

Table 11: Linkage Position Agency-Wise

	No. in 000's of SHGs		Bank Loan (Rs. Crore)	
	2004-05	2005-06	2004-05	2005-06
i) Commercial Banks	843 *52.1	1177 *53.1	4159	6987
ii) Regional Rural Banks	564 *34.8	740 *33.1	2100	3322
iii) Credit Cooperative Banks	211 *13	310 *13.9	640	1087
Total	**1618**	**2239**	**6898**	**11398**

* Figures are % to total.

Source: NABARD.

Table 12: Linkage Position Model-Wise

	As at March 31, 2005		As at March 31, 2006	
	No. of SHGs per 1000	Bank Loan Rs. Crore	No. of SHGs per 1000	Bank Loan Rs. Crore
1	2	3	4	5
i) SHGs promoted, guided and financed by banks.	343 *21.2	1013 *14.7	449 *20.1	1637 *14.4
ii) SHGs promoted by NGOs/Government agencies and financed by banks.	1158 *71.6	5529 *80,2	1646 *73.5	9200 *80.7
iii) SHGs promoted by NGOs and financed by banks using NGOs/formal agencies as financial intermediaries.	117 *7.2	356 *5.2	143 *6.4	561 *4.9
Total	**1618**	**6898**	**2239**	**11398**

* Figures are % to total.

Source: NABARD.

i. Report of the Internal Group to Examine Issues Relating to Rural Credit and Microfinance – Reserve Bank of India

In India, the institutional framework for advancing credit to the rural areas consist of cooperative credit institutions, domestic banks and Regional Rural Banks

(RRBs). At the micro level, several measures including establishment of the Lead Bank Scheme, directed lending for the Priority Sectors, banking sector's linkage with the Government sponsored programmes have been targeted at the poor. Later on the SHG-Bank linkage programme and introduction of the Kisan Credit Card were initiated. Further, the National Bank for Agriculture and Rural Development (NABARD) and other apex level institutions have made serious efforts in meeting the needs and demands of the rural sector.

The Committee felt that, however, there are wide gaps in the availability of banking services in the rural areas. Though the Primary Agriculture Credit Societies (PACS) have a deep and wide presence in rural India, their impact has been minimal and has concentrated in a few states only. The Committee also felt that the decline in productivity of the rural branches of the commercial banks, fragility of the co-operative credit structure and weakness of RRBs witnessed since the early 90s, further accentuated the problem of inaccessibility of banking services for a large part of the rural population. Furthermore, as the banking sector showed propensity towards larger size accounts to cut down on transaction costs, the number of loan accounts of small borrowers with credit limit range of less than Rs.25,000 has decreased over time.

After reviewing the state of affairs the Committee explored various options and felt that two models could be adopted namely the "Business Facilitator Model" and the "Business Correspondent Model". Under the first model, it is envisaged that a large number of institutions/persons, who currently interface between the rural poor and banks, can be leveraged to provide such support services under well defined terms and conditions by way of contractual arrangements. These agencies may be NGOs, Farmers Clubs, Functional Cooperatives, IT-enabled rural outlets of corporate entities, Postal agents, insurance agents, well functioning Panchayats, etc. The banks may also leverage a large number of Rural Multipurpose Kiosks, and Village Knowledge Centres set up under private or Government initiatives under this Model. Under the latter model, properly identified "Business Correspondents" under contractual arrangement may be allowed to function as "pass through" agents. Besides the functions described under the first model, the correspondents would provide other value added services, such as: i) disbursal of small value credit; ii) recovery of principal/collection of interest; and iii) sale of micro insurance/mutual fund products/pension products.

The Committee also recommended rating of Micro Finance agencies, regulation issues, capital adequacy issues and also setting up of a Micro Finance Development and Equity Fund (MFDEF).

ii. Report of the Internal Working Group on RRBs – Reserve Bank of India

On reviewing the performance of RRBs, the Committee recommended merger of RRBs in a state, either sponsored by the same bank or sponsored by different banks. Their other recommendations included change in sponsor banks, capital infusion to improve capital adequacy and designing an exit route for RRBs whose performance did not improve within a period of three years.

The committee also deliberated on various issues pertaining to governance, business development and human resources. Their recommendations in these areas include:

i) Appointment of a Chairman from the open market through a transparent process;

ii) Broad-base the Board through inducting professionals such as agricultural experts, bankers, management experts, etc.;

iii) Develop an appropriate recruitment policy providing for greater flexibility and freedom to recruit competent and skilled staff from the open market;

iv) Sponsor bank to post appropriate number of specialized staff to help the RRBs in professionalising their advances portfolio, risk management, etc.;

v) Evolve an appropriate incentive to structure and career planning to increase the productivity and profitability of RRBs;

vi) Provide relevant training for skill upgradation and information technology; and

vii) Introduction of new products and streamlining of business processes.

iii. Report of the Advisory Committee on Flow of Credit to Agriculture and Related Activities for the Banking System – Reserve Bank of India

The agricultural sector continues to be the single largest provider of livelihood to people in India. Further, the production base continues to comprise predominantly of small and marginal farmers. Thus, in order to attain agricultural growth at

4 percent per year and also its equitable spread across regions and classes of farmers as per the National Agricultural Policy, it is necessary that cost-effective mechanisms of delivery of credit to the agricultural sector is evolved. From the equity point of view, the cost of credit must be affordable by the vast majority of its potential users who are agriculturists. The Committee looked at the demand and supply side issues and also institutional and regulatory issues and came up with policy recommendations.

Their recommendations include:

- Integration of investment and production credit and increase in scales of finance;
- Strengthening the linkages between production and marketing;
- Finance for land reclamation, schemes of improved water management and dryland farming development;
- Processing and export-oriented farming;
- New commodities exchange mechanisms to provide opportunity to hedge and mitigate risks;
- Training of human resources in lending institutions;
- Outsourcing of credit-related tasks to development agents such as SHGs, NGOs, members of panchayati raj institutions, village functionaries, farmers' clubs etc;
- Recognising and noting tenants' and sharecroppers' rights in land records to help provide these groups access to bank credit. Service Area Approach to be mandatory only for government-sponsored schemes;
- Format of village surveys to be changed in view of current realities; and
- Service area monitoring and information system to be modified and strengthened to include information on new products introduced since its inception.

Their other recommendations involved reduction in costs, NPA norms and capital adequacy issues. The Committee also gave detailed recommendations with respect to merger of RRBs, reorientation of NABARD and also RIDF.

iv. Report of the Task Force on Revival of Cooperative Credit Institutions – Government of India

While outlining the significant role of Co-operative Credit Institutions in India, the Task Force deliberated on the reasons for their impairment and also why these institutions have not been able to deliver and in the process have themselves become financially weak. The policy recommendations of the Task Force were drawn from their experience and they include:

- Special financial assistance to wipe out their accumulated losses and strengthen capital base;
- Institutional restructuring to make for democratic, member driven, autonomous and self-reliant institutions;
- Radical changes in the legal framework to empower the RBI to take action directly in matters and to the extent deemed appropriate for prudent financial management of banks; and
- Qualitative improvement in personnel in all tiers and at all levels through capacity building and other interventions leading to an increase in overall efficiency.

The report also detailed out the restructuring of PACS and the desired role of NABARD.

As against a Tenth Plan Target of Rs.7,36,750 crore flow of credit to the agricultural sector, in the years 2002-03 and 2003-04 only Rs.70,810 crore and Rs.86,981 crore respectively, was achieved. This led the government to announce a 30 percent rise in credit in the year 2004-05 over 2003-04 and this responsibility was given to PSBs, private sector banks, RRBs and co-operative banks. NABARD was asked to advise the District Level Technical Committees to review the scales of finance required to meet the credit needs of the agriculturalists. Accountability was fixed with the sponsors of RRBs.

During the year 2004-05, the rates of interest on farm loans up to Rs.50,000 were reduced to 9 percent and at times to 8.5 percent. To minimse the incidence of under-financing, the scale of crop finance has been revised and recovery of loans in cases of drought has been postponed.

Of the various recommendations made by the Committees, many of them have been adopted and are various stages of implementation. These include waiver of security margins on loans upto Rs.50, 000, providing loans for storage facilities, investment by banks in securitised assets in agriculture under the priority sector, revising NPA norms for agriculture, appointing direct selling agents by banks, making Kisan Credit Cards – ATM-enabled, restructuring of farm loans at reasonable rates of interest, ensuring that institutions lending to MFIs determine the rate of interest charged to their clients on a cost plus and reasonable margin basis, introduction of negotiable warehousing receipt system, reduction in stamp duty in connection with agricultural loans and restructuring of RRBs through merger, amalgamation and consolidation.

4. Conclusion

The purpose of this chapter was to provide an overview of the state of the rural financial sector in India and to set the tone of this book. The other papers in this book have been selected to provide the reader with a deeper understanding of each issue and also results of some specific studies, both in India and abroad. It is expected that the papers would convey to the reader the importance of rural financial sector development and the extent of progress that India has made in this regard.

(Tamal Datta Chaudhuri is a Faculty at Icfai Business School, Kolkata. He can be reached at tamal5302@yahoo.com).

2

SPEECH

Rural Banking: Review and Prospects*

The paper highlights that a piecemeal approach to rural finance will not work and a comprehensive approach to various issue have to be taken. Although efforts have been initiated, the author however, maintains that non-institutional credit still continues; the credit deposit ratio is low in rural areas; the performance of many public sector banks has been inadequate; and the co-operative credit sector has not delivered. The paper concludes by stating that any plan for growth in agricultural credit has to address the four deficits namely public investment and credit deficit, infrastructure deficit, market economy deficit and knowledge deficit.

Dr. Kotaiah, Mrs. Nandita Ray, Mr C S Reddy, Prof. Mahendra Dev and Distinguished guests,

I am grateful to the organisers for giving me an opportunity to deliver the first Smarajit Ray memorial lecture. Mr. Ray, about a couple of years younger to me in age and a valued colleague in the civil service, had been one of my close friends

* The first Smarajit Ray Memorial Lecture delivered by Dr. Y V Reddy, Governor, Reserve Bank of India, organised by the Andhra Pradesh Mahila Abhivruddhi Society, Hyderabad on December 16, 2006 at the Centre for Economic and Social Studies, Ameerpet, Hyderabad.

for almost four decades. He was a self-effacing person with courage of conviction in servicing the cause of the poor with great integrity and objectivity. I also happen to know his wife, Mrs. Nandita Ray, particularly in terms of her association with the Centre for Economic and Social Studies. Together, they worked for a better society and the betterment of the downtrodden. Given his simplicity and humility, it was difficult for many to believe that Mr. Ray had been a student of the elite Presidency College, Kolkata; Delhi School of Economics and London School of Economics. It is said that he inherited his courage of conviction from his father Mr. Ranajit, who was also of the Indian Civil Services.

Since this is the first in the series of lectures, I will recall in brief Mr. Ray's major achievements.

First, and perhaps the foremost is his pioneering role in the development of women's help groups in Andhra Pradesh, which led the SHG movement to become the most impressive mass movement in this area.

Second relates to his innovations in the organisation of the drought prone area programme, specially in terms of people's participation.

Third is his contribution to the programme of "back to school" which specifically targetted the children who were school dropouts and majority of whom were scheduled castes in the rural areas.

Fourth, he prepared a useful document on integrated irrigation management and also helped in resettlement and rehabilitation of the project oustees.

Fifth, he helped to set up the Environment Research and Training Institute, which focused on consultancy, and training in a wide range of environment-related issues – perhaps, the first of its nature at the state level.

I have been a silent admirer of his contributions and achievements in these diverse fields. However, I had a closer interaction with him in my personal and professional capacity very recently. He visited Mumbai in March 2005, to attend the Sachin Choudhury memorial lecture and at that time, I spent almost a full day with him, both in my office and at home. I was deeply impressed by his commitment to issues relating to micro finance. This prompted me to follow it up with a meeting with all people concerned with the micro finance movement involving NGOs in Andhra Pradesh at the Reserve Bank of India, Hyderabad in June, 2005. Mr. Ray helped in organising this meeting, which gave me a deep insight into the issues involved. In a sense, therefore, Mr. Smarajit Ray was a catalyst for my getting deeply involved in the matters relating to micro finance and thus, both RBI as an institution and I, at a personal level, are, therefore, indebted to him. This first memorial lecture is, thus, our way of acknowledging the inspiration that we derived from his personal conduct and his professional work.

Considering the deep interest that he had shown during his life time and the relevance of that work to the RBI, I have chosen to speak on the subject of Rural Banking. After a brief review of the past and recent efforts, the current perceptions on outcomes are noted. I will then mention the national policy directions, followed by, what I would call, New Realities. I will conclude the lecture with a few issues that need to be addressed in the days ahead.

Review of Efforts

It is useful to recall that rural banking was traditionally a monopoly of the money lenders, till the colonial government enacted Co-operative Societies Act in 1904 with a view to making the co-operatives as premier institutions for disbursement of credit. The Process of a three-tier structure commenced in 1915. Government was also providing agricultural loans usually called Takkavi loans, which have since been discontinued. The RBI Act vested a unique responsibility of rural credit to the central bank. All India Rural Credit Survey (1951) of the RBI opined that the co-operatives were "utter failure" in providing rural credit, but added they had a vital role in agriculture credit. The Imperial Bank was nationalised as SBI, which was visualised as a vehicle for rural banking. A rural credit survey of 1966 also concluded the ineffectiveness of co-operatives but stressed the importance of their succeeding. Many State governments legislated the registration and regulation of money lenders but with little emphasis on implementation. Nationalisation of banks in 1969 gave a boost to expansion of banks and banking in rural areas. The Reserve Bank hived off a part of its role in agricultural credit to a separate national level institution, viz., Agriculture Refinance and Development Corporation (ARDC) in 1975. Soon thereafter, a legislation was enacted to create

Regional Rural Banks, with participation from Central and State governments and the nationalised banks, which have their network spread almost all over the country. Subsequently, the ARDC was converted into NABARD, which continued to get the lines of credit from the World Bank. The World Bank's lines of credit were, however, discontinued on the ground that functioning of co-operatives had been less than acceptable. Simultaneously, the directed credit in the form of priority sector lending continued and the administered interest rate regime lasted.

During the reform period, capital was infused into the RRBs and the NABARD. While the priority sector lending continued, the administered interest rate regime was dismantled. To make up for the shortfall in the priority sector lending by the banks, the Rural Infrastructure Development Fund (RIDF) was initiated to ensure the envisaged flow of bank resources to agriculture through the intermediation of the NABARD and the State governments. A system of Special Agricultural Credit Plan was also introduced. Innovations in the area of rural credit included Kisan Credit Cards and encouraging bank-SHG linkages. It may also be of interest to note that many District and State Co-operative Banks are yet to meet the applicable minimum capital requirements.

More recently, since 2004, vigorous efforts have been made to more than double the credit flow to agriculture. Emphasis has been laid on sound credit culture, effective credit delivery and appropriate credit pricing. New instruments for financial inclusion such as General Credit Cards and no-frills accounts were initiated. Micro finance programme was intensified and new guidelines for business facilitator model were issued. Use of technology for rural banking is being encouraged. Special Area Plans for banking in several states such as Uttaranchal, North-Eastern States, Chattisgarh, Bihar and Andaman-Nicobar have been formulated to suit the local conditions. In terms of institutional development, consolidation of the RRBs, revamping of the urban co-operative banks as per the vision document, revival of rural co-operative credit structure as per the Vaidyanathan Committee recommendations, a plan for restructuring of long-term lending institutions for agriculture, and a revisit to the prescriptions relating to the priority sector lending are underway. While a Working Group to review the legislations of various States in regard to money lending has been formed, another Working Group is looking into the relief measures for the distressed farmers. Above all, as per the Government of India announcement in 2005, it has been decided to subsidise the commercial banks and NABARD to enable provision of short-term credit at 7% interest rate to the major segment of the farmers.

In brief, there have been vigorous and determined efforts towards expansion of rural credit, especially through rural banking.

Current Perception of Outcomes

The litmus test of any effort is the outcome, and perhaps even more important, the perceptions of the outcomes. These can be summed up as follows:

First, the non-institutional credit still continues as far as rural areas and agriculture sector are concerned.

Second, the credit-deposit ratio shows that despite the intermediation of banks, the ratio continues to be low in the rural area.

Third, the all-in costs of credit from banks, after factoring in timeliness, transaction-costs, access, etc., appears high for agriculture relative to private corporate sector even after accounting for the risks as reflected by the level of actual non-performing assets.

Fourth, the performance of some of the public sector banks in rural and agricultural lending is also inadequate while that of most of the private and foreign banks is even lower, despite considerable expansion of the scope of priority sector lending.

Fifth, credit-system in rural areas finds it difficult to cope with the rising demands of commercialised agriculture and in any case, there are few credible risk-mitigation measures for the borrowers resulting in greater distress to the farmers in areas with significant presence of commercial crops.

Sixth, while there has been notable progress in micro finance, it is, mostly confined to the states with fairly well-developed banking system. Further, the cost of credit at around 20 to 30% also appears high.

Seventh, the co-operative credit system is, in most parts, dormant and it is commented that the three-tier structure helps finance the bureaucracy rather than benefiting the farmers. Similarly, in many parts of the country, RRBs are less active though in some others they are expanding.

Eighth, while there has been significant growth in rural credit in the recent years, its medium-term sustainability is contingent upon growth in agriculture and improvements in the institutional settings.

In brief, the perceptions on the outcomes of vigorous and varied efforts to expand the reach of rural banking, seem to be less than expected.

Perhaps it's time we ask ourselves some questions.

First have our strategies, in terms of institutions and strategic directions, been flawed all along? Have we run out of ideas in this regard? Is our thinking on rural credit has fallen behind the emerging realities in the economy? Is there a need for distinguishing between the cause and the effect as also between the symptom and the disease? Is it lack of credit availability or want of commercial viability of agriculture that is constraining the credit-flow, or is it a complex combination of both? While we may not be able to answer many of these questions satisfactorily, I submit that we need to keep asking these right questions.

New Policy Directions

Answers to some of the complex questions relating rural credit may be found in the most recent policy directions. The National Development Council approved a week ago "An Approach to the 11th Five Year plan" which contains extensive references to the future policy directions. Some extracts from the document may be in order.

On Objectives and Challenges

"One of the major challenges of the 11th Plan will be to reverse the deceleration in agricultural growth from 3.2% observed between 1980 and 1996-97 to a trend average of around 2.0% subsequently".

"To reverse this trend, corrective policies must not only focus on the small and marginal farmers who continue to deserve special attention, but also on middle and large farmers who suffer from productivity stagnation arising from a variety of constraints".

"A second green revolution is urgently needed to raise the growth rate of agricultural GDP to around 4%".

On Financing Development

"The 11th Plan must ensure that our policies are sufficiently flexible to support the development of micro finance. Interest rates in the micro finance sector have to be significantly higher than in the banking sector reflecting the much higher cost of doing business. It is important to remember that most micro-finance institutions charge rates which are much lower than rates charged by money lenders".

On Agriculture Sector Policy

"The failure of the organised credit system in extending credit has led to excessive dependence on informal sources usually at exorbitant interest rates. This is at the root of farmer distress reflected in excessive indebtedness".

"There is evidence that farm debt is increasing much faster than farm incomes and the larger issue of the overhanging debt stock, as distinct from credit flow, has not even been on the agenda except of a few State governments. Admittedly, there are limits to the extent that banks can be expected to play a purely social role in today's more competitive environment. However, too conservative an approach on settling debt that has turned bad, due to contingencies of poor weather or prices, is not even prudential banking if this serves only to show bank balance sheets to be better than they are, and prevents profitable new lending. There are several suggestions, ranging from a Stabilisation Fund to be run by the Centre for automatic write-off under some specified conditions, to the setting up by States of standing professional Debt Commissions to examine individual debt (including to non-institutional sources) on a case-by-case basis for one time settlement. The 11th Plan will examine in details the impediments which now stand in the way of social and developmental banking and suggest innovations that can improve access and speed up one-time settlements while maintaining credit discipline and financial prudence".

"As farmers adopt new and untried technology, and increase input intensities, they also face larger risks."

"These and related issues of risk management are again largely non-plan areas but need to be addressed during the 11th Plan. This should ideally be done by concentrating on innovations in design which could help expand insurance in a manner that is financially viable without excessive subsidy."

It is also useful to extract some of the statements of Prime Minister Dr. Manmohan Singh, on the subject in the meeting of National Development Council on 9th December 2006.

"The 11th Plan must give top priority to redressing the weaknesses in the agricultural sector. Growth in the agricultural sector has been less than 2% per annum since the middle of the 1990s. With about half of the rural population still dependent on it for most of their income we cannot expect inclusive growth if we do not revitalise agriculture. It is important to recognise that the problem is not distributional, with the better off farmers doing well while the small farmers and the landless face hardships. Though the weaker groups clearly face more difficulties and need special attention, agriculture as a whole is in crisis. We should, therefore, focus on achieving higher productivity and incomes for all farmers in both crop and non-crop agriculture."

"The Approach Paper calls for corrective action in several dimensions of agriculture. Water is a critical input for agriculture and we need to re-examine all aspects of the water economy. We are not spending enough on irrigation and what we are is not being utilised efficiently."

"In addition to investment in irrigation, we must take steps to conserve water and promote artificial recharge in rain fed areas."

"Other issues on the agriculture agenda identified in the Approach Paper relate to the need for focused research in specific crops, farming systems and dry land farming practices, improved extension work to close the knowledge deficit affecting farm productivity; better seeds and inputs; enhanced facilities for credit, including revamping the co-operative credit system; initiatives to support agricultural diversification with effective marketing solutions; and completing the unfinished agenda of land reforms etc."

The Four Deficits

Before concluding this section, I would like to invite your attention to landmark observations made by the Prime Minister in his address at 2nd Agriculture Summit on October 18, 2006, wherein he develops the four deficits theme.

"When we review our agricultural situation, it is clear that there are four deficits we need to bridge. These four deficits are (i) the public investment and credit deficit; (ii) the infrastructure deficit; (iii) the market economy deficit; and (iv) the knowledge deficit. Taken together they are responsible for the development deficit in the agrarian and rural economy."

"However, we need more thinking on the credit front. While the financial system should do more for the credit needs of farmers, we need to raise some questions. What do farmers need – a lower rate of interest or reliable access to credit at reasonable rates? Is our existing institutional framework adequate for meeting the requirements of our farmers who are a diverse lot? Do we need to create new institutional structures such as SHGs, micro finance institutions, etc, to provide improved and reliable access to credit? Or do we need to bring in money lenders under some form of regulation? It is necessary that we find answers to these questions in the near future".

New Realities

It is useful to recognise that there are unprecedented structural changes in the fast-growing domestic economy and rapidly-integrating global economy. These throw up what may be called new realities but these have to be met (a) without losing sight of large population currently dependent on agriculture; and (b) the medium-term trend towards lower share of GDP generation in agriculture. Thus, while some short-term actions may be warranted to be sensitive to aspirations and expectations in rural areas, medium to longer-term strategies have to take into account what may be termed as new realities, though some of them are old realities with greater relevance now and in future. There is some recognition of these in the Approach Paper to 11th Five Year Plan, to which there was detailed reference earlier in the speech. Kindly let me elaborate on the theme here:

First, there is a continuum of agricultural and non-agricultural activities, in terms of inputs, outputs, supply chains, etc, in an emerging, highly-commercialised and globalising agriculture.

Second, there is a spectrum of financial services such as deposit taking, lending, insurance, pension, mutual finds, etc, and there exist several financial intermediaries which need to complement and compete with each other even in rural areas. Banks and banking are a part of this emerging larger whole of the financial institutions and their activities.

Third, there is a clear trend towards rural-urban continuum in economic linkages and the process of integration needs to be facilitated in the interests of growth and equity. Hence, segmentation of these through public policies or procedures should, at best, be an exception than the rule.

Fourth, distinction between productive and non-productive or consumption end, becomes blurred and in any case, consumption smoothening is essential. The cash flow and risk management become more relevant relative to ensuring and monitoring end use of funds.

Fifth, today's technology provides immense opportunities to the financial intermediaries to reach a large section of population, assess and price risks better, and minimise transaction costs. Naturally, this would need considerable business re-engineering.

Finally, there are dramatic changes in demand for food and other articles and supply of related inputs that need to constitute some of the basic elements of a new approach. These aspects of a new approach have been comprehensively and succinctly brought out in a paper by my colleague Dr. Rakesh Mohan, titled "Agricultural Credit in India: Status, Issues and Future Agenda", (*RBI Bulletin*, November 2004). I do not want to repeat them here.

Issues

The new policy directions by NDC and the Prime Minister clearly indicate the criticality of improving the credit system but rightly position it as one of the four deficits that need to be addressed to manage the crisis of stagnation in the Indian agriculture. Agriculture development has to be led by ensuring commercial viability, which has to be enabled by an appropriate credit system. In other words, credit can be a substitute for longer-term commercial viability only if a price is paid in the financial sector and fiscal sector. At the same time, costly or inadequate credit system may constrain growth and commercial viability. The main issues in this regard, therefore, are related to, what may be called, policies complementary to credit or financial services for upliftment of rural economy. Illustratively these are:

First, fiscal policy could play an enabling role in two ways in terms of (a) targetting the poor for subsidy; and (b) enhancing public investment while encouraging private investment that would benefit the rural economy. Perhaps to make agriculture commercially viable, costs and benefits of continuing with the existing allocation of resources for subsidising water, power and fertilizer need to be assessed *vis-à-vis* bestowing focused attention to providing funds for risk mitigation, investments for enhancing supply, ensuring quality and rationalising availability.

Second, trade policy, both domestic and external, should facilitate commercialising of agriculture and thus, enhance the scope for investments. Restrictions to trade within the country at a time when economy is opening up, may, at times, be less than optimal. As mentioned, the savings in rural areas and agriculture are now transmitted by the banking system to urban areas and nonagriculture, often, for want of commercially viable avenues in rural areas. Besides, banks have to improve their own risk-assessment, pricing and credit-disbursement procedures on an urgent basis.

Third, major bottleneck is inadequate arrangements for risk mitigation, be it in regard to quality or timeliness of inputs especially seed, fertilizer, water, power or price of outputs. The risk mitigation for natural calamities or vagaries of weather is often discretionary, based on assessment and response of public policy. Risk mitigation mechanisms will make credit disbursal also less risky.

Fourth, there are attitudinal aspects that need to be considered. It is often said that fiscal support to manufacturing industry is called incentive, while similar support to agriculture is called subsidy. It may be worthwhile considering institutional arrangements and incentive framework that would facilitate attitudinal changes.

Fifth, financial sector as a whole, and banking system in particular, may have to consider paradigm shift in strategies and processes consistent with new thinking, as urged by the Prime Minister and the NDC. Reserve Bank and the whole of banking system stand in readiness to serve this worthy cause of ensuring development of rural-agrarian economy by integrating it with the vibrant services and manufacturing sectors.

Let me conclude by thanking the organisers for giving me the opportunity to share my thoughts on this subject, which affects a major part of our country's population. I would also like to place on record my deep appreciation of the initiatives taken by the organisers in instituting the Memorial Lecture Series and want to assure them of my whole-hearted support to this worthy initiative.

Thank you.

3

NABARD's Innovations in Rural Development

A K Bandyopadhyay

To achieve rural development and provide easy finance to the rural areas, NABARD has initiated several actions. Major among them are: exploring innovative investment opportunities, creating infrastructure base, creating leadership and entrepreneurship, educating the rural masses, building sound network of rural financial institutions and building research and development activities.

The three key words in the theory of innovation originally developed by Joseph A Schumpeter are innovation, entrepreneur and risks, which are inextricably bound up with each other. Innovation means "doing new things or the doing of things that are already being done in a new way". It is a tool in the hands of an entrepreneur, by which he exploits changes as an opportunity for achieving his goal. While doing so, he will invariably take risks as a matter of challenge and prowess.

The entrepreneur is an economic man, who organizes, supervises and speculates a business enterprise. He also tries to maximize his profits by innovations.

Source: Professional Banker, September 2005. This article earlier appeared in the book titled, "Innovations in Banks", published by the Icfai University Press.

According to Schumpeter, economic development consists of "employing resources in a different way" in doing a new combination of means of production. The entrepreneur locates ideas and puts them into effect in the process of economic development. Innovation, thus, occurs through:

- Introduction of a new good;
- Introduction of a new method or technique of production;
- Opening of a new market;
- Exploration of new sources of raw materials; and
- Reorganization of an industry.

Entrepreneur is the innovator and the supply of 'innovative entrepreneurs' depends on the necessary social and economic overheads. Thus, entrepreneur is one who starts an industry, undertakes risk and also performs the managerial functions of decision-making and coordination. However, in the context of developing countries like ours, entrepreneurship may be either innovator or imitator. To Arthur Dewing, entrepreneur is a critical input of socio-economic development and his main function is to promote ideas into business.

Principles of Innovations

- It begins with thinking, i.e., an analysis of opportunities;
- The entrepreneur goes out to look, to ask and to listen regarding his product;
- It is simple but focused;
- It starts small; and
- It is market-driven.

Characteristics of an Entrepreneur

A successful entrepreneur must be a person with technical competence, initiative, good judgment, leadership qualities, self-confidence, creativity, honesty and tactfulness. He should have a clear objective as to the exact nature of the business, the nature of the goods to be produced and related activities to be undertaken. Emotional stability, good personal relations and consideration to the problems of the staff members are some of the important personality factors that contribute to the success of an entrepreneur. The major functions of an entrepreneur are: Innovation, planning production, risk taking, managing enterprise, deciding the project, earning profit, raising finance, ability to deal with situations.

Innovation as a Tool for Rural Development

Since independence, several quantitative and qualitative measures have been undertaken in the country to mitigate poverty and achieve improvement in the field of agriculture and rural development. However, our achievements in the field of agriculture and rural development fall short of the requirement. Even after 58 years of independence and 54 years of planning, 29 crore people are still living below the poverty line, and out of these, 1.21 crore people are landless. Therefore, new strategy in the form of innovation must be adopted.

Improvement of human capital, institutional set-up and infrastructure are the pillars of development. It is an undeniable fact that the rural poor have skill, labor and zeal to work and amass wealth, but they lack ideas, entrepreneurship and capital. Further, available natural resources are sufficient to provide a decent standard of living to the rural masses in our country. Therefore, for achieving improvement in agriculture and rural development, the people and institutions at the grass roots level must be sensitized and suitable steps must be initiated to create a favorable business climate, where the poor have a say.

Village Panchayat, rural youth clubs, schools, credit institutions and Non-Governmental Organizations are the major agents of development at the grass-root level. Though most of the villagers depend on agriculture for their livelihood, inadequate water supply, traditional cropping practice and non-remunerative price for the produced crops make the lives of the farmers miserable. Farmers are also not getting proper guidance or education regarding utilization of local manpower or resources, skill up-gradation and awareness.

NABARD and Innovation

The National Bank for Agriculture and Rural Development (NABARD), an apex financial institution has been working closely with rural development. Provisioning refinance to eligible financial institutions and undertaking related activities to achieve rural prosperity through credit are the core mandate of this organization. Some important innovative actions initiated by NABARD for achieving rural prosperity are as follows:

Explores New/Innovative Investment Opportunities

The investment credit is being provided by NABARD for a variety of purposes. The Bank has encouraged the adoption of water management devices like drip irrigation, sprinkler irrigation as well as programs like watershed development. Special thrust has also been given to investments in farm mechanization. With a focus on diversification of lending, the banks are encouraged to finance investments in plantation and horticulture, etc., through refinance support. Investments in allied activities such as dairy, poultry, fisheries, etc., are also encouraged. A beginning has also been made in direct lending through co-financing with financial institutions.

For reducing poverty and achieving rural prosperity, knowledge dissemination, skill updation and grounding of laboratory experiments on farm sector need expansion. Diversification, commercialization and market-driven agricultural production are the key factors for achieving higher production and productivity. It would also help in generating more employment and income. Group approach would promote collective action, responsibility and knowledge sharing. It also lowers the extension cost in the field of agricultural development. Though a small size holding is a major limitation in the direction of diversification, commercialization and growth, NABARD's initiatives of Farmers' Club, Self-Help Groups (Group approach), Contract farming, Corporate farming and the policy of attracting private bodies into agri-business would definitely sort out these limitations.

Creates Infrastructure Base

Recognizing inadequate storage capacity as one of the major infrastructure bottlenecks of agricultural reforms, NABARD in collaboration with GoI has been encouraging investments in construction, modernization and expansion of cold storages and rural godowns. Setting-up of market yards, agri-clinics and agri-business centers are some other innovative activities undertaken by NABARD. For promotion and development of industries in rural areas, NABARD has been developing rural clusters.

The bank has identified 65 clusters spread over 18 States and has so far launched promotional programs in 55 clusters. Also to strengthen rural industries, one of the initiatives taken by NABARD was the launching of District Rural Industries Projects (DRIP). As of March 2003, the project has been extended to 61 districts. Besides, a special fund, viz., Rural Infrastructure Development Fund (RIDF), has been set up with NABARD for providing loans to State Governments and State-owned Corporations for completion of on-going projects relating to agriculture and rural development.

Creating Leadership/Entrepreneurship

Recognizing lack of entrepreneurial skills in rural areas, NABARD has designed a special program, viz., Rural Entrepreneurship Development Program (REDP). The bank has also set up a Rural Promotion Corpus Fund for supporting developmental and promotional activities of tiny, cottage and village industries for creating employment opportunities in rural areas. The cumulative number of REDPs supported since the commencement of the program in 1990 stood at 5,465, benefiting 1.51 lakh rural youths.

As a step towards women empowerment, NABARD has introduced many programs like ARWIND (Assistance to Rural Women In Non-farm Development), MAHIMA (Marketing of Non-Farm Products of Rural Women) and Self-Help Groups (SHGs). Whereas ARWIND scheme has been introduced for meeting both promotional and credit needs of women entrepreneurs supported by VAs/NGOs, cooperatives and other registered institutions, MAHIMA has been introduced for supporting agencies engaged in marketing of products produced by rural poor women. Besides, in order to strengthen the institutional capabilities in addressing gender issues in credit and support services, a scheme providing grant support for setting up Women Development Cells (WDCs) in RRBs and cooperative banks has been introduced in 1995. So far, 66 RRBs, 27 DCCBs, four SCBs and three SCARDBs have been supported for the establishment of WDCs.

Educates the Rural Mass

Understanding exploitation of local resources, production of market-driven products and up gradation of skills are the vital elements of personal development. NABARD, through workshops, training programs and formation/nurturing of village level community-based organizations (like Village Watershed Committees) has been providing guidance/education, skill and insight in the mindset of rural people. NABARD has also taken a creative initiative in bringing about an attitudinal change amongst borrowers in their outlook towards the concept of credit through the launching of Vikas Volunteer Vahini (VVV) program in 1983. During the year 1998-99, NABARD introduced the Kisan Credit Card (KCC) Scheme in conjunction with cooperative banks, scheduled commercial banks and RRBs to smoothen and strengthen the credit delivery system and more particularly, to make available timely and hassle-free crop loans to the farmers.

Understanding the great merit/ability of Self-Help Groups (SHG) to inculcate the sound habits of thrift and banking among the poor, NABARD ventured in promoting SHGs in India in 1987. As a corporate strategy, it was launched in 1992-93. This SHG-bank linkage program has been built around a simple but basic aspect of human nature – the feeling of self-worth. Without adopting any target-approach, NABARD has promoted and linked 3,97,464 number of Self-Help groups enabling many poor families to access sustainable financial services from the banking system by the end of the year 2003-04. Today, it has expanded to become the largest microfinance program in the world in terms of its outreach, extending banking services to people hitherto unserved by the banking system. The Government of India has also accorded top priority to Self-Help Groups as an instrument of achieving the mission of poverty alleviation.

Builds Sound Network of Rural Financial Institutions

NABARD undertakes institutional development process specifically for the cooperative credit structure and regional rural banks. With the introduction of financial sector reforms in 1991, NABARD has taken upon itself the task of institution building and strengthening of these rural financial institutions to place them on par with other financial institutions.

Credit Planning

With the objective of exploring existing potential for development and evolving an appropriate mechanism through which such potential could be harnessed with credit support over a specified time frame, NABARD undertakes credit planning, i.e., Potential Linked Plans (PLPs), on an annual basis. NABARD has been preparing PLPs for each district, co-terminating with Five Year Plan periods of GoI and updating them after taking into account the available fresh or updated information, latest developments and insights during the implementation.

With a view to enhance organizational learning with reference to the field realities and to establish a two way communication process between NABARD and the field functionaries besides ensuring effective coordination among various agencies involved at the district level, NABARD has also set up District Development Managers (DDMs) offices in select districts since 1989. Over the years, DDMs have become an important link between governmental agencies, RFIs, NGOs/Voluntary Agencies (VAs) and other agencies involved in agriculture and rural development.

Research and Development Activities

NABARD has set up a Research and Development Fund to support research studies, surveys, seminars, conferences, symposia, workshops, etc., in the area of agriculture and rural development. Recommendations of such funded seminars are internalized for modifying the developmental policies and programs of NABARD from time to time.

Conclusion

Rural development is a delicate issue. It requires changing the mindset of the rural masses. Sufficient attention must be given in arousing an interest in the mindset of the rural masses by dissemination of innovative ideas, creating leadership and people-friendly means, which would help in speeding up the process of development at the grass-root level.

(A K Bandyopadhyay is the Chief General Manager at the Department of Economic Analysis and Research, NABARD Head Office, Mumbai.)

4

Microfinance in India: Coming of Age

V Vipin Sharma

This paper starts with a brief background of the SHG movement in India and the value chain in the bank-SHG linkage program is elaborated upon. The relationship between SHGs, NGOs and Self-Help Promoting Institutions and the various sources of funds are discussed. The paper also discusses the scale which the sector has been able to attain, and the pace at which it has grown consistently over the last few years.

April 1992:

It was the first time that Hanuman Van Vikas Samiti's Raj Karan Yadav sat across the branch manager of the Sakroda branch of Mewar Aanchalik Gramin Bank in the Udaipur district of Rajasthan. A group of women had accompanied Raj Karan to negotiate for a loan for their SHG[1]. The brokering of this small loan of Rs.3,000 was a protracted process both for the reluctant banker as well as for the SHG members. It took a full day – copious paper work, many thumb impressions and detailed discussions. This was among the first SHG loans given

1 SHGs are the primary affinity groups of 15-20 rural poor women who come together on weekly/fortnightly/monthly-basis to save and borrow loans from banks, and to rotate these among their members for petty and emergent purposes.

Source: Chartered Financial Analyst, November 2005. This article earlier appeared in the book titled, "Rural Credit and Microfinance", published by the Icfai University Press.

by a bank in India and a part of a pilot project initiated by NABARD to link 500 SHGs in the country.

August 6, 2005:

Malik the CEO of Biswa, an MFI from Sambhalpur, sits comfortably in a hotel lobby in Bhubaneswar discussing a Rs.30 cr bank loan with visitors from ICICI Bank, Mumbai. The meeting lasts about an hour, and once Malik submits a few more documents, the deal will be finalized.

The Origin

After NABARD was carved out of the Reserve Bank of India in 1982, the apex financial institution for the development of agriculture and rural areas was constantly challenged to strengthen the rural credit delivery system so as to enable the rural poor to access small loans from formal financial institutions. With perhaps one of the most impressive institutional infrastructures, this should not have been a difficult task, particularly given the fact that most of the banks were government-owned.[2] To supplement credit provision in the rural areas, Regional Rural Banks (RRBs) were established across the country in 1975, in addition to the already existing institutional infrastructure of the cooperative and land development banks. Coupled with stringent statutory priority-sector lending obligations, the flow of finance to the rural poor under this regime should not have been an issue. However, the only loans going to the poor seemed to be under the subsidy-linked IRDP[3] of the Government of India.

Although the program had a long run, its impact with wrong identification of 'beneficiaries', leakages, misuse of subsidies, and low recoveries, was at best marginal. The program never found favor with the bankers, who lent under extreme pressure from the state governments. Few other avenues for the poor existed, which resulted in their reliance upon the ubiquitous local mahajan for their credit requirements. Despite the infrastructure, large poverty-alleviation programs and statutory obligations, almost 65% of the poor were still borrowing from informal resources.

---

2 In 1969, 19 banks were nationalized, with 6 more in 1974.

3 Integrated Rural Development Program was initiated by the Government of India in 1972 as a large national poverty alleviation program in which the poor were provided with income generating assets through a mix of subsidy from the government and loans from banks.

Linkage Banking and other Microfinance Models

The year 1992 marks the formal beginning of microfinance in India. Although its growth was cautious and erratic in the initial years, in the last half-decade, the microfinance sector has grown at a fairly significant pace. From a pilot project, it became a full-fledged program; and today, the linkage-banking model is known, particularly in the NGO sector, as the 'SHG movement'.

Linkage-banking is the predominant national model. Many actors are involved in making the program operational. The primary stakeholders are the poor women who come together as an SHG. These SHGs are broadly promoted by NGOs, who, for the purpose of the program, are called Self-Help Promoting Institutions (SHPIs). For promoting SHGs, the SHPIs are usually provided with small grants from NABARD; the government also provides grants in case the purpose of promotion of SHGs is for their participation in the 'Swarnajayanti Gramin Swarojgar Yojana'; or under large multilateral funded programs like 'Swashakti' or DPIP or 'Swayamsiddha' or by bilateral donors. The size of grants for SHG promotion differs from agency to agency ranging between Rs.60,000 under the recently concluded 'Swashakti' Project to Rs.3,900 that NABARD provides. In recent years, a few banks like Canara Bank and ICICI Bank, too have started providing SHG promoting grants to NGOs. Bank branches link the SHGs with loans. As per the current guidelines from NABARD, the loans are linked to the savings made by an SHG and can go up to four times the level of these savings. Under the linkage-banking model, typically the SHGs get loans at an interest rate of 8-9% and, in turn, lend it to their members between 18-24%. Their lending rate is fixed as per the by-laws agreed to by the SHG members.

Banking Infrastructure in India

Bank	Bank Branches			
	Total	Rural	Semi-Urban	Urban
Commercial Banks (27)	46,068	19,266	10,900	15,902
Foreign Banks (40)	237	0	2	235
Other Scheduled and Non-scheduled Banks (35)	5,420	1,143	1,776	2,501
RRBs (196)	14,483	12,062	2,045	376
Total	**66,208**	**32,471**	**14,723**	**19,014**

Till recently, the program was primarily supported by the public sector banks, but in the last couple of years, there has been a lot of interest among private-sector and multinational banks as well. In the last half-decade, several NGOs also have shed their traditional social intermediation role and have begun to undertake financial intermediation. Among these, there are a few like BASIX, SPANDANA, SHARE, CASHPOR, ASA which have established themselves as commercial MFIs (NBFIs)/Grameen replicators. There are about 100 such MFIs in the country now. While SEWA is an urban cooperative bank model, the BASIX group also has a Local Area Bank. Another model that has emerged in the country is the aggregation of SHGs into federations. This has particularly become popular in Andhra Pradesh and was made possible by the introduction of the Mutually Aided Cooperative Act 1995. There are no clear guidelines, as yet, on lending by banks to community-based federations. The schematic, presented in the following paragraphs, represents the structural arrangements for the delivery of microfinance services in India.

The Current Status

Despite a slow-growth rate in the initial period, as of 2005, India today has the highest number of poor being served by the microfinance Sector (25 million),

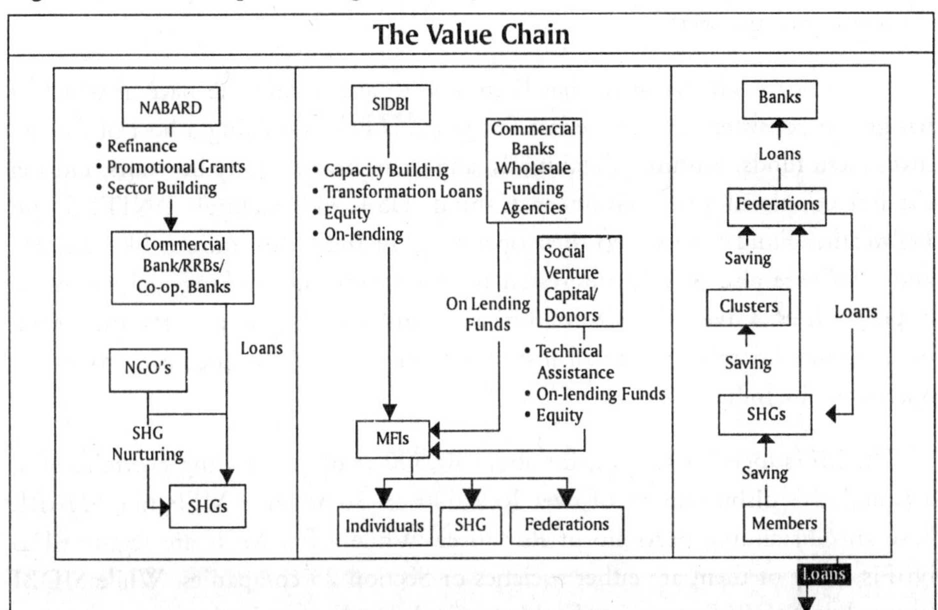

having overtaken its neighboring Bangladesh, one of the first countries to have adapted microfinance route as an effective poverty-alleviation strategy. Here is a snapshot view of the SHG-bank linkage program.

Bulk of the SHG linkage targets have been achieved through the public-sector banks, and even today, 73% of all microfinance loans are provided by these government-owned banks. However, in the past few years, the private-sector and the multinational banks, despite the lack of rural bank branches and understanding of rural areas or the rural clients, and with their very upmarket, urbane culture, have shown a keen interest in microfinance. To overcome constraints of infrastructure, these banks have evolved innovative mechanisms and models to expand their microfinance portfolio. ICICI Bank, among the newcomers, has been the most aggressive. The ICICI Bank through its 'partnership model' has already achieved an outstanding of Rs.720 cr and among all commercial banks, has the second largest microfinance portfolio after SBI. It plans to achieve a portfolio of about Rs.2,000 cr by the end of this year. Other private-sector banks like HDFC Bank (Rs.175 cr), UTI Bank (Rs.100 cr), IDBI Bank, etc., too are looking at microfinance as a serious business opportunity. Among the multinational banks, ABN AMRO Bank (Rs.85 cr), Standard Chartered Bank (Rs.15 cr), and HSBC (Rs.12 cr), among others, have also developed their own strategies and models for lending to the sector.

The scale which the sector has been able to attain, and the pace at which it has grown consistently over the last few years, is now attracting a host of foreign investment funds, venture capital funds, and even private-equity investors. During the last couple of years, Grameen Capital, USA, Lok Capital, UNITUS and Bellweather Fund have set up their operations in India. Institutions like the IFC and CDC are also getting interested in this sector and looking at investment opportunities. Given the size of India's population below poverty line, even international microfinance retail institutions like FINCA are preparing to set up operations in India.

The MFIs together account for about Rs.500 cr of outstanding portfolio with a cumulative disbursement of over Rs.1,600 cr. Some large MFIs like SHARE have an outstanding portfolio of Rs.370 cr. While a few MFIs are registered as NBFIs, most of them are either societies or Section 25 companies. While SIDBI (through its SIDBI Foundation for Micro Credit) is the apex institution supporting the growth of MFIs in the country, a few large bilateral-funded programs like CASHE (Credit and Savings for Household Enterprises) being implemented by CARE India, too support the incubation of community-based microfinance institutions. Almost 90% of all microfinance clients are in the rural areas, with most of the urban poor being left out of this program.

Policy Shifts

In the last one year, the sector has seen a lot of action. Moving beyond setting targets for NABARD to link SHGs to banks, the Union Finance Minister, in his last budget speech, made some major announcements for the sector. For the first time, certain legitimacy was given to the growing contribution of the MFIs. To start with, he expanded the scope of the Microfinance Development Fund to include equity, and doubled the fund size to Rs.200 cr. The fund will be managed by an independent board comprising of representatives from both financial as well as NGO sector. He also announced the opening up of the External Commercial Borrowing (ECB) route for the MFIs to allow cheaper foreign funds for the sector. In addition, he also allowed banks to channel their services through banking correspondents. And, finally, responding to the demands of the sector, he announced the introduction of a legislation for the sector. While this is seen as a major achievement for the sector, there still remain demands, particularly of the MFIs for deposit collection, lowering the entry barriers for registration of NBFCs, and a legislation that allows a defined institutional space to the microfinance institutions.

Microfinance Landscape	
No. of SHGs Linked to Banks	1.67 million
Cumulative Loans Disbursed by Banks	Rs.6,878 cr
Total Loans Disbursed by Commercial Banks during the Last Year (2004-05)	Rs.2,800 cr
No. of Participating Banks	560
• Commercial Banks	48
• RRBs	196
• Cooperative Banks	316
No. of Bank Branches Lending to SHGs	35,294
No. of NGOs and other Agencies Associated	1,000 (Approx.)
Average Member Level Loan-size	Rs.3,024
Average Loan-size for SHGs	Rs.46,000

Future Challenges

While the sector has grown significantly in the last half-decade, several challenges still remain. Microfinance still reaches only about 10 to 12% of the poor in the country. Sixty-seven percent of the population in the country have no bank accounts and 80% have never taken a loan from a formal source. About 40% continue to borrow from informal sources. The demand and supply gap is still huge. As per estimates, it varies between Rs.50,000 to 1,50,000 cr and only 20% are currently met through the program. Regional skew is another area of concern. Almost three-fourths of all microfinance clients are located in the four southern states. Andhra Pradesh, with over 5,00,000 SHGs, accounts for almost a third of all clients in the country. Large parts of the northern and northeastern states are still underserved by the sector. NABARD has identified 13 states for special focus in the coming years. Financial deepening also requires urgent attention. With an average loan size of about Rs.3,000, the loans can, at best, serve consumption smoothening. For asset acquisition, new models and greater conviction is required

SHG-Bank Linkage Programme

(Amount in Rs.Crore)

Year	Total SHGs Financed by Banks (Numbers in '000)		Bank Loans		Refinance	
	During the Year	Cumulative	During the Year	Cumulative	During the Year	Cumulative
1	2	3	4	5	6	7
1999-00	81.78 (147.9)	114.78 (247.9)	136 (138.6)	193 (238.6)	98 (88.5)	150 (188.5)
2000-01	149.05 (82.3)	263.83 (129.9)	288 (111.8)	481 (149.2)	251 (156.1)	401 (167.3)
2001-02	197.65 (32.6)	461.48 (74.9)	546 (89.6)	1,026 (113.3)	396 (57.8)	797 (98.8)
2002-03	255.88 (29.5)	717.36 (55.4)	1,022 (87.2)	2,049 (99.7)	622 (57.1)	1,419 (78.0)
2003-04	361.73 (41.4)	1,079.09 (50.4)	1,856 (81.6)	3,904 (90.5)	705 (13.3)	2,124 (49.7)
2004-05	539.39 (49.1)	1,618.48 (50.0)	2,994 (61.3)	6,899 (76.7)	968 (37.3)	3,092 (45.6)

Note: Figures in parentheses indicate percentage variations over the previous year.

from the banks. The sector needs to grow beyond meeting survival credit/ subsistence credit needs of the poor and provide for sustainable livelihoods. Linking credit with enterprises/livelihoods finance is a new focus area. Through the program, there are few opportunities for long-term loans, and there are very few investments in product development. Within microfinance, it is largely microcredit services that the poor are being offered. Large population of the poor is not covered by any microinsurance product. Although both NABARD and SIDBI have assigned allocations for capacity building, these are released in driblets and are far short of the requirements for upscaling the program.

Impact

There are very few studies that empirically support the claim that microfinance is helping the poor in asset acquisition and moving out of poverty. However, the big contribution of the sector has been the organization of the poor, particularly women, to access critical financial services. Since 90% of the SHG members are women, the program has had an impact not just in economic terms, but also in terms of the improvement in social indicators, resulting in double bottom lines. Empirical evidence shows that the mobility of women associated with the microfinance programs have increased, resulting in greater awareness and confidence amongst them. An impact assessment of CARE's microfinance program 'CASHE' demonstrates that microfinance program results in better health and nutrition, greater role of women in household decision-making, and their empowerment to contribute to the community decision-making process. With women having access to financial resources, they also influence critical decisions like sending the girl child to school. The households have also been able to report higher levels of assets, though the change from the baseline is only marginal. Overall, microfinance clearly is a path towards empowering the most marginalized among the poor to take charge of their lifecycle-related requirements. Through microfinance, they are better positioned to access not only financial services, but also resources, markets, and their entitlements. While microfinance is looked upon as a financially viable approach to address economic vulnerability, more importantly, it has demonstrated the potential of building the social capital of the poorest communities.

(V Vipin Sharma is Program Director, Microfinance, CARE India.)

5

Microfinance in India: Empirical Evidence, Alternative Models and Policy Imperatives

Rajaram Dasgupta

One of the reasons for the lacklustre performance of both public and private sector banks in extending credit to weaker sections is their high level of NPAs. While credit under the Swarnjayanti Gram Swarozgar Yojna scheme across states has been extended in proportion to the poor in the population, this is not so in the case of Self-Help Group (SHG) credit that has been growing at the rate of 120 percent per annum. However, growth in SHG credit has been uneven. The southern states are seen as SHG-developed states while Bihar and Madhya Pradesh are among those characterised as SHG-backward. But besides the SHG model in extending credit to weaker sections, other different models exist for extending microcredit to the poor and weaker sections.

Source: Economic and Political Weekly, March 19, 2005, (www.epw.org). © EPW. Reprinted with permission.

A paradigm shift is required from 'financial sector reform' to 'microfinance reform'. While the priority sector needs to be made lean, mandatory microcredit must be monitored rigorously. Simultaneously, space and scope have to be properly designed for providing competitive environment for microfinance services. Extensive database needs to be created by the RBI for understanding microfinance.

1

Microfinance (MF) is a financial service of small quantity provided by Financial Institutions (FI) to the poor. These financial services may include savings, credit, insurance, leasing, money transfer, equity transaction, etc., that is, any type of financial service, provided to customers to meet their normal financial needs: lifecycle, economic opportunity and emergency (Dasgupta and Rao 2003) with the only qualification that (i) transaction value is small; and (ii) customers are 'poor'.

Besides, size and clientele group, what makes microcredit different from normal credit is that the latter is 'walk-in' and the former is 'walk-out' business for the FI. Unlike normal credit, microcredit is limited with collateral substitute and credit plus services. Microcredit thus becomes distinct from other regular credit where not only credit amount is small and clientele is poor, but also credit is provided with 'collateral substitute' instead of traditional collateral and non-financial services for increasing the productivity of credit.

To some extent, microcredit is not a new concept in India. Priority sector credit in general and weaker section credit in particular was actually a kind of microcredit. But in the 1990s during the banking reforms, the definition of priority sector underwent a sea change (Dasgupta 2002). So far as microsaving services are concerned, these are indeed recent with the advent of Self-Help Group (SHG) movement. Microinsurance, however, is still in experimental stage, till now 'microsavings' has been a proxy for 'microinsurance'.

It is only the savings and credit aspects of microfinance that have, therefore, been addressed so far in India. Moreover, information with regard to credit only is available. RBI provides information on agriculture and weaker section credit through different Scheduled Commercial Banks (SCBs). The National Bank for Agriculture and Rural Development (NABARD) provides information with regard to those SHGs, which are linked, with NABARD through the refinance scheme. Weaker section credit of FIs includes SHG credit, however, information provided by NABARD does not cover the entire SHGs.

This paper attempts to examine the trend of (i) Agriculture Microcredit (AGMC); (ii) Weaker Section Microcredit (WSMC); and (iii) SHG Microcredit (SHMC) in Section II. Section III discusses different models for microfinancing. Policy imperatives have been discussed in Section IV so that all the models discussed in Section III can become functional and microfinance services are accessible to all the eligible poor.

II

Disbursement of short- and long-term agriculture credit to farmers by SCBs increased from Rs.10 billion in 1980-81 to Rs.42 billion in 2001-02 at 1980-81 price, more than four times in just 20 years (Table 1). Disbursement per hectare increased from Rs.72.3 in 1980-81 to Rs.275.13 in 1999-2000, less than four times in 19 years.

Table 1: Trends in Disbursement by Scheduled Commercial Banks in Agricultural Sector in India

Year	Disbursement (Rs. Billion)	Disbursement (Rs. Billion) in 1980-81 Price	Disbursement as Percent of GDP from Agriculture	Disbursement as Percent of Input Cost	Disbursemnet Hectare (Rs.) 1980-81 Price
1980-81	10.1	10.1	2.4	6.7	72.3
1985-86	22.4	17.9	3.2	9.7	126.9
1987-88	29.4	20.4	3.5	10.6	150.2
1990-91	39.1	21.4	2.9	10.0	149.8
1993-94	45.6	18.4	2.1	8.2	129.1
1995-96	76.6	25.9	2.8	10.6	182.0
1999-00	140.1	38.9	3.3	13.6	275.1
2001-02	163.0	42.1	3.4	13.7	–

Source: RBI, CSO.

The disbursement as a percent of Gross Domestic Product (GDP) from agriculture has increased from 2.4 in 1980-81 to 3.4 in 2001-02 after declining during the period, 1987-88 to 1993-94. Disbursement as a percent of total input to agriculture increased from 6.7 in 1980-81 to 13.7 in 2001-02, after declining during the same above period which formed the years of economic reform followed by the period of financial sector reform. Agriculture sector, therefore, suffered comparative credit crunch during the initial years of financial sector reform. What is, however, of concern is that less than 15 percent of input cost is financed by the SCB credit assuming that entire credit is for inputs which however is not the case.

In 1995-96 only 3.7 million out of 93 million of SM farmers (5.22 percent) had been disbursed agricultural credit by SCBs (Table 2). This share has declined from 5.67 percent in 1985-86. Within the total spectrum of farmer borrowers, percent of SM farmer borrower has declined from 74 to 69 percent during 1980-96, while the percent of SM farmers has increased. There is thus a shift from SM farmers although disbursement per hectare to this group of farmers has increased from Rs.97 to Rs.230 at 1980-81 prices. This trend of intensive rather than extensive credit helps Formal Financial Institutions (FFIs) to maintain their mandatory credit ratio at a lower transaction cost.

Total agricultural outstanding amount at current prices has increased from Rs.38 billion in 1980-81 to Rs.648 billion in 2001-02 (Table 3). But what is important to note is that share of direct finance to farmers after reaching a peak of 93 percent in 1990-91 has come down to 68 percent in 2000-01 before increasing to 72 percent in 2001-02. This is why SM farmers have suffered. Dasgupta (2002) had argued earlier that because of redefinition of the priority sector, it would be easier for the banks to fulfil the target of 40 percent set by the priority sector and 18 percent of agricultural lending at the cost of SM farmers. PSBs account for more than 96 percent of WSMC provided by all SCBs (Table 4). PSBs together provide slightly more than 7 percent of NBC to the WSMC portfolio whereas PVSBs provide less than 2 percent of NBC only.

Table 2: Credit to Small and Marginal Farmers by Scheduled Commercial Banks

Year	Land holdings ('000 Number)			Land Area ('000 Hectares)					
	Small and Marginal Farmers	Total	Percent of Small and Marginal Farmers	Small and Marginal Farmers	Total	Per Cent of Small and Marginal Farmers	Per Cent of Small and Marginal Farmers Extended Credit	Per Cent of Small and Marginal Farmers Borrower to Total Farmer Extended Credit	Disbursement Per Hectare to Small Marginal Farmers (Rs 1980-81 Price)
1970-71	49110	70490	69.7	33830	162120	20.9	–	–	–
1976-77	59250	81570	72.6	38410	163340	23.5	–	–	–
1980-81	66190	88970	74.5	42900	163800	26.2	4.5	74.3	97.1
1985-86	74070	97160	76.2	47750	164560	29.0	5.7	76.3	203.8
1990-91	82080	105290	78.0	53330	165620	32.2	5.1	78.0	224.3
1995-96	92822	115579	80.3	58843	163357	36.0	5.2	68.6	229.7
2001-02	–	–	–	–	–	–	–	66.2	–

Source: CMIE, RBI, CSO.

Table 3: Total Finance to Agriculture by Scheduled Commercial Banks

(Rs. Billion)

Year	Direct Finance	Indirect Finance	Total Finance	Total Finance in 1980-81 Price	Percent of Direct Finance
1980-81	28.88	8.83	37.71	37.7	76.58
1985-86	91.6	14.25	105.85	85.4	86.54
1990-91	161.45	11.89	173.34	97.2	93.14
1999-00	364.66	129.68	494.34	137.1	73.77
2000-01	404.85	188.25	593.1	158.7	68.26
2001-02	465.81	182.38	648.19	167.3	71.86

Source: RBI.

The performance of all PSBs, however, is not uniform. WSMC portfolio for BOM, COR, DEN, OBC, UCO, SBH, SBS and SBT,[1] was less than 5 percent of NBC in March 2004. Very few banks, viz., ALB, IB, IOB, PNB,[2] SYN, SBM, SBP and also ANB have achieved the target of 10 percent in 2004 and most of them are concentrated in southern region. ALB and PNB have been making efforts to improve their performance in last four years at the risk of having more Non-Performing Assets (NPA). ANB, IOB, SYN, SBM and SBP have been improving their NPA in WSMC. Except SBP, all others have concentration in the southern region. These banks of southern region and also SBP seem to be dealing with weaker section portfolio on commercial lines.

1 Abbreviations refer to Bank of Maharashtra, Corporation Bank, Dena Bank, Oriental Bank of Commerce, United Commercial Bank, State Bank of Hyderabad, State Bank of Secunderabad, State Bank of Travancore, respectively.

2 Allahabad Bank, Indian Bank, Indian Overseas Bank, Punjab National Bank, Syndicate Bank, State Bank of Mysore, State Bank of Patiala, Andhra Bank, respectively.

Table 4: Weaker Section Credit by Commercial Banks

Name of the Bank	Concentration of Lead Banks in Regions	Weaker Section Credit (Rs. Bn) 2001	Weaker Section Credit (Rs. Bn) 2002	Weaker Section Credit (Rs. Bn) 2003	Weaker Section Credit (Rs. Bn) 2004	Per Cent of Weaker Section Credit to Net Bank Credit 2001	Percent of Weaker Section Credit to Net Bank Credit 2002	Percent of Weaker Section Credit to Net Bank Credit 2003	Percent of Weaker Section Credit to Net Bank Credit 2004	Percent of NPA of Weaker Section Credit 2001	Percent of NPA of Weaker Section Credit 2002	Percent of NPA of Weaker Section Credit 2003	Percent of NPA of Weaker Section Credit 2004	Annual Growth of Weaker Section Credit during 2001-04 (Percent)	Annual Growth of Net Bank Credit during 2001-04 (Percent)
Allahabad Bank (ALB)	C	6.10	7.53	7.40	15.75	6.43	7.04	5.84	10.11	17.36	14.67	26.24	18.32	52.7	21.4
Andhra Bank (ANB)	S	7.83	8.94	11.09	12.43	11.74	9.63	10.13	9.89	19.64	23.49	5.19	6.31	19.6	29.5
Bank of Baroda (BOB)	W&C	12.66	16.01	19.24	19.15	7.08	7.46	7.89	7.88	25.91	26.22	20.54	16.15	17.1	11.9
Bank of India (BOI)	E&C	10.27	16.00	17.00	23.93	5.09	7.20	5.87	8.58	20.60	27.16	24.77	26.53	44.4	12.7
Bank of Maharashtra (BOM)	W	3.94	6.11	4.95	5.30	5.86	7.64	5.29	4.69	26.24	30.58	30.99	30.19	11.5	22.7
Canara Bank (CAN)	S	19.11	19.30	21.45	26.26	8.66	7.50	6.12	5.89	24.37	23.16	19.26	16.04	12.5	34.0
Central Bank of India (CBI)	E&C	9.12	9.33	16.89	20.90	5.12	4.48	7.44	9.3	29.81	15.77	28	34.83	43.0	8.7
Corporation Bank (COR)	S	1.62	2.06	1.87	3.30	2.48	2.30	1.97	2.83	25.33	14.18	18.77	14.41	34.5	26.1
Dena Bank (DEN)	W	2.63	2.53	2.94	3.43	3.64	3.34	3.54	3.64	NA	23.00	35	19.51	10.1	10.1
Indian Bank (INB)	S	7.44	8.45	10.29	12.31	9.21	10.01	10.02	10.05	22.76	23.89	24.75	23.13	21.8	17.2

Contd...

Contd...

Indian Overseas Bank (IOB)	S	10.60	12.95	15.83	19.72	12.43	12.11	10.82	10.86	10.46	8.26	4.43	3.60	28.7	37.7
Oriental Bank of Commerce (OBC)	N	4.81	4.92	5.18	7.66	4.19	3.42	3.25	3.89	3.27	14.28	13.46	9.97	19.8	23.8
Punjab & Sind Bank (PSB)	N	2.69	2.66	3.18	3.79	5.51	9.79	5.31	6.06	12.18	13.38	12	0.00	13.7	9.4
Punjab National Bank (PNB)	N&C	24.00	32.63	40.60	50.36	8.83	5.09	10.16	10.82	14.84	15.29	13.14	23.49	36.6	23.8
Syndicate Bank (SYN)	S	9.80	10.95	13.15	16.92	10.16	10.17	10.04	10.12	13.51	20.98	18.58	12.30	24.2	24.5
UCO Bank (UCO)	E&N	4.39	5.69	6.84	8.31	4.93	5.73	4.61	4.3	48.19	44.34	27.42	20.48	29.8	39.0
Union Bank of India (UNB)	C	7.84	10.87	13.16	19.07	5.18	6.09	5.66	6.61	34.70	26.47	22.31	21.89	47.7	30.2
United Bank of India (UBI)	NE	3.90	4.57	4.62	4.75	6.11	4.67	5.91	5.58	44.89	24.21	22.73	13.68	7.3	11.1
Vijaya Bank (VJB)	S	3.51	3.87	3.94	6.57	7.31	6.81	5.57	6.26	NA	14.33	18.33	11.18	29.1	39.6
State Bank of Bikaner & Jaipur (SBJ)	N	3.83	4.40	5.32	5.77	7.68	7.22	7.91	6.86	12.34	NA	29.2	10.50	16.8	22.9
State Bank of Hyderabad (SBH)	S	4.96	7.71	6.16	4.89	7.42	7.79	6.33	4.38	19.72	19.00	13.48	4.59	–0.5	22.4
State Bank of India (SBI)	AI	68.47	70.52	66.44	95.72	7.68	10.01	5.78	7.2	27.52	26.11	24.61	31.24	13.3	16.4

Contd...

Contd...

State Bank of Indore (SBN)	C	2.19	2.97	3.91	4.17	6.47	6.96	7.55	6.35	26.62	15.74	10.69	6.42	30.1	31.3
State Bank of Mysore (SBM)	S	4.31	4.61	5.07	5.72	11.75	10.90	10.85	10.04	14.84	13.27	13.57	9.07	10.9	18.4
State Bank of Patiala (SBP)	N	6.47	7.67	9.29	12.51	10.01	10.02	9.4	10.03	4.63	26.87	18.58	12.56	31.1	31.0
State Bank of Saurashtra (SBS)	W	1.45	2.30	2.59	2.28	4.02	5.73	5.7	4.18	7.08	23.32	14.38	6.64	19.2	17.1
State Bank of Travancore (SBT)	S	4.11	4.21	4.66	4.93	12.16	10.74	6.29	4.95	11.00	8.07	11.97	13.33	6.7	64.9
Total Public Sector Banks	–	248.05	289.75	323.04	415.89	7.28	7.30	6.76	7.44	22.51	21.71	19.39	18.90	22.6	21.4
Total Private Sector Banks	–	9.59	11.42	12.23	14.95	1.7	1.80	1.5	1.3	19.7	10.3	16.8	12.20	18.7	32.6
Total Indian Commercial Banks excluding RRBs	–	257.64	301.17	335.27	430.84	6.5	6.50	5.9	6.4	22.5	19.4	17.6	15.90	22.4	22.9
Percent Share of Public Sector Banks	–	96.28	96.21	96.35	96.53	–	–	–	–	–	–	–	–	–	–

N – North; E – East; NE – North-east; C – Central; W – West; S – South; AI – All-India.

Source: RBI.

BOB has been marginally increasing its share of WSMC and also reducing its NPAs. CBI too has been increasing the WSMC share but at the risk of increasing NPA. WSMC portfolio of other banks has either been fluctuating or decreasing although they are below the 10 percent target level. CAN, COR, UCO, SBS and SBH which have been making efforts in reducing NPA have been reducing their exposure to this segment. OBC with average level of NPA has been decreasing its exposure to the weaker section, although it is already too low.

At the industry level although for PSBs, the growth of WSMC and NBC has been almost equal, for PVSBs the growth of NBC is much higher than that of WSMC. The NPA level seems to be one of the factors affecting disbursement to weaker sections. Except for IOB, no other PSB has less than 10 percent of NPA in WSMC. Correlation between percent of NPA in the previous year and WSMC exposure among the public sector banks as expected, is negative (Table 5). What, however, is to be noted is that this correlation amount is declining. Banks are now guided by other factors like transaction costs too.

Table 5: Correlation between Percent of NPA in Weaker Section Credit and Percent of Weaker Section Credit in NBC

Per Cent of Weaker Section Credit in the Year	Per Cent of NPA of Weaker Section Credit in the Year	Correlation Coefficient
2002	2001	–0.33
2003	2002	–0.21
2004	2003	–0.13

Information on Swarnjayanti Gram Swarozgar Yojna (SGSY) has been given in Table 6. Sixty percent of this credit in 2004 had been disbursed in the eastern and central region, which account for 64 percent of the poor in India. Proportions of poor people and SGSY credit in the states have been found to be highly correlated (0.91). However, correlation coefficient between SGSY credit per poor and recovery rate is only 0.21. SGSY credit, because of the directive of central and state governments, is distributed in proportion to the poor, and not as per the recovery rate.

There is, however, a different scenario for SHMC. Compared to 22.4 percent of annual growth of WSMC during 2001-04, SHMC has grown at the rate of 120 percent per annum (Table 7).

Table 6: State and Region-Wise Information on Poverty and SGSY Credit in 2003

	Total Poor (000)	Poverty (Percent)	Percent Distribution of Poor	SGSY Disbursement	Percent Distribution (Rs. Billion)	Per Capita SGSY Credit Disbursed to poor (Rupees)	SGSY Recovery percent
State							
Haryana	1796.7	8.2	0.7	0.235	2.1	131.0	52.0
Himachal Pradesh	450.9	7.2	0.2	0.100	0.9	222.7	59.1
Punjab	1455.7	5.8	0.6	0.135	1.2	93.0	52.2
J and K	432.6	4.0	0.2	0.000	0.0	0.0	32.2
Rajasthan	8783.0	14.8	3.4	0.521	4.6	59.3	43.4
Assam	9965.0	35.9	3.8	0.346	3.0	34.8	33.7
Bihar	48894.0	42.9	18.7	2.333	20.5	47.7	37.6
Orissa	17834.7	47.2	6.8	0.689	6.1	38.6	32.0
West Bengal	22251.1	26.9	8.5	0.411	3.6	18.4	44.1
Madhya Pradesh	23806.9	37.6	9.1	1.713	15.1	72.0	31.6
Uttar Pradesh	53949.1	30.9	20.6	1.678	14.8	31.1	53.9
Gujarat	6999.2	13.3	2.7	0.261	2.3	37.3	51.7
Maharashtra	24861.5	24.8	9.5	0.948	8.3	38.1	41.1
Goa	44.7	3.1	–	0.010	0.1	228.4	60.8
Andhra Pradesh	11727.6	15.1	4.5	0.733	6.4	62.5	72.2
Karnataka	10611.3	19.5	4.1	0.632	5.6	59.6	52.0
Kerala	3955.6	12.1	1.5	0.291	2.6	73.6	60.3
Tamil Nadu	13453.1	21.2	5.1	0.324	2.8	24.1	67.2
Pondicherry	188.5	18.8	0.1	0.007	0.1	37.7	66.8
All-India	261460.9	26.0	100.0	11.369	100.0	43.5	45.8
Region							
North	12918.8	10.5	4.9	0.992	8.7	76.8	–
North-east	9965.0	28.1	3.8	0.346	3.0	34.8	–
East	88979.7	37.8	34.1	3.433	30.2	38.6	–
Central	77756.0	33.0	29.6	3.391	29.8	43.6	–
West	31905.3	20.7	12.2	1.219	10.7	38.2	–
South	39936.0	17.4	15.4	1.988	17.5	49.8	–

Table 7: Contribution of Different Segments of FFIs in the SHG Movement

Bank	Cumulative Number of SHGs Provided with Bank Loan upto March 2001	Cumulative Number of SHGs Provided with Bank Loan upto March 2004	No. of New SHGs Provided with Loan during 2001-02	No. of New SGHs Provided with Bank Loan during 2003-04	Cumulative Bank Disbursed upto March 2001 (Rs. mn)	Cumulative Bank Loan Disbursed upto March 2004 (Rs. mn)	Bank loan Disbursed during 2001-02 (Rs. mn)	Bank Loan Disbursed during 2003-04 (Rs. mn)	Annual Growth Rate (percent) in Number of SHGs Lent during 2002-04	Annual Growth (percent) in Disbursement of SHG Credit during 2002-04	Annual Growth (percent) Having been Financed (Cumulative) during 2001-04	Disbursement per SHG during 2001-02 (Rs. mn)	Disbursement per SHG during 2003-04 (Rs. mn)
Total Public Sector Bank	118855	516697	146956	168329	2741.7	20195.5	2887.3	9650.4	7.3	117.1	111.6	0.020	0.057
Total Private Sector Bank	5391	21725	3045	9032	226.0	2352.8	154.0	1402.9	98.3	405.4	101.0	0.051	0.155
Regional Rural Bank	84775	405998	82137	128658	1564.2	12782.6	1895.3	5510.8	28.3	95.4	126.3	0.023	0.043
Cooperative	12773	134671	27133	55712	274.2	3711.2	520.7	1991.3	52.7	141.2	318.1	0.019	0.036
Total	221794	1079091	259271	361731	4806.1	39042.1	5457.3	18555.3	19.8	120.0	128.8	0.021	0.051
No. of SHGs Provided Repeat Loan	–	–	–	171669	–	–	–	–	–	–	–	–	–
Total SHGs Provided Loan during the Year	–	–	–	533400	–	–	–	–	–	–	–	–	–
SHARE (percent)													
Total Public Sector Bank	53.6	47.9	56.7	46.5	57.0	51.7	52.9	52.0	–	–	–	–	–
Total Private Sector Bank	2.4	2.0	1.2	2.5	4.7	6.0	2.8	7.6	–	–	–	–	–
Regional Rural Banks	38.2	37.6	31.7	35.6	32.5	32.7	34.7	29.7	–	–	–	–	–
Cooperatives	5.8	12.5	10.5	15.4	5.7	9.5	9.5	10.7	–	–	–	–	–

Source: NABARD.

Number of SHGs having been financed by FFIs has increased from 0.2 million in 2001 to 1.1 million in 2004 at the rate of 128 percent per annum. Number of SHGs financed during a year has increased from 0.26 million in 2001-02 to 0.36 million in 2003-04 with an annual growth of 19.8 percent. All this information relates to SHGs refinanced by NABARD only. In the absence of any centralised information on SHMC, information provided by NABARD has been used for analysis.

PSBs and Regional Rural Banks (RRBs) account for 48 and 38 percent respectively of cumulative SHGs lent so far and 52 and 33 percent of cumulative credit to them (Table 7). The rest is by PVSB and district central cooperative banks (DCCB). During 2003-04, PSB, PVSB, RRB, and DCCB financed 46.5, 2.5, 35.6 and 15.4 percent, respectively of 0.36 million SHGs. Their share in the credit of Rs.18.6 billion during the same year has been 52, 7.6, 29.7 and 10.7 percent, respectively. PSBs and RRBs are thus the major financiers to SHGs.

Not only the number of SHGs being extended credit has increased, the amount of disbursement too has increased from Rs.0.02 million in 2001-02 to Rs.0.05 million per SHG in 2003-04 (Table 7A). There is thus, both extensive and intensive expansion of SHG credit. Firstly, the recovery rate has been very high. According to NABARD (2003-04) report on SHG bank linkage, it has been more than 95 percent (there is no published information on either recovery rate or NPA level of SHG credit). Secondly, the SHGs because of their inherent capacity building mechanisms, increases its credit absorption capacity. During 2003-04, whereas 67.8 percent of SHGs were financed for the first time, 32.2 percent were financed for the second or third time. In 2002-03 these percentages were 69.1 and 30.9 respectively. Thus, there seems to be an increase in the share of the 'old' SHGs in the total number of SHGs financed. This again indicates the 'willingness' of the FFIs to repeat credit to older SHGs, which have already been financed. This indicates the possibility of a stable credit relationship between SHGs and FFIs. This was not the case with government-sponsored credit schemes (Pulley *et. al.*, 1989).

The annual growth rate of new SHGs lent during a year, however, is negative for ANB, BOI, BOM, DEN, INB, OBC, SBH and SBS (Table 7A). ANB, INB and SBH having concentration in southern region are already doing business with a large number of SHGs. This is not the case with other five banks. OBC and SBS are facing negative growth in credit too. Among the states, Gujarat and Andhra Pradesh face negative growth in SHG linkage (Table 8). No state, however, faces negative growth in SHG credit.

Table 7A: Trend in SHG Movement for Public Sector Banks

Bank	Annual Growth Rate (percent) in Number of SHGs Lent during 2002-04	Annual Growth (percent) in Disbursement of SHG Credit during 2002-04	Annual Growth (percent) in SHGs Having Been Financed (Cumulative) during 2001-04	Disbursement per SHG during 2001-02 (Rupees)	Disbursement per SHG during 2003-04 (Rupees)
ALB	64.4	249.0	370.1	9855.2	25768.6
ANB	-17.9	79.7	82.3	19880.8	80251.9
BOB	1.0	84.6	93.5	16385.4	43216.3
BOI	-3.7	33.3	94.3	22979.5	41373.5
BOM	-11.3	94.1	64.7	17096.6	63723.8
CAN	86.4	174.5	110.5	28091.9	46221.0
CBI	28.3	110.6	125.1	25843.0	53034.9
COR	7.0	89.9	118.7	22936.2	56268.7
DEN	-36.8	63.4	113.4	6001.9	51625.4
INB	-2.9	115.7	162.6	23432.4	82446.2
IOB	1.7	107.9	95.5	19528.8	59657.9
OBC	-26.4	-18.7	111.8	26226.9	34816.2
PSB	238.4	209.6	3208.3	48372.1	43548.4
PNB	114.7	336.0	850.4	17904.3	41959.3
SYN	5.8	154.4	93.4	20755.4	76063.6
UCO	34.6	93.6	243.7	17801.8	30202.0
UNB	12.6	141.7	135.1	17701.1	54168.8
UBI	5.2	354.2	139.4	2629.2	19264.5
VJB	286.1	349.9	114.6	25530.9	30374.7
SBJ	13.5	58.1	239.5	13232.5	22529.8
SBH	-7.2	113.1	75.0	16288.8	62048.6
SBI	17.7	151.2	125.9	18570.8	55206.2
SBN	385.5	218.5	181.9	52284.0	32232.5
SBM	126.2	164.6	144.4	31912.8	38876.2
SBP	103.9	99.0	396.0	53888.9	52166.1
SBS	-49.2	-40.1	984.5	6600.4	79333.3
SBT	14.2	71.2	59.6	29172.6	55050.6

So far as spatial distribution of SHG and SHG credit is concerned, it is completely at variance with SGSY credit although both are poor and SHG-centric. Whereas the eastern and central region accounted for more than 60 percent of SGSY credit in proportion to the poor, the southern region accounted for

Table 8: Business with New SHGs

State	No. of New SHGs Provided with Bank Loan during 2001-02	Bank Loan during 2001-02 (Rs. Million)	No. of New SHGs Provided with Bank Loan during 2003-04	Bank Loan during 2003-04 (Rs. Million)	Annual Growth (percent) for SHGs Provided Bank Loan during 2001-04	Annual Growth (percent) of SHGs Loan during 2001-04
Haryana	433	21.72	820	76.99	44.7	127.2
Himachal Pradesh	2524	48.6	4353	144.32	36.2	98.5
Punjab	296	16.37	806	42.96	86.1	81.2
Jammu and Kashmir	97	1.9	352	11.62	131.4	255.8
Rajasthan	6948	120.24	11104	271.18	29.9	62.8
Assam	748	9.66	7229	123.09	433.2	587.1
Bihar	1282	19.09	8085	186.73	265.3	439.1
Orissa	11665	125.96	35316	764.43	101.4	253.4
West Bengal	8404	68.75	19038	299.96	63.3	168.2
Madhya Pradesh	4069	68.31	11824	292.87	95.3	164.4
Uttar Pradesh	11490	170.51	25514	841.79	61.0	196.8
Gujarat	4567	21	2099	93.78	-27.0	173.3
Maharashtra	9151	243.31	10470	439.08	7.2	40.2
Goa	57	4.43	66	6.83	7.9	27.1
Andhra Pradesh	117352	2670.92	104238	7529.92	-5.6	91.0
Karnataka	18413	347.54	41688	1396.04	63.2	150.8
Kerala	5134	148.3	12716	584.19	73.8	147.0
Tamil Nadu and Pondicherry	30100	1204	52002	5094.82	36.4	161.6
All-India	259271	5457.3	361731	18555.31	19.8	120.0

Source: NABARD.

63 percent of SHGs and 79 percent of SHG credit in 2004 (Table 9) with only 15.4 percent of the poor. Within the southern region, Andhra Pradesh accounts for 35.79 percent of SHG and 44.32 percent of SHG credit followed by Tamil Nadu, which account for 14 percent of SHGs and 24 percent of SHG credit. In contrast, Assam, Bihar, MP and UP account for a much less share of SHG and SHG credit *vis-à-vis* the share of poor. The average credit to SHG in 2004 has been Rs.36,196. High volume credit of Rs.50,000 or more per SHG has been extended in Haryana, Punjab, Goa and Tamil Nadu. Average volume of credit between Rs.25,000 to 50,000 has been extended in J & K, Bihar, Maharashtra, Andhra Pradesh, Karnataka and Kerala. However, considering the average size of SHG and the average family size as 5, whereas less than 10 percent of poor families in Haryana and Punjab have been extended SHG credit, in Himachal Pradesh, Andhra Pradesh, Karnataka and Tamil Nadu more than 70 percent of poor families have been extended credit by FFIs.

Table 9: State and Regional Distribution of SHG Credit

	Cumulative Number of SHGs Extended Credit Upto 2004 through				Cumulative Amount (Rs. Million) of Credit Provided to SHGs Upto 2004			Percent Distribution Total	Percent Distribution of SHG 2004	Percent Distribution of SHG Credit 2004	Credit per SHG (Rs.) 2004	SHG Credit per Poor (Rs.) 2003	Percent of poor Families Extended Credit Through SHG 2003	Per Cent of SGSY Disbursement to SHG Disbursement in 2002-03
	Commercial Banks	Regional Rural Banks	Cooperative Banks	Total	Commercial Banks	Regional Rural Banks	Cooperative Banks							
State														
Haryana	744	1563	37	2344	78.69	66.61	1.13	146.43	0.22	0.38	62470	83	9.96	339.00
Himachal Pradesh	5156	2281	5791	13228	99.95	45.01	170.09	315.05	1.23	0.81	23817	707	222.54	58.81
Punjab	724	216	708	1648	36.33	16.26	30.37	82.96	0.15	0.21	50340	58	8.61	338.50
J and K	606	371	263	1240	15.7	6.46	14	36.16	0.12	0.09	29161	86	22.10	0.00
Rajasthan	12476	16996	4374	33846	254.02	381.36	98.36	733.74	3.14	1.88	21679	85	29.49	112.55
Assam	1809	8529	368	10706	61.21	102.46	4.92	168.59	0.99	0.43	15747	17	8.20	761.32
Bihar	13038	15722	133	28893	439.88	278.36	4.32	722.56	2.68	1.85	25008	15	4.51	601.81
Orissa	25959	43506	8123	77588	413.51	723.4	137.92	1274.83	7.20	3.27	16431	72	33.05	134.97
West Bengal	10676	13946	27063	51685	111.32	208.41	284.84	604.57	4.80	1.55	11697	28	17.66	134.76
Madhya Pradesh	12370	19365	5156	36891	313.63	292.17	73.51	679.31	3.42	1.74	18414	29	11.86	474.24
Uttar Pradesh	32927	52586	4605	90118	774	1212.4	97.54	2083.94	8.36	5.34	23125	39	12.79	154.49
Gujarat	9826	4595	1553	15974	146.24	80.4	27.86	254.5	1.48	0.65	15932	37	17.39	162.27
Maharashtra	18769	12514	7252	38535	655.47	319.95	160.68	1136.1	3.58	2.91	29482	46	11.80	135.95
Goa	208	0	98	306	11.18	0	7.03	18.21	0.03	0.05	59510	419	52.76	89.63
Andhra Pradesh	246123	130470	8983	385576	11426.04	5546.91	310.84	17283.79	35.79	44.32	44826	1493	249.73	7.52
Karnataka	38605	37087	28174	103866	1006.79	1094.73	734.66	2836.18	9.64	7.27	27306	271	74.35	43.91
Kerala	21378	5365	6985	33728	785.91	135.72	307.43	1229.06	3.13	3.15	36440	314	64.65	45.13
Tamil Nadu and Pondicherry	86463	39894	24829	151186	5892.3	2256.98	1240.9	9390.19	14.03	24.08	62110	695	83.98	7.71
Region														
North	19706	21427	11173	52306	485	516	314	1314	4.86	3.37	25128	104	30.95	129.26
North-east	1809	8529	368	10706	61	102	5	169	0.99	0.43	15747	17	8.20	761.32
East	49673	73174	35319	158166	965	1210	427	2602	14.68	6.67	16451	30	13.54	285.41
Central	45297	71951	9761	127009	1088	1505	171	2763	11.79	7.09	21756	36	12.50	234.30
West	28803	17109	8903	54815	813	400	196	1409	5.09	3.61	25701	45	13.08	140.21
South	392569	212816	68971	674356	19111	9034	2594	30739	62.59	78.83	45583	779	128.14	12.32
All-India	**537857**	**405006**	**134495**	**1077358**	**22522**	**12768**	**3706**	**38996**	**100.00**	**100.00**	**36196**	**152**	**31.43**	**55.55**

Source: NABARD.

All the states have been classified on the basis of credit per SHG and percent of poor families financed through SHG channel. There emerges seven groups of states: (a) Goa and Tamil Nadu with high volume (Rs.50,000 or more per SHG) and high penetration (50 percent or more poor families extended credit); (b) Andhra Pradesh, Karnataka and Kerala with average volume (Rs.25,000-50,000) and high penetration; (c) Himachal Pradesh with low volume (less than Rs.25,000) and high penetration; (d) Rajasthan and Orissa with low volume and average penetration; (25-50 percent); (e) Haryana and Punjab with high volume and low penetration (less than 25 percent); (f) J & K, Bihar and Maharashtra with low volume and average penetration; and (g) Assam, West Bengal, Madhya Pradesh, Uttar Pradesh and Gujarat with low volume and low penetration.

What is clear from Table 10 is that microcredit is more SHG-centric in a, b and c groups of states; but more SGSY-centric in e, f and g groups of states. The group d comprising Rajasthan and Orissa lies in between these two sets with equal emphasis on SHG and SGSY.

In the absence of state level of recovery or NPA data, correlation between SHG credit and its recovery level could not be ascertained. Statewise data, however, shows the following interesting correlation coefficients (Table 11).

If the FFIs have to increase the SHG credit per poor, it is better to cover more poor families through SHG (correlation 0.92) rather than increasing the credit per SHG (correlation .42). In this context, what is of concern is that SHG movement is more active where poverty ratio is less (correlation -.31) whereas the opposite is expected.NABARD provides district wise distribution of SHGs, which have been financed. If there is widespread distribution of SHGs in districts within a state, the percent of SHGs financed in each district should be 'equal'. Otherwise, there is concentration of SHGs in few districts. Table 12 gives an indication of districts where SHGs are concentrated within a state. Percent of SHGs financed in top 10 percent of districts has been estimated. States where top 10 percent of districts cover (i) less than 30 percent of SHGs are 'widespread'; (ii) 30-50 percent of SHGs, 'average spread'; and (iii) more than 50 percent of SHGs 'low spread'. Based on these and other characteristics discussed earlier, Andhra Pradesh, Karnataka, Kerala and Tamil Nadu may be categorised as SHG developed states

Table 10: SHG Credit in Different Types of States

Type of State	SHG Credit Per Poor (Rs.)	Percent of SHGs Extended Credit in Top 10 Percent of Districts	Percent of SGSY Credit to SHG Credit
A	687.4	17.5	7.9
B	811.9	16.3	13.9
C	698.7	32.4	58.8
D	75.5	22.4	124.3
E	70.5	25.1	338.8
F	25.5	42.7	295.8
G	32.4	29.5	225.2

Table 11: A Set of Correlation Coefficients

Variable 1	Variable 2	Correlation Coefficient
Percent of Poor Families Financed through SHG	SHG Credit Per Poor	0.92
Percent of Poor Families Financed through SHG	Percent of Poor in the State	–0.31
Credit Per SHG	SHG Credit Per Poor	–0.42

Table 12: Concentration of SHGs in Different States

States	Percent of SHGs Expected in a District Distribution (Widespread)	Districts with Relatively High Concentration of SHGs within the State (Figures in parenthesis indicate Percent of SHGs in the District)	Top 10 Percent Districts Financing Percent of SHGs
Haryana	5.3	Gurgaon (41)	31.03
Himachal Pradesh	7.7	Kangra (24), Mandi (26)	32.50
Punjab	5.9	Fatehgarh (20)	20.40
J & K	7.1	Jammu (30), Kathua (25)	38.50
Rajasthan	3.1	Ajmer (21), Tonk (9)	34.56
Assam	4.3	Sonitpur (34)	42.17
Bihar	2.6	Gaya (19), West Champaran (24)	63.70
Orissa	3.2	None	17.91
West Bengal	5.3	Nadia (18)	25.65
Madhya Pradesh	2.2	Dhar (13), Jhabua (24)	57.50
Uttar Pradesh	1.4	Allahabad (4), Moradabad (5), RaiBareli (5)	20.59
Gujarat	4.0	PanchMahal (14),Sabarkantha (17)	31.25
Maharashtra	3.0	Chandrapur (24)	33.00
Goa	50.0	None	13.60
Andhra Pradesh	4.5	None	14.03
Karnataka	3.7	Dakkhin Kannada (14)	20.83
Kerala	7.1	None	15.96
Tamil Nadu and Pondicherry	3.6	None	18.20

Source: NABARD.

with (i) high SHG credit per poor; (ii) high penetration among poor through SHG; and (iii) widespread coverage of poor and Bihar and Madhya Pradesh may be classified as SHG backward states with (i) low SHG credit per poor; (ii) low penetration among poor through SHG; and (iii) lowspread coverage of poor. More effort is required in the latter group.

III

In spite of the optimism generated in some of the states with regard to SHGs, the fact remains that the commercial banks fall short of mandated 10 percent of NBC to weaker sections. At the same time 40 percent of rural credit which is mostly micro credit is met by Informal Financial System (IFS) (RBI 2000). The problem with IFS is with regard to high interest rates and the limited scope of the credit. The former is mainly because of scarcity of capital and monopolistic market; the latter is because of the knowledge risk. Both together limit the risk absorbing capacity of the IFS. The informal moneylenders extend credit mainly for traditional short-term needs. They cannot take part in the long-term investment credit.

The IFS, however, is quite efficient because it (i) provides at anytime, doorstep service; (ii) accepts deposits of any amount; (iii) extends credit of any amount for any purpose; and (iv) does not demand complex formalities. The FFIs lack in these aspects although they have large capital and greater risk absorbing capacity with them.

The IFS operates in a localised market, and has the full information about its clients. Because of its low cost structure and compact command area, the transaction cost is low. The FFIs on the other hand operating from a remote area lack the above informal advantages. This increases both transaction costs and default risks. All these factors come in the way of the development of a stable relationship between FFIs and the microcredit clients. What has, therefore, been advocated in different expert circles (Dasgupta 2001) is a linkage between formal and informal systems or an informal approach by formal system. Different FFIs including Non-Government Organisations (NGOs) and Micro Finance Institutions (MFIs) in India are practising different models.

All these models have been depicted in the Figure. In the organisational approach, the FFIs are lenders to either the ultimate borrower or to the informal system or the NGOs. In the collaborative approach the big FFIs deal with small FFIs or MFIs that are yet to be rigorously defined.

Figure: Models of Microfinance

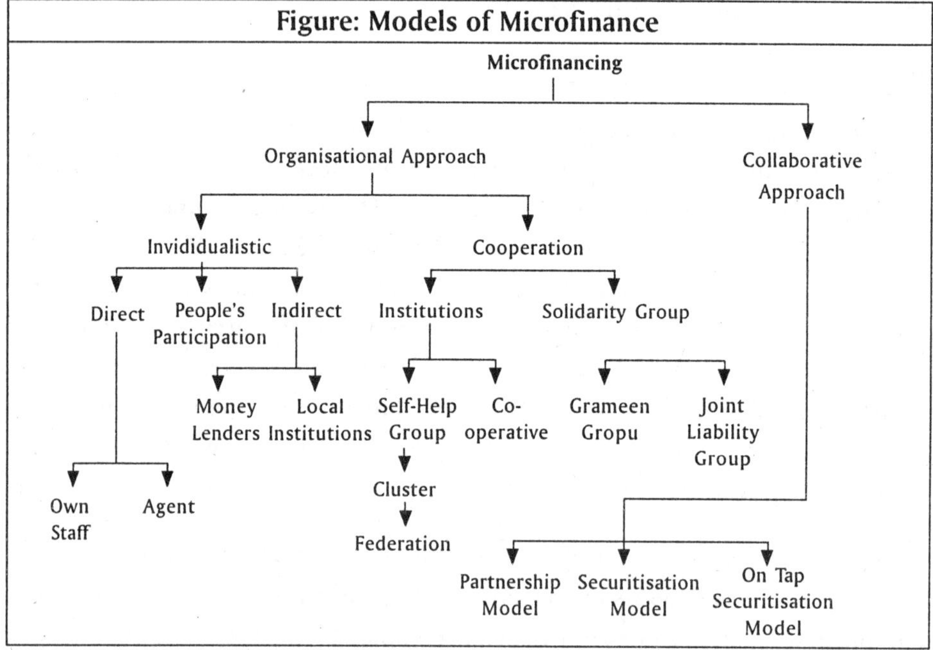

The organisational approach (see chart) has been discussed by Dasgupta and Rao (2003). Direct approach through own staff is not cost effective for the FFIs. Microfinance services are both labour-and travel-intensive process because of intensive monitoring and large size of the clientele group of small unit value. The FFIs and even MFIs, however, can adopt the 'agent' approach which has been to a large extent successful (Basu and Jindal 2000). In the case of the 'moneylender' approach it is more important to enhance the supply of credit and increase the number of moneylenders to bring competitiveness which would bring down the interest rate instead of policing it.

For SHG credit, there are three different models. In Model I SHGs are formed and extended credit by the banks; in Model II SHGs are formed by the NGOs but credit extended by the banks; in Model III NGOs in addition to forming SHGs, avail bulk loan from banks for lending to SHGs.

Table 13 provides the modelwise distribution of credit. At the aggregate level Models I, II and III account for 20, 72 and 8 percent of SHGs and 14, 81 and 5 percent of SHG credit respectively. Southern and northern regions depend less on Model I and more on Model II. In contrast other four regions especially north-east and east depend more on Model I. Share of Model II is much less in these two regions. Not much organic relationship has yet been established between banks and non-bank SHGs there. In these regions, RRBs and cooperatives are proportionately more active in SHG credit. These small FFIs presumably form SHGs on their own and do not depend upon NGOs and hence adopt Model I.

Table 13: Modelwise Percent Distribution of SHGs and SHG Credit in 2004

	Model I SHG (Number)	Model II SHG (Number)	Model III SHG (Number)	Model I SHG Credit (Amount)	Model II SHG Credit (Amount)	Model III SHG Credit (Amount)
States						
Haryana	24.8	75.2	0.0	18.5	81.5	0.0
Himachal Pradesh	2.5	97.5	0.0	0.8	99.2	0.0
Punjab	25.9	74.1	0.0	23.3	76.7	0.0
Jammu & Kashmir	1.7	98.3	0.0	0.9	99.1	0.0
Rajsthan	19.7	80.3	0.0	18.8	81.1	0.1
Assam	74.3	16.2	9.5	82.9	12.5	4.6
Bihar	4.9	95.1	0.0	3.0	97.0	0.0
Orissa	47.8	35.4	16.8	49.9	36.9	13.2
West Bengal	82.1	0.9	17.0	86.1	0.8	13.1
Madhya Pradesh	30.2	67.7	2.1	29.4	68.2	2.3
Uttar Pradesh	28.3	66.0	5.7	36.2	59.2	4.6
Gujarat	7.4	91.2	1.5	8.8	89.5	1.7
Maharashtra	36.6	62.7	0.7	33.9	65.7	0.4
Goa	35.6	64.1	0.3	30.3	69.6	0.1
Andhra Pradesh	0.6	98.5	1.0	0.5	99.0	0.6
Karnataka	46.7	32.1	21.2	50.3	28.9	20.8
Kerala	16.7	39.7	43.6	19.2	48.8	32.0
Tamil Nadu and Pondichery	8.3	83.1	8.6	10.3	85.6	4.1
Region						
North	15.3	84.7	0.0	14.1	85.8	0.1
North-east	70.5	20.7	8.9	72.6	21.7	5.7
East	50.9	33.9	15.1	45.0	43.2	11.9
Central	28.4	67.6	4.0	31.6	65.0	3.4
West	28.1	71.0	0.9	29.3	70.1	0.6
South	10.2	81.9	7.9	8.8	86.4	4.8
All-India	20.2	72.0	7.8	14.1	81.1	4.9

Source: NABARD.

Table 14 provides the modelwise distribution of credit in different types of states. In A and B groups of states Model I is less important vis-à-vis other groups of states, D, E, F and G. In former two groups commercial banks are more active than RRBs and cooperatives together. A much more contrasting picture emerges in Table 15 where above distributions has been highlighted for 'SHG-developed states' and 'SHG-backward states'. In the former group, Model I is much less important and commercial banks are much more dominant in financing SHGs. Opposite is the case for 'SHG-backward states'. Also, Model III is more influential in SHG-developed states.

Table 14: Influence of Different Models of SHG Lending and Different Financial Institutions in Different Types of States

Type of States	Percent of Credit in 2004 through			Percent of SHGs Extended Credit in 2004 by		
	Model I	Model II	Model III	Commercial Banks	RRBs	Cooperatives
A	10.3	85.6	4.1	57.2	26.3	16.5
B	8.2	86.8	5.1	58.5	33.1	8.4
C	0.8	99.2	0.0	39.0	17.2	43.8
D	38.5	53.1	8.4	34.5	54.3	11.2
E	20.2	79.8	0.0	36.8	44.6	18.7
F	26.7	73.0	0.3	43.9	42.5	13.7
G	41.2	53.5	5.3	32.1	49.6	18.3

Table 15: A Few Characteristics of SHG Developed and Backward States

SHG Status of States	SHG Credit per Poor (Rs.)	Percent of Poor Families Extended Credit through SHG	Percent of Credit through			Percent of SHGs Financed by		
			Model I	Model II	Model III	Commercial Banks	RRBs	Cooperatives
Developed	4040	87	8.8	86.4	4.8	58.2	31.6	10.2
Backward	103	4	20.5	78.0	1.5	37.6	56.3	6.1

This indicates that in the SHG-developed states, the commercial banks depend upon NGOs especially for development of SHGs and to a very small extent for financial intermediation. In the SHG-backward states where RRBs and cooperatives are more dominant, commercial banks depend on their limited organisational resource for both development of SHGs and extending credit. SHG credit per poor is much less there. The FFIs lack social mobilisation skill for the development of SHGs. It is, therefore, important to develop the NGO and MFI sector for increasing SHG credit especially in areas where microcredit is more required.

In the securitisation model, MFIs assign existing microfinance receivables to FFI, share risk and continue to service the portfolio. This helps the FFI to do business in unfamiliar areas, and helps the MFIs to extend credit in their areas familiar to them, without bothering for capital adequacy ratio. In the on-tap securitisation model, the FFIs provide advance purchase consideration to MFIs to build portfolio and then purchase the asset as in these curitisation model. This takes care of the initial resource problem of MFIs. In any case, the FFIs evaluate NGOs, MFIs and also the portfolio. If necessary they develop and strengthen these NGOs and MFIs. Foreign banks, which are not mandated to extend WSMC, should be asked to adopt this model to extend micro credit. This is going to be important even for the SCBs which are gradually withdrawing from rural areas (Table 16).

Table 16: Offices of the SCBs

Year	Rural	Semi-urban	Urban	Metro	Total
1993	35389	11465	8562	5753	61169
2004	32200	15023	10917	8922	67062

Source:RBI.

IV

What has thus been observed in earlier sections is that per capita credit to the poor extended by the FFIs is too small, although there is a big demand. More importantly, most of the FFIs fall short of the mandatory requirement. One of the reasons identified in the earlier sections is higher proportion of NPA because of information gap and inadequate monitoring. This arises because of higher transaction cost. An answer has been found in group lending and linking with informal systems but this is yet to be widespread. Policy reform is the necessary condition for this. This demands a paradigm shift from 'financial sector reform' to 'microfinance reform'.

In this reform process, microfinance has to be the focal point. All issues related to definition and scope, financial architecture, capital structure, prudential norms, management information system, personnel policy, legal aspects, regulatory and supervisory role, support and capacity building mechanism, monitoring the mandatory requirement and incentive schemes, etc., need to be addressed. The task force (1999) constituted by NABARD has made recommendations for MFIs. However, a comprehensive policy is required for microfinance in which both FFI and MFI have to take part.

The first task is to define microfinance in terms of quantity and clientele group. At the current level of prices it may be less than Rs.25,000 per poor person. The old classification of priority sector needs to be scrapped, and new focused segments need to be identified on the basis of (i) their role in the economy; and (ii) the inclination level of the FFI towards that segment in the light of transaction cost, risk and profitability (Dasgupta 2002). The scope of mandatory credit then has to be narrowed down to microcredit segment only, and mandate has to be with reference to deposit levels instead of NBC. All the SCBs and foreign banks must then be brought under the ambit of this mandatory credit. The FFIs, however, need to be given free hand in (i) designing delivery mechanism; (ii) formulating personnel policy; and (iii) fixing the interest rate without any interference. Scope has to be created for competition, which only can bring down the interest rate. Tax incentives will encourage the FFIs to go beyond mandatory level.

For better monitoring and planning, a good management information system needs to be developed. Responsibility of collecting and publishing the microfinance information must lie with RBI, which can capture all types of microcredit. Information on NPA and recovery needs to be collected both bankwise and statewise; besides, information on micro savings and micro deposit too must be collected.

At the same time effort is required to develop the NGO-MFI sector, without which, as argued earlier, microfinance cannot spread widely. The task force (1999) has already dealt adequately with this aspect. Licensing procedure of local area banks needs to be made faster and rigorous. Capital requirement needs to be reduced; capital adequacy ratio may be increased. The government has to take cognisance of the task force report seriously, consult RBI, initiate public debate and legislate appropriate policy for developing micro finance sector by creating space for competition in the absence of which India may emerge as a tall economic tower with weak foundations, that in the long run, will not be sustainable.

Acknowledgement

Author is thankful to Sukhbeer Singh and Shainaz Baig for their contribution.

(Rajaram Dasgupta can be reached at dasgupta@nibmindia.org).

References

Basu, K and K Jindal (eds) (2000): *Microfinance: Emerging Challenges*, Tata McGraw Hill Publishing Company, New Delhi.

Central Statistical Organisation (2003): *Statistical Abstract India*, CSO, New Delhi.

National Accounts Statistics, CSO, (various years), Delhi.

Centre for Monitoring Indian Economy (2004): *Agriculture*, CMIE, Mumbai.

Dasgupta, Rajaram (2001): "An Informal Journey through Self-Help Group", *Indian Journal of Agricultural Economics*, Vol 56, No 3.

– (2002): "Priority Sector Lending: Yesterday, Today and Tomorrow", *Economic and Political Weekly*, October 12, Vol 37, No 41.

Dasgupta, Rajaram and K Dinker Rao (2003): "Microfinance in India: Issues, Challenges and Policy Options", *Savings and Development*, Vol 2, No. XXXVII.

National Bank for Agriculture and Rural Development (1999): *Task Force on Supportive Policy and Regulatory Framework for Microfinance*, NABARD, Mumbai.

Progress of SHG Bank Linkage in India, NABARD, Various years, Mumbai.

Parikh, Kirith S and R Radhakrishna (ed) (2004): *India Development Report* 2004-05, Oxford, Delhi.

Pulley, R V *et. al.*, (1987): "Making the Poor Crediworthy: A Case Study of Integrated Rural Development Programme in India", World Bank Discussion Paper 58, The World Bank, Washington, DC, US.

Reserve Bank of India (2000): "All India Debt and Investment Survey, 1991-92", "Incidence of Households", Reserve Bank of India Bulletin, February.

"Report on Trend and Progress of Banking in India", Various years, Mumbai.

"Handbook of Statistics on the Indian Economy", Various years, Mumbai.

Rao, K Dinker (2004): *Swaranjayanti Gram Swarozgar Yojana*, Working Paper, NIBM, Pune.

6

Access, Use and Contribution of Microfinance in India: Findings from a National Study

Frances Sinha

Microfinance is making a significant contribution to both the savings and borrowings of the poor in the country. The main use of microcredit is for direct investment. While the presence of Micro Finance has increased the borrowing options for the poorer clients, it seems not (yet) to have significantly affected the terms and conditions of different informal credit providers.

There is a diversity of approaches to microfinance in India, involving banks, government agencies and NGOs. In most of these approaches, groups are used as intermediaries for financial transactions, though there are different ways of working with groups. On the basis of these differences, the models of microfinance delivery may be broadly classified as the Self-Help Group model (SHGs) and the Grameen replication model (Grameen). Mutually Aided Cooperative Societies (MACS) can be included in the SHG category as the primary cooperatives often consist of smaller SHG type groups which are expected to be relatively autonomous. In both these models, the group is

Source: Economic and Political Weekly, April, 2005, (www.epw.org).

expected to assume joint liability for loans taken by its clients, but there are significant differences in service delivery. A small number of Microfinance Institutions (MFI) also follow the individual banking approach.

Group-based MFIs target women as clients. In the SHG model, groups can mature to be relatively autonomous. Clients organise their own meetings, take decisions on financial transactions, circulate their savings as internal loans, and group leaders/office bearers guided by MFI staff play a significant role. In the Grameen model MFI staff play the main role in weekly meetings and transactions, focusing on a regular annual cycle of credit. Products and interest rates vary between MFIs. SHG loans start at Rs.5,000 with Effective Interest Rate (EIR)[1] usually in the range of 24-27 percent. Grameen loans sometimes have a lower loan size at the start and the EIR is in the range of 32-42 percent. MFIs following the Individual Banking (IB) model generally have male clients, higher loan sizes (Rs.15,000 and above) linked often to economic activities and production cycle-linked individual transactions, including daily collections. There are few independent women clients, though women may be involved in these MFIs through affiliated groups or with add-on savings accounts in client families. The operational features of various models of microfinance are presented in Table 1.

Table 1: Operational Features of Different Microfinance Models in India

Operational Features	SHG Banking	Grameen	Individual
Clients	Primarily women	Primarily Women	Primarily Men
Groups	15 to 20 clients per group into 'centres' of 4-6 groups.	Usually 5 clients per group (organised into 'centers' of 4-6 groups)	Individual clients
Service Focus	Savings and credit	Credit – regular cycle	Credit
Role of MFI Staff	Guide and facilitate (groups may develop autonomy)	Organise (groups dependent on staff)	Organise
Meetings	Monthly	Weekly	Individual transactions – often daily
Savings deposits	Rs.20-100/month	Rs.5-25/week	Flexible
Interest on Savings	Bank rate (4.25 percent) + profit share	6-9 percent	6 percent +
Initial Loan Size	Rs.5-10,000	Rs.2-5,000	Rs.5-15,000 Rs.35,000[a]

Contd...

1 The Effective Interest Rate (EIR) converts all financial costs to the borrower (such as interest, fees) into an annual declining balance interest calculation.

Contd...			
Effective Interest Rate (Usual Range)	24-28 percent	32-38 percent	23-38 percent
Insurance	At a very preliminary stage: usually loan linked, some Life and Health; Sometimes, links to national companies		
Development services	Some Associated Programmes	A Few Small Social Projects	Enterprise Support.
Source: EDA Rural Systems, 2004.			

In this paper we analyse the performance of 20 MFIs from across the country representing all the three models in terms of use of their services by clients. The paper is divided into four sections. The profile of the study sample and methodology are presented in Section I. Section II explores the scope of outreach of microfinance in terms of access and use by clients of services and contribution to the financial needs of client households. Starting with a summary overview of access, the section profiles the use and contribution of different microfinance services: microsavings, microcredit, insurance and non-financial services. Credit use analysis is based on 'actual use' reported by clients for the two years prior to the time of the survey. In Section III we discuss the impact of microfinance service on clients' dependence on informal sources of credit. The Section IV raises some issues on equity in the context of microfinance intervention.

1. Sample and Methodology

The MFIs are selected in such a way that the sample reflects the main models of microfinance delivery and their relative presence in different regions of India. The study covered the states of Andhra Pradesh, Tamil Nadu, Karnataka, Kerala, Uttar Pradesh, Rajasthan, Assam and Manipur. They also represent variations in structure, age, rural/urban presence and microfinance approach (Table 2).

From each MFI, two to six clusters (villages or urban areas) having a minimum of 20 clients were randomly selected from village/area lists. All MFI clients within a cluster were surveyed for a client sample size of at least 130 per MFI (providing a statistical confidence level of 95 percent for each MFI model at the regional level). The sample covers 83 clusters in nine states: 71 rural clusters and 12 urban clusters. The rural clusters reflect varying market contexts, categorised as accessible, remote and semi-rural/semi-urban. Accessible rural clusters are the

Table 2: Profile of Sample MFIs				
Profile	**SHG**	**Grameen**	**IB**	**All**
MFIs from south (No.)	7	3	2	12
MFIs in north and east (No.)	2	3	3	8
All MFIs (No.)	9	6	5	20
Number of sample clients	2,447	1,950	1,216	5,613
Clients per MFI ('000)	23	24	30	13
Active borrowers per MFI ('000)	11	4	23	10
Proportion of clients as active borrowers (per cent)	47	15	76	85
Number of MFIs with client savings	15	4	6	3
Client savings per MFI (Rs. million)	20	14	15	49
Savings per client (Rs.)	1,200	1,000	500	10,100
Loan per client (Rs.)	9,200	6,300	5,300	21,100
Portfolio outstanding per MFI (Rs. million)	39	22	71	30
Repayment Rate (percent)	94	91	97	96

ones with a pucca road and close to a main road, well connected by public transport to the nearest main market, primary and secondary schools and some health facilities (primary health centre, regular visits from government nurse). Remote villages have kuccha access road, infrequent transport facility, distant markets and basic or no education and health facilities. Semi-rural areas are market towns, with population of 4,000 to 25,000 and substantial levels of non farm activity. The urban clusters are located mainly in slum areas of cities – smaller cities such as Tirupati and Guntur in the south, and the larger ones such as Kanpur, Jodhpur and Howrah in the north/east. In each cluster, all MFI clients present at the time of the field visit were interviewed using a questionnaire. In all 4,235 clients in 3,908 households were covered in the survey.

The study was designed in such a way as to capture the effect of poverty status of clients and level of their involvement in microfinance. Poverty assessment was carried out based on wealth rank categories that are comparable across different areas whilst reflecting local perceptions and a range of indicators of economic status (including housing quality, assets, type of employment, incidence of ill health, alcoholism). Five wealth categories – very poor, poor, borderline and non-poor ('self-sufficient' and 'surplus') – were identified through participatory research conducted in all clusters. The assessment, therefore, included more than income poverty.

A number of factors can be thought of as being relevant to measuring the involvement of clients like number of loans availed from MFI, number of loans availed from group (in the case of SHGs), length of association with MFI, total amount of loans availed, amount of savings with MFIs and/or group, regularity in attending group meetings, etc. However, after the field research it was clear that the first three factors, i.e., number of loans from MFI, number of loans from group and length of association with MFI, could sufficiently explain client involvement. Hence, client involvement in a microfinance programme is defined in the study as a function of these three factors, and an index of involvement has been worked out for each client household as follows:

$$\frac{(2 * \text{number of years with programme}) + \text{number of MFI loans} + \text{number of group loans}}{\text{Maximum number of years } (=20) + \text{maximum number of loans (MFI} + \text{group} = 27) \text{ in the entire sample}}$$

The maximum number of years of client participation in the sample has been found to be 20 years and the maximum number of loans availed by any single household, 27. Thus, the numerator for the index is 47 for all households. The index score varies between 0 and 1. Three levels of involvement – 'low', 'medium' and 'high' – are defined by applying a cut-off proportion of one-third to the normalised distribution of index scores.

For each MFI, non-client households were sampled in all the clusters. The non-client: client ratio worked out to be 1:2.8. These households were used as a 'quasi-experimental' comparison group, purposively selected to match the client sample primarily in terms of wealth rank, and secondarily, as far as possible, in terms of other features. The study also used a number of qualitative tools including focus group discussions, case studies (typical cases of clients and dropouts), key informant interviews and interviews with other financial players (like managers of the nearest bank branch, moneylenders, etc.).

II. Microfinance Services

Nearly all group-based MFIs have a stated policy that only one member per family could become a client. Table 3 shows that this is mostly, but not always, observed in practice. In the IB model, 3 MFIs with men as primary clients actively

Table 3: Number of Clients per Household in MFI

Model	Clients	Households	Percent of Households with		
			1 client	2 clients	3-4 clients
SHG/Grameen	3,160	3,020	96.4	3.1	0.5
IB	1,075	888	83.4	13.3	3.3

Note: Excludes one IB MFI which does not offer a savings product.

Source: Survey data, for the entire period of membership with MFI.

encourage additional family members (often women) to open savings accounts Hence, 17 percent of the IB sample households have more than one member as an MFI client.

Apart from borrowing from sample MFIs, 3 percent of client households have borrowed from other microfinance programmes (like groups supported by other NGOs or groups promoted under government schemes). Such clients are more in the south – 5 percent of the sample – where there is a concentration of microfinance activity. As against this only 0.5 percent of clients in the northern sample had loans from other programmes.

Microcredit

Households borrow for a variety of different purposes. We have classified these as investment use (referring to directly productive use in non-farm enterprise, animal husbandry, and agriculture) and other household purposes (covering a range of family expenses, including medical costs, debt redemption, housing, household purchases, family events and education). Of these, health, debt redemption and costly family events (marriages) often come as financial shocks for the household and involve an element of risk. Loans taken for such purposes are, hence, treated as risk loans in subsequent discussion.

Average credit intake for the overall sample does not vary much between clients and non clients both in terms of amount and shares, except in the case of investment (Table 4). However, the share of borrowing shows considerable variation between clients and non-clients in the very poor category, indicative of the increased access to credit by MFI members.

Table 4: Average Borrowing by Use (over 2 years)

Use	Client		Non-Client	
	Average	Per Cent of Total Borrowing	Average	Per Cent of Total Borrowing
Total credit	12,500		10,000	
Investment	9,000	39 (29)	9,000	29 (10)
Medical	2,000	28 (33)	2,500	28 (39)
Emergency/house repair	1,000	20 (33)	1,000	15 (29)
Housing	10,000	19 (20)	10,000	15 (12)
Food/HH spend	2,000	15 (19)	2,000	12 (13)
Marriage	10,000	14 (16)	12,500	13 (10)
Other life cycle events (birth, death, etc.)	2,000	14 (15)	2,000	12 (14)
School	2,000	12 (10)	2,000	9 (5)
Household assets	2,850	11 (7)	3,000	8 (5)
Debt repayment	5,000	10 (13)	10,000	4 (5)

Note: The data pertains to 19 MFIs, excluding the sector cooperative in which the average investment borrowings are extremely high. Bracketed figures are for the wealth category 'very poor'.

Source: Survey data.

In the SHG model, group loans account for about 70 percent of the members' borrowings. Table 5 presents the data on average loans by MFI model and client involvement level. Average loan size is smaller for group-based MFIs compared to the IB model, even in the case of high involvement clients. This reflects the differential credit absorption capacity of clients across models.

Table 5: Client Borrowing by Model and Level of Involvement

Clients' Borrowing	SHG	Grameen	IB
From MFI			
Number of Borrowers (No.)	491	1,246	607
Average Borrowing (Rs.)	6,000	7,000	15,000
Of high Involvement Clients (Rs.)	10,000	11,000	31,000
From Group			
Number of Borrowers (No.)	953	140	77
Amount per Borrower (Rs.)	3,000	1,400	10,000
Of high Involvement Clients (Rs.)	4,000	1,800	13,750

Source: Survey data.

As reported by clients, 77 percent of the loans overall have been used for productive investment. This percentage varies between 57 percent for the SHG model and 86 percent for IB/Sector cooperative (Table 6). Interestingly, except in the case of IB/Sector cooperative, there is a perceptible difference between the actual reported use of loans and what the MFIs have in their records. Insistence of Grameen MFIs on productive use of loan is reflected in the high percentage of loans recorded as investment in the official records. However, only 79 percent of Grameen loans were reported by clients as being so used. The gap between reported and recorded use of credit is very small in the case of IB and specific cooperative which also emphasise on production credit. Table 6 reflects the fact that MFIs following SHG model give more freedom to the members in the matter of credit use.

Table 6: Percentage of Investment Loans by Model

	Percentage of Loans Used for Investment			
	All	SHG	Grameen	IB
Use Reported by Clients	77	54	79	86
Use Recorded by MFI	85	67	97	90

Note: Internal group loans are not included.

Source: Survey data.

Credit Use across Wealth Ranks

Use of microcredit (both MFI and group) for different wealth ranks is analysed in Table 7. The data reinforce the fact that compared to the better-off, poorer

Table 7: Use of Microcredit across Wealth Rank Categories

	Overall	Very Poor	Poor	Borderline	Non Poor
Number of clients (No.)	3,908	309	1,110	1,347	1,142
Average loan size (Rs.)	7,000	5,000	6,000	6,900	10,000
Percentage of use Direct investment	63 (21)	47 (16)	56 (14)	64 (24)	72 (30)
Risk needs	17 (39)	29 (47)	22 (45)	17 (37)	10 (27)
Housing	7	9	8	6	7
Education	3	1	2	3	3
Other household purchases	10 (26)	14 (26)	11 (27)	10 (23)	8 (28)
Total	100	100	100	100	100

Note: Bracketed figures are percentages for SHG model MFIs.

Source: Survey data.

households borrow smaller amounts and are more likely to borrow for household expenses. This is most evident in the SHG model where clients have more flexibility in loan use.

Microsavings

Microsavings are primarily a means of collateral for micro credit, and in some IB, MFIs savings deposits may be adjusted for final instalment of repayments. Over time they are also a form of 'saving up'.[2] Group-based MFIs tend to 'lock in' the savings and a client may have to leave the programme if she decides to withdraw her savings.[3] As high as 97 percent of client households (after excluding members of the IB model which does not offer any savings product) have savings with the MFI programme (Table 8). In the group-based MFIs where clients are required to save amounts varying from Rs.20 to Rs.50 per month, savings per head works out to be Rs.600 to Rs.1,700. In the IB sample, with higher savings amounts and more product options, average saving amount works out as Rs.3,700, increasing to Rs.9,300 for high involvement clients. Savings in the group-based MFIs, – indicating, perhaps, the facilitative role of their organisational dynamics – nevertheless contribute 74 percent to total household savings compared to a 47 percent contribution for IB households. Figure 1

Table 8: Microsavings of Client Households

Microsaving	Sample	SHG	Grameen	IB
Clients who save (percent)	97	97	99	97
Average savings (Rs.)	1,000	1,100	600	3,700
Contribution to household savings (percent)	70	74	74	47
High involvement clients				
Average savings (Rs.)	1,600	1,700	1,200	9,300
Contribution to household savings (percent)	71	79	73	45

Source: Survey data for 19 MFIs, excluding 1 IB MFI with no savings product.

2 Rutherford (1999) outlines the following three forms of saving (1) Saving up – depositing small amounts now in exchange for a lump sum to be enjoyed in the future; (2) Saving down – a lump sum enjoyed now in exchange for a series of savings, or repayment instalments, to be made in the future; (3) Saving through – a lump sum to be enjoyed at some unspecified future time in exchange for a series of savings made both now and in the future. MFI savings are a mechanism which reflects all these forms, although the withdrawal of savings (from 'saving up') can lead some clients to drop out of the programme. See Rutherford, S (1999), *The Poor and Their Money*, Oxford University Press, New Delhi.

3 See EDA Rural Systems (2004), "The Maturing of Indian Microfinance: A Longitudinal Study", Chapters 7 and 10.

indicates that savings with MFIs form the major part of total household savings for all clients, except non-poor client households who have access to alternative saving mechanisms.

Figure 1: Share of Microsavings in Household Savings

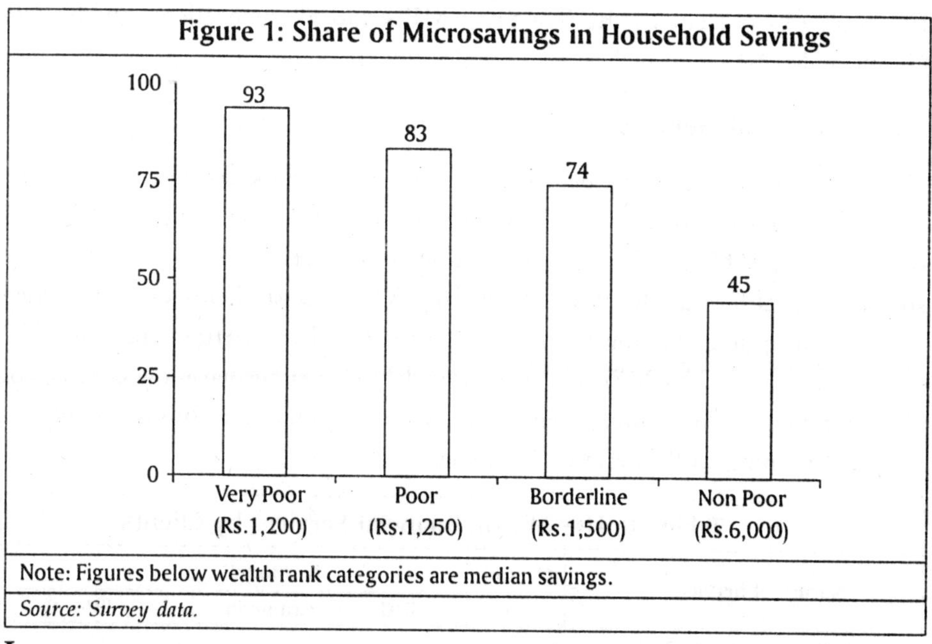

Note: Figures below wealth rank categories are median savings.

Source: Survey data.

Insurance

Insurance coverage as a service through the MFIs is at a nascent stage. Overall 11 MFIs in the sample offer life insurance products covering 48 percent of clients (Table 9). Life insurance coverage is the highest in the Grameen sample

Table 9: Access to Insurance through Microfinance

Clients	Sample	SHG	Grameen	IB
No. of sample MFIs offering life insurance	11	4	2	5
No. of clients in these MFIs	2,217	681	765	771
Percentage with life insurance	48	35	78	29
Clients in sample with asset insurance (percent)	5	4	3	12
No. of sample MFIs offering asset insurance	8	5	2	1
No. of clients in these MFIs with asset loan	603	151	43	409
Percent borrowers with asset insurance	32	40	100	22

Source: Survey data.

(78 percent) and lowest in the IB sample (28 percent). Only 8 MFIs offer asset insurance products. This is usually linked to loans that are taken for purchase of assets like animals and houses. Across models 32 percent of clients have asset insurance (40 percent in the five SHG MFIs and all such clients in the two Grameen MFIs).

Non-Financial Services

Only six MFIs (five SHG model MFIs and one sector cooperative that follows the IB model) offer enterprise related support and five (four SHG model MFIs and one Grameen MFI) are linked to local development programmes, mainly in the spheres of health and education (Table 10). Whilst most clients of group-based MFIs receive initial training in group procedures and transactions, non-financial programmes offered by MFIs or by associated NGOs either have low coverage or do not target microfinance clients. The sector cooperative, interestingly, has provided training to 85 percent of its clients.

Table 10: Use of Non-financial Services by Clients

Nature of Service	Overall	By Model		
		SHG	Grameen	IB[a]
Enterprise training/support				
MFIs offering service	6	5	–	1
No. of clients	1,047	879	–	168
Percent of clients reporting use	5	3	–	85
Linked Social Development Programmes/Projects				
MFIs linked	5	4	1	–
No. of clients	1,014	766	248	–
Percent of clients reporting use	5	9	3	–

Note: [a] data relating to the sector cooperative among IB MFIs.

Source: Survey data.

III. Informal Credit Sources

Informal financial markets across India offer a wide range of products to meet local demand. Finance companies and chit funds offer both savings and credit services, where as local money-lenders and pawnbrokers offer credit with varying terms and conditions, usually with an option of one-time repayment. Interest rates depend on the amount borrowed and the urgency of the situation (smaller the amount and greater the urgency, higher is the interest rate). Late repayment invites compounded interest. Friends and relatives are also an important source of credit, which is often interest free.

In this we analyse the extent of use of informal sector financial services by MFI client households. Table 11 which summarises the access, terms and

Table 11: Access to Informal Credit Sources by Microfinance Clients

Informal Credit Providers	Access by Client Households (Percent)	Loan Terms and Conditions		
		Loan	Effective Interest Rate (Percent)	Loan Amount and Repayment Conditions
Moneylenders/ Private financiers/ Pawnshops/Pawn-brokers	36	Any purpose loan	26 – 200	Rs.500 –1 lakh; payable in 3-24 months usually in a one-time balloon repayment.
		Weekly loan	41 – 200	Rs.1 – 10,000 repayable daily/ weekly up to a maximum of 100 days.
		Gold/Silver loan	26 – 61	Up to Rs.50,000 or 50 percent of gold value or 25 percent of silver value payable in a balloon repayment.
ROSCAs/Chit funds	2	General loan	19 –57	Usually Rs.2,000 Up to Rs 1 lakh (urban); up to Rs.30,000(rural) – monthly
Friends/relatives	32	General loan	0	Up to Rs.50,000 (urban); up to Rs.20,000(rural) with a flexible repayment option.

Source: Survey data and FGDs.

conditions of informal sector borrowing shows that 36 percent of the client households have borrowed from money-lenders over two years prior to the survey. Nearly one-third borrowed from personal informal sources (friends/relatives). These are usually at little or no cost. A small percentage of client households reported having taken loans from ROSCAs or 'chittis'. These have been mostly found in the southern states.

Moneylenders and pawnshops are more costly in direct terms, sometimes charging very high annual interest rates of 60-200 per cent, especially, when the amounts are small and (<Rs.5,000) are urgently required. The survey data reveals a significant difference between regions in the average annual interest rate paid by households on their borrowings from costly informal sources or CIS (Table 12). The rates are found to be very high for the sample of the north/east (especially rural) in comparison with the southern sample. This difference probably

Table 12: Annualised Average Interest on Loans from CIS

Region		Average Interest (Percent)	Average Loan Size (Rs.)
South		41	11,000
	Rural	39	11,000
	Urban	47	11,410
North/East		66	6,000
	Rural	69	5,400
	Urban	60	8,000

Note: (1) Average interest rate is weighted against the average amount borrowed; (2) Independent means test shows statistically significant difference between south and north for clients.

Source: Survey data.

reflects two features: the greater variety and outreach of informal money-lenders/finance companies in the south, and the difference in amounts borrowed. As we mentioned earlier, smaller loans are offered at higher interest rates. Households in the southern region borrow larger amounts compared to the north/east.

Interestingly, the study found a lower incidence of borrowing from CIS by client households compared to non clients – 38 percent and 58 per cent respectively (Table 13). Also, the percentage of households borrowed at very high interest rates ($\geq$ 60 percent per annum) is comparatively lower (14 percent) in the case of

Table 13: Sources of Credit by Wealth Rank

Status Rank	Wealth	No. of Borrowers	Share in Credit by Source			
			MFI (Percent)	Formal (Percent)	CIS (Percent)	PIS (Percent)
Client	Overall	3,674	87	8	38 (14)	36
	Very poor	290	88	5	36	31
	Poor	1,032	86	3	40	34
	Borderline	1,282	87	10	42	35
	Non-poor	1,070	87	12	31	40
Non-client	Overall	1,069	–	17	58 (23)	55
	Very poor	100	–	8	63	52
	Poor	348	–	9	66	48
	Borderline	361	–	20	62	57
	Non-poor	260	–	27	40	63

Note: Bracketed figures are percentage of households borrowing at very high interest rates of over 60 percent per annum.

Source: Survey data.

clients as compared to non clients (23 percent). Twenty per cent of such households among clients and 35 per cent among non-clients belong to scheduled castes/scheduled tribes. It thus appears that though involvement in microfinance has not affected access to formal credit (individual loans), it has helped clients reduce dependence on moneylenders and other costly sources of credit.

The terms and conditions of different informal credit providers in the MFIs' operational areas have remained more or less the same after the latter's intervention, in some cases, for several years. The former operate on the basis of their local knowledge – lending to people they know, or introduced by people they know. Locally accessible – often virtually at the doorstep of the borrower – they can provide loans of varying amounts, without formal guarantees or surety, and with relatively flexible repayment schedules. For these reasons, clients continue to approach moneylenders for credit. MFIs are not geared to operating in this way. Although most MFIs compete on cost, they usually lack the flexibility, timeliness and adequacy of funds that informal sources can offer. Moreover, MFI outreach relative to the local population and overall credit needs is not high. For both these reasons, even where MFI clients have reduced their use of informal financial sources, the overall demand has not gone down substantially.

Contribution of Different Providers to Credit Needs

As we have seen above, households depend on multiple sources to meet their fund needs. In the case of clients of various microfinance programmes, MFIs have come to constitute a convenient source of credit flow. In terms of its contribution, microcredit contributes 42 percent of aggregate client household borrowings reported over the previous two years (Table 14). The balance comes mainly from moneylenders, while some funds come from Personal Informal Sources (PIS) – friends and relatives. For the client households, this proportion is almost similar across the different wealth rank categories. The contribution of CIS to the total borrowings of the non-clients is much higher at 43 percent than that for clients (30 percent).

Table 14: Distribution of Household Borrowings by Source (over two years)

Wealth Rank	Total Borrowings (Rs. Million)	MFI	CIS	PIS	Bank
All Clients	89.67	42	30	18	10
Very poor	3.07	46	28	20	5
Poor	16.38	47	34	15	4
Borderline	25.11	39	35	19	7
Non poor	45.10	41	26	18	14
Non-clients	20.18	–	43	34	22

Source: Survey data.

Credit Providers: A Comparative Perspective

Having explored the different credit needs and providers, we now attempt to compare alternative credit providers based on feedback from clients and non-clients canvassed through FGDs. We have scored this feedback to arrive at the relative position of microfinance in the credit market (Table 15 and Figure 1). While this is an illustrative explanation, it serves to show how Microfinance is rated in relation to other major providers like banks (higher on all parameters barring cost) and moneylenders (higher on cost and repayment terms). MFIs score less well on credit purpose and timeliness, and sometimes on repayment terms. Overall, groups emerge as a preferred option. As groups mature and the savings fund accumulates, members are able to quickly access internal group loans of varying amounts and for varying purposes at a relatively low cost, while the interest goes back into the group fund.

Table 15: Comparison of Alternative Credit Providers

Different Credit Providers	Client Assessment in Terms of					
	Purpose	Amount	Access	Speed	Cost	Repayment Terms
MFI	Average, sometimes inflexible	Small medium	Variable	Slow	Low to moderate	Moderately flexible
Group	Very flexible	Small+	Good	Quick	Low to high	Flexible
Friends/relatives	Very flexible	Small to medium	Average	Quick	Low to moderate	Flexible
Pawnbrokers	Very flexible	Small large	Good	Very Quick	Moderate to high	Flexible
Moneylenders	Average	Small to large	Average	Quick	Moderate to very high	Not flexible
Banks	Average	Large	Low	Slow	Moderate	Moderately flexible

Source: FGDs.

IV. Some Issues in Equity

Equity issues are explored in this section by comparing access and quantum of micro-borrowings by wealth rank of client households. The data indicates uniform access by all wealth ranks in the Grameen model, but significantly lower access by poorer clients to MFI loans in the SHG and IB models. Interestingly, this pattern is reversed in the case of group loans, suggesting that poorer clients may be considered less creditworthy for MFI loans whereas they are able to access (smaller) group loans that match their credit absorption capacity.

In group-based microfinance programmes, an issue often raised is whether group leaders use their position to influence group decisions (mainly in loan allocation) in their favour. Group leaders tend to be better off than other group members and more educated, the latter being a requirement if they are to handle and manage group records and accounts. Nevertheless, one-third of group leaders in our sample were poor or very poor, and many had no schooling – over half in the Grameen sample and one-third in the SHG sample (Table 16).

Table 16: Profile of Group Leaders – SHG and Grameen Models

Wealth Rank	N	Very Poor	Poor	Borderline	Non-Poor
Group Leaders	375	6	29	38	26
Other Members	2,537	10	34	37	18
Schooling	N	No schooling	Completed primary	Completed secondary	Graduate
Group Leaders	375	42	47	9	2
Other Members	2,537	65	29	4	1

Note: Relates to households with only women clients.

Source: Survey data.

The data comparing access and quantum of borrowings by group leaders show a pattern in favour of group leaders. They are likely to access more microcredit and also to borrow more than other members (Table 17). This is partly due to group leader households being more likely to have more than one client (7 percent compared to 3 percent of other households), which is against the programme norm of one client/household in the group-based MFIs. However, over time, older members begin to catch up, especially in group-borrowings. Though the difference still remains, it is considerably reduced.

Table 17: Access to Microcredit-Comparing Group Leaders and Others

Model	Loans	Overall	Recent (<2yrs)	Older (2-4yrs)	Oldest (>5 yrs)
SHG	Average number of MFI loans	1.6	2.0	1.5	1.3
	Amount borrowed by group leaders.	10,000	6,000	10,000	10,000
	Amount borrowed by other members.	5,000	5,000	6,000	9,000
Grameen	Average number of MFI loans	1.2	1.2	1.1	1.2
	Amount borrowed by group leaders.	10,000	6,000	12,000	14,000
	Amount borrowed by other members.	7,000	5,000	10,000	10,000

Notes: Client households with male clients are excluded as men's loans tend to be higher.

Data relates to seven SHG MFIs and two Grameen MFIs where members' savings are circulated as group loans.

Source: Survey data.

V. Concluding Observations

Microfinance is making a significant contribution to both the savings and borrowings of the poor in the country. The main use of microcredit is for direct investment. There is of course some fungibility, depending on household credit requirements at the time of loan disbursement, despite MFI insistence on loan use for enterprise which is the most pronounced in the Grameen model. The performance of the SHG model is exceptional in providing a savings-based mechanism for internal group credit to meet household needs. This mechanism also serves (though not always) to facilitate access to credit by poorer clients, who are more likely to need small amounts of credit for immediate household purposes but appear less creditworthy for larger MFI loans.

While the presence of Microfinance has increased the borrowing options for the poorer clients, it seems not (yet) to have significantly affected the terms and conditions of different informal credit providers. In terms of accessibility, capability to provide loans to meet borrowers' demand, willingness to lend without security, and flexibility of repayment schedules, they are still considered valuable even by microfinance clients. Most of the MFIs are not yet ready to offer this extent of

Figure 2: Credit Providers: A Scored Comparison

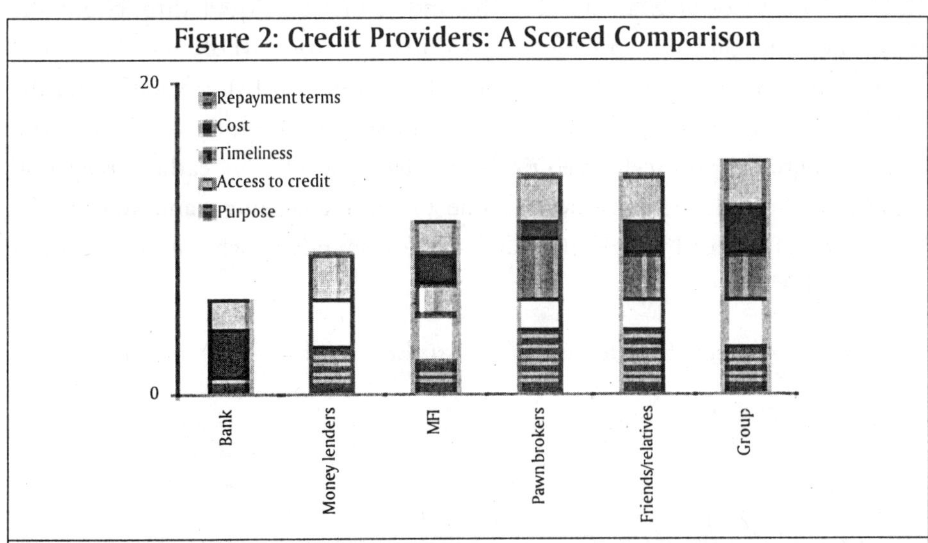

Note: Scale 4 = maximum; 3 = high; 2 = average, 1 = somewhat; 0 = nil. Maximum possible score = 20.

Source: FGDs.

flexibility and provide timely and adequate credit, though many of them do compete on cost. Another reason why Microfinance has not been able to make a significant mark on the local financial landscape is their relatively low outreach – relative to the local population and to overall credit needs.

The practical absence of non-financial support services is perhaps surprising given the ongoing debate about 'Microfinance plus' services. It partly reflects the trend in MFIs to focus on finance as part of their drive towards attaining organisational sustainability. But even when MFIs do have a link to social development programmes, their coverage is relatively limited and notsystematically integrated with the Microfinance programme.

Acknowledgement

This paper draws on some of the findings of a baseline study undertaken for the SIDBI Foundation for Micro-Credit (SFMC). Many people have contributed to the design and implementation of the study. The research was undertaken by a team from EDA Rural Systems, Gurgaon, including Amitabh Brar, Meenal Patole, Nand Kishor Agrawal and Nishant Tirath. We were associated with David Hulme (IDPM, University of Manchester, UK) and Jennefer Sebstad throughout the study, and were guided by an Advisory Committee from SIDBI, DFID, NIRD (S Rajakutty), SEWA (Renana Jhabvala), IIM Ahmedabad (M S Sriram) and the JNU (Amit Ray). I thank all for very substantive contributions, and also thank Tara Nair both for the excellent editing of the paper and for her earlier association in parts of thestudy. Thanks are also due to the management and staff of the MFIs who participated in the study and 4,000 respondents who are the focus of the research.

(Frances Sinha can be reached at francessinha@edarural.com).

7

Impact of Self-Help Groups on Formal Banking Habits

Mahendra Varman P

Deposits are foundations upon which banks thrive and grow. The twin objectives of a commercial bank, i.e., acquiring deposits and advancing credit cannot be attained without good banking habits of the people. Therefore, people's banking habits seem to be a major factor that affects sustainability of the banks concerned. In microfinancing in India, Self-Help Groups (SHGs), which recently came into existence as informal organisations, are linked to banks and its members are mainly women. This paper makes a modest attempt to examine whether there is any association between the growth of SHGs and the increase in female bank deposit accounts and whether SHGs have a tendency to influence account holding in formal banks. In the process, the paper tries to trace the socio-economic factors that determine deposit and credit account holdings (banking habits) in formal banks, among individuals and households.

Source: Economic and Political Weekly, April 23, 2005, (www.epw.org).

I. Introduction

Deposits are foundations upon which banks thrive and grow. They are unique items on a bank's balance sheet that distinguish them from other types of business organisations. The ability of a bank's management and staff to attract checking and savings accounts from business and individuals is an important measure of the bank's acceptance by the public. Deposits provide most of the raw materials for bank loans and thus represent the ultimate source of bank profits and growth. Deposits generate cash reserves, and it is out of the excess cash reserves a bank holds, that new loans are created (Rose 1998). Important indicators of management effectiveness in any bank are whether or not deposited funds have been raised at the lowest possible cost and whether enough deposits are available to fund those loans the bank wishes to make. This last point highlights the two key issues that every bank must deal with in managing its deposits: (i) where can the bank raise funds at the lowest possible cost; (ii) how can management ensure that the bank always has enough deposits to support the volume of loans; and (iii) other financial services demanded by the public. However, it is very essential to know that the twin objectives of a commercial bank, i.e., acquiring deposits and advancing credit cannot be attained without good banking habits of people. Therefore, banking habits seem to be a major factor that affects profitability, productivity and sustainability of banks.

Banks are the backbones of trade and commerce, playing the intermediary role of capital formation and supply thereof. Unless the rural population, constituting more than 72 percent of the total population of the country, are brought under the banking network, banks as well as economic objectives will remain unrealised. Therefore, a planned course of action should be formulated to habituate rural people to banking transactions. Banks' credit creation, i.e., how much banks can lend and at what rate of interest depends upon the cost of deposits and the amount of deposits acquired. More important is the number of deposit accounts, because it ensures that the probability of account holders withdrawing cash at a time decreases as the number of deposit account increase, thereby creating an advantage for banks in terms of increasing the size of the loanable fund.[1] So the higher number of deposit accounts the greater is the advantage to banks. The number of deposit accounts depends on the number of

[1] This logic comes from the banker's assumption that not all depositors withdraw cash at one point of time.

deposit account holders. If the number of deposit account holders have to be increased then banking habits have to be inculcated in higher proportion of the population.

However, there are social, economic and psychological barriers in the way of inculcating banking habits. Rural people with low income and lack of knowledge of available banking facilities can do little for the growth of banking habits on their own. For this a concrete effort is needed to be taken up by society, the government and by bankers themselves to enhance the standard of rural people with regards to banking habits. Due to high transaction cost; the perception of risk in serving the rural population who are unable to provide collateral, articulate their case for or submit proper deposit/loan proposals, the urban orientation of banks, the lack of flexibility in terms of operation, ignorance and the lack of exposure to banking services, etc., banks were finding it difficult to inculcate banking habits and provide access to banking services, which proves to be costly (Madeshwaran and Dharmadhikari 2001). If it is difficult for formal banks to change their strategy such that inculcation of banking habits and accessibility of banking services to the poor increase, is it not possible for the upcoming microfinancing SHGs to do so, such that majority of the poor can access formal banking services?

II. Achievements of Microfinance SHGs

Microfinance programmes are important institutional devices for providing small credit to the rural poor in order to alleviate poverty. Microfinancing programmes through SHGs, introduced and expanded by Non-Governmental Organisations (NGOs) in several parts of India, have the potential to minimise the problem of inadequate access of banking services to the poor (Rajasekhar 2000). They can also influence savings. Likewise many studies (Rajasekhar 2000, Kumaran 2001, Hashemi 1996, Lathif 2001, Kaladhar 1997, Majumdar 1997, NABARD 2002) highlight that SHGs have inculcated savings habits in the poor. Reviewing the available literature reveals a limited number of studies being done on microfinancing SHGs and their impact on rural poor, especially with reference to India. Many of the studies (Lathif 2001, Khandkar 2000) reveal that increased availability of micro-credit to the poor through microfinancing SHGs will enable rural households to take up larger productive activities, empower the poor women, decrease the dependence on exploitative local moneylenders and increase savings.

Khandkar (2000) while estimating the impacts of microfinance on savings and borrowings found that micro-credit not only increases involuntary savings, but also induces voluntary savings. A study by National Bank for Agriculture and Rural Development (NABARD), which covered 560 SHG member households from 223 SHGs across 11 states, showed many positive results on the impact of participation of rural poor in the SHGs. It shows that there have been perceptible and wholesome changes in the living standards of SHG members in terms of ownership of assets, borrowing capacities, income generating activities, income levels and increases in savings. It traces out that almost all members developed savings habits in the post-SHG situation as against only 23 percent of households who had this habit earlier. It indicates that the average annual saving per household registered an increase over threefold [NABARD 2002]. However, the study nowhere mentions the basis of measurement of the change in savings and borrowing habits. Whether they are measured in terms of the number of bank deposits and credit account holders or in terms of any other forms of savings and borrowings is not clear. Other studies (Khandkar 2000, Rajasekhar 2000, Kumaran 2001, and Lathif 2001) measure the impact of microfinance on household savings and borrowings in SHGs only and not in formal banks.

Since most of the SHGs are linked to formal banks for their deposit and loan mobilisation, it is a researchable issue, as to whether the informal microfinance intervention through SHGs has had any impact on the deposit and credit accounts in the formal banks. With this backdrop, this study tries to examine the association between the operation of SHGs and formal banking habits,[2] especially among the females. In the process, it traces out the socio-economic factors that determine individual and household formal banking habits and analyses the impact of SHG operation on individual and household banking habits

III. Data Sources and Methodology

The major sources of secondary data used for analysing the trends and patterns of various banking variables among the states and over the years are: various publications of Reserve Bank of India (RBI), NABARD, All India Census and

2 Formal banking habits of an individual/household is to operate banking transactions with an element of regularity. Regularity here refers to mean creation and establishment of economic relationship by the person with a bank through opening up a bank account and continuing thereafter. For the purpose of the study a bank customer has been defined as having either a savings bank account or a time deposit.

Centre for Monitoring Indian Economy (CMIE). Population information for the year 2001 was taken from the 'Provisional Population Totals' published by Census of India, 2001. The projected population for the intermediate years, starting from 1996 to 2000 were taken from 'Population Projections for India and States, 1996-2016' published by Census of India, 1991. Since the available secondary data was insufficient to answer the questions evolving out of the discussion, required data was collected from two appropriately sampled villages of Tamil Nadu. A purposive sampling of two villages has been done wherein the villages surveyed needed to have certain characteristics so that the impact of micro-credit SHGs on banking habits could be clearly captured. Accordingly, two villages, viz., Kavarayapatty and Pottapatty were selected as sample areas. Though the villages are sampled ones, the number of cases came from a census that was conducted in both the villages. Kavarayapatty has a total population of 103 households and Pottapatty has 114. Out of the two villages surveyed one village (Kavarayapatty), happens to be a less experienced village in terms of the number of years of operation of SHGs (two years). This village belongs to Dindigul district. The other village (Pottapatty) had a comparatively larger exposure to SHG operation (six years) and it belongs to Madurai district of Tamil Nadu. Information regarding household characteristics, economic status, banking habits and participation in SHGs were some of the important variables that were needed for our analysis. A structured questionnaire was used to collect such information from households and individuals. Primary data was collected during the period January to February, 2003. All the questions in the questionnaire were of the objective type. On this basis, Sections IV, V and VI empirically trace out and explain the relationship between bank accounts and the growth of SHGs, and the criteria by which one can assess the impact of SHGs on bank account holdings.

IV. Trend of Banking Habits during the Period 1996-2001[3]

Banking statistics, till 1995, give information on deposits and credit (number of accounts as well as amount) of all scheduled commercial banks according to states. But from the year 1996, banking statistics issues have subdivided deposits according to ownership category, viz, individuals – males and females (Table 2). Thus, there is scope to analyse the trend and pattern of individual deposit accounts of scheduled commercial banks in various states and regions.

---

3 The data regarding deposit accounts, categorised on the basis of the gender of the account holder is available only from the year 1996. For a comparison here, the period of reference is taken from 1996.

Table 1: Statewise Number of Accounts per 1,000 Population, 1996 to 2001

States/Regions	Credit Accounts per 1,000 Population						Deposit Accounts per 1,000 Population					
	1996	1997	1998	1999	2000	2001	1996	1997	1998	1999	2000	2001
Northern Region	43.82	45.05	41.85	45.26	48.79	55.96	510.1	520.1	525.4	533.6	546.6	559.8
Haryana	45.28	45.22	41.93	43.78	50.18	51.04	465.6	467.4	477.0	482.9	500.5	506.2
Himachal Pradesh	43.21	46.04	44.97	56.18	58.32	57.33	588.9	593.1	605.1	625.3	640.5	647.2
Jammu and Kashmir	34.52	27.61	27.99	30.19	29.89	34.26	385.7	415.5	423.9	433.8	452.3	475.4
Punjab	55.37	57.44	51.22	56.86	64.01	66.60	743.1	754.0	763.9	782.2	793.3	791.6
Rajasthan	36.12	38.54	36.32	35.50	37.17	37.35	250.5	254.0	264.3	272.0	280.1	290.0
Chandigarh	72.77	87.30	70.17	104.34	165.39	189.81	1692.7	1746.0	1770.4	1853.6	1902.5	1797.1
Delhi	57.87	59.13	54.72	69.19	69.33	127.29	1208.3	516.9	1204.7	1189.1	1212.1	1278.8
North-eastern Region	42.44	41.59	39.90	33.79	33.77	27.53	279.2	288.8	280.1	285.4	269.9	273.0
Assam	38.01	38.18	36.12	28.53	27.33	23.95	278.2	296.0	301.7	299.3	290.9	291.7
Tripura	119.02	102.39	100.99	90.25	108.74	68.94	325.9	338.7	306.5	328.9	313.4	314.0
Eastern Region	55.34	49.85	49.41	41.47	43.11	36.90	298.0	307.8	306.0	307.8	311.4	321.4
Bihar	60.98	55.12	53.49	43.75	41.14	24.95	314.1	320.6	304.8	306.3	310.8	221.1
Orissa	76.80	65.40	66.68	59.44	64.70	54.43	227.6	241.0	242.7	250.3	252.9	267.2
Sikkim	38.23	36.51	35.20	27.75	31.45	25.90	220.2	218.3	235.0	236.6	231.3	247.9
West Bengal	58.44	54.13	54.00	44.93	49.86	42.78	413.5	428.5	438.7	438.8	443.1	453.0
Central Region	38.81	38.45	36.27	34.45	34.92	35.74	285.4	316.3	326.2	330.7	333.3	349.7
Madhya Pradesh	52.41	51.58	47.05	43.05	44.65	36.08	324.5	327.2	332.4	327.9	332.0	268.7
Uttar Pradesh	40.73	40.46	38.76	37.41	37.55	35.88	359.5	368.2	381.5	390.0	392.5	381.8
Western Region	42.81	43.05	40.64	46.59	47.25	44.62	425.6	428.4	431.4	437.3	447.6	468.1
Goa	74.21	77.85	74.55	81.85	94.49	85.57	1559.5	1523.1	1563.2	1621.2	1685.3	1776.8
Gujarat	39.37	41.22	40.36	39.37	42.12	43.01	388.2	400.8	408.5	413.9	429.2	451.4
Maharashtra	44.17	43.55	40.37	49.82	49.25	44.95	428.5	426.9	426.6	432.5	439.6	458.2
Southern Region	91.21	91.76	89.36	88.93	93.43	88.40	464.4	458.1	460.6	470.2	482.6	499.9
Andhra Pradesh	86.38	87.02	82.36	84.22	86.64	82.54	344.1	351.4	358.6	372.4	388.9	406.3
Karnataka	82.23	83.82	79.51	82.11	96.50	84.14	480.9	473.1	470.4	477.2	487.9	513.1
Kerala	105.61	111.07	114.23	108.61	111.47	116.21	617.9	616.9	632.6	641.5	645.8	645.5
Tamil Nadu	97.43	94.44	93.63	90.35	89.94	84.96	517.0	492.6	486.0	493.9	505.6	525.3
Pondicherry	91.37	93.44	88.51	97.55	95.50	90.36	599.7	614.1	654.1	634.9	672.6	691.1
All-India	**55.28**	**54.25**	**52.26**	**51.02**	**53.03**	**51.07**	**382.4**	**386.8**	**390.2**	**395.9**	**402.6**	**417.5**

Source: RBI, Basic Statistical Returns, 1996 to 2001.

The number of credit accounts overall is decreasing over the years and across the states. It can be seen from Table 1 that, on an average, the credit account per 1,000 population[4] for all-India is also declining over the years. The all-India average was 55 accounts per 1,000 population in the year 1996, it gradually declined and came down to just 51 credit accounts per 1,000 population by the end of year 2001. A state level analysis reveals that the range of variation in credit account holdings is much wider. Whereas the lowest is Assam, around 40 credit accounts per 1,000 population, the highest is in Kerala, which has always been above 100 credit accounts. Except for a few states such as Haryana, Punjab, Chandigarh, Delhi, Gujarat and Kerala, all other states show a downward trend of credit accounts per 1,000 population over the years. The states which come

Figure 1: Flow Chart Indicating the Procedure for Access to Formal Credit

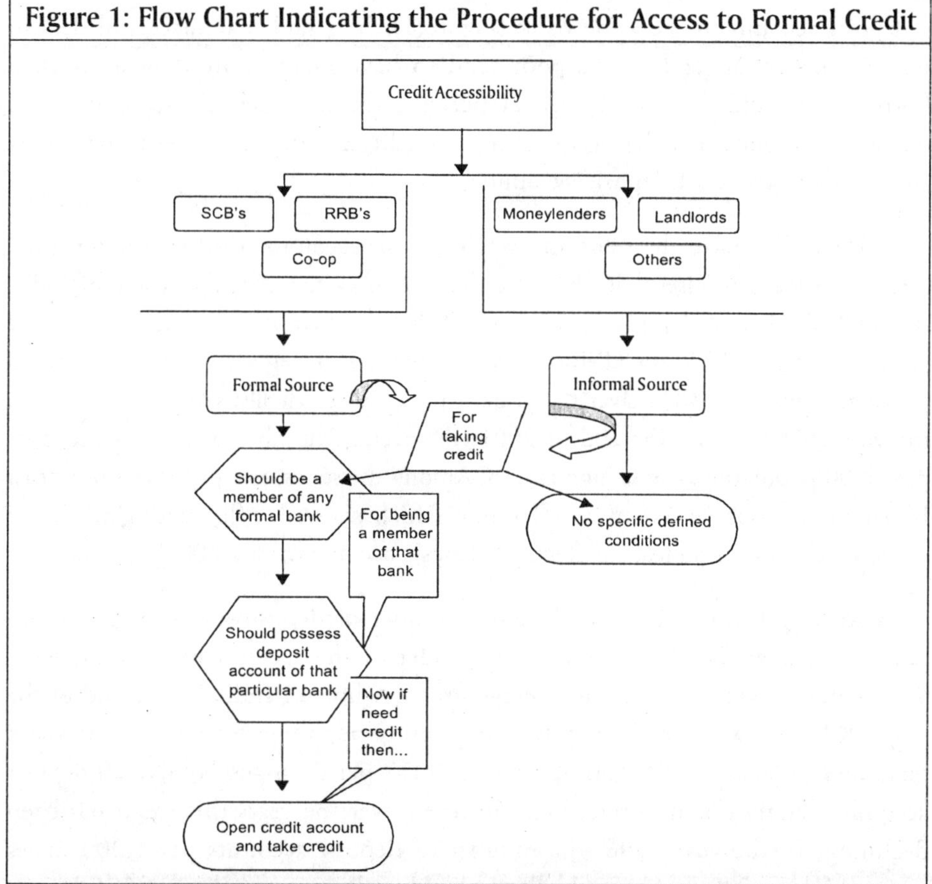

4 For standardising the number of deposit and credit accounts, the total population is taken into account since there is no age limit to hold an account. This method is followed everywhere in this paper.

under the higher number of credit accounts per 1,000 population are Haryana, Himachal Pradesh, Punjab, Chandigarh, Delhi, Tripura, Orissa, Goa, Andhra Pradesh, Karnataka, Kerala, Tamil Nadu, and Pondicherry. It is interesting to observe that most of the states that have contributed to a higher number of credit accounts per thousand population (on an average, more than 50) seem to be economically and socially developed states. So, what determines the number of credit account holding per 1,000 population among the states?

The credit account holding in formal banks is conditional on the deposit account holding. For holding a credit account, an individual or a group (SHG) should be a member of the bank. Most important is that an individual or group can be a member of that particular bank only on the condition that they possess a deposit account in the same bank (Figure 1). It is said that successful deposit taking banks that lend to the poor tend to have many more depositors than borrowers (Pischke *et. al.,* 1996). Hence, the trend of deposit accounts has a major role to play in analysing the trend of credit accounts. Now, let us have look at the trend of overall deposit accounts.

Table 1 also traces the trend of overall deposit accounts per 1,000 population, statewise. One can observe in the table that on an average, for the whole of India, the total number of deposit accounts per 1,000 population is increasing over the years. In the year 1996 the all-India average number of deposit accounts per 1,000 population was just 382. Over the years it increased gradually, going up to 395 in the year 1999, and by the end of 2001, the average number of deposit accounts per 1,000 population was as high as 418. Among the states, except for few northeast Indian states such as Assam and Tripura, which showed a fluctuating trend, all other states had an increasing trend of deposit accounts per 1,000 population.

A striking feature appears when the number of deposit accounts per 1,000 population is analysed on the basis of gender of the account holder (Table 2). The analysis reveals that, on an average for the whole of India by the end of the year 2001 there were nearly 575 deposit accounts accruing to males per thousand males, which is above the national average (417 per thousand) of overall deposit accounts per thousand population. However, over the years this trend has been declining. In the year 1996, the number of deposit accounts per 1,000 males was as high as 598 but it gradually declined and came to a low of 575 by the

Table 2: Statewise Number of Deposit Accounts per 1,000 Males/Females, 1996 to 2001

States/Regions	Deposit Accounts per 1,000 Males						Deposit Accounts per 1,000 Females					
	1996	1997	1998	1999	2000	2001	1996	1997	1998	1999	2000	2001
Northern Region	794.5	776.4	764.55	757.88	751.37	737.29	269.8	280.4	289.3	295.7	303.3	308.1
Haryana	736.6	708.0	710.37	708.07	683.80	675.07	244.4	260.0	261.6	269.7	283.4	271.0
Himachal Pradesh	856.1	799.7	802.70	804.47	785.54	866.01	304.0	333.3	324.2	330.3	339.4	383.3
Jammu and Kashmir	630.5	652.5	635.93	637.24	656.00	641 .63	200.6	218.8	231.7	232.2	226.8	262.5
Punjab	1110.6	1079.0	1071.21	1079.25	1060.83	1010.17	402.9	438.7	453.7	471.4	484.4	486.3
Rajasthan	420.1	411.5	419.26	423.35	421 .69	412.40	106.7	110.9	118.0	123.7	127.9	130.9
Chandigarh	2555.0	2356.7	2335.51	2446.09	2445.59	2256.88	1073.1	1266.1	1190.9	1165.8	1124.7	1036.4
Delhi	1797.9	1762.5	1621.34	1510.07	1466.85	1534.86	755.1	639.9	712.9	694.7	700.3	766.3
North-eastern Region	446.9	447.9	421 .60	425.22	381.66	384.40	124.1	128.4	123.4	123.3	121.1	127.8
Assam	448.4	465.8	464.31	459.22	426.89	417.33	117.5	124.6	126.3	123.5	125.9	128.9
Tripura	470.9	477.9	410.10	425.50	386.51	446.17	131.9	138.2	126.5	131.8	123.5	155.6
Eastern Region	494.4	508.3	496.89	492.39	481 .60	476.70	135.6	134.7	135.2	137.0	142.9	136.8
Bihar	416.4	421.2	397.15	392.23	385.23	326.83	115.4	112.5	104.3	103.7	105.8	96.6
Orissa	390.7	407.3	400.09	409.13	400.76	41 1 .55	76.9	82.0	88.8	92.6	97.5	102.9
Sikkim	342.4	315.8	316.36	302.82	315.07	364.31	104.8	117.6	129.0	132.3	112.4	99.1
West Bengal	639.1	663.4	666.41	657.00	640.98	666.44	188.5	187.0	195.4	199.3	210.4	194.0
Central Region	495.9	498.6	499.90	498.94	479.80	495.22	148.7	148.3	155.6	157.3	165.3	170.3
Madhya Pradesh	385.1	395.6	387.01	380.27	362.92	387.01	110.0	92.4	97.0	95.1	110.3	123.1
Uttar Pradesh	546.9	546.0	551 .92	553.48	533.32	535.06	167.6	175.6	184.1	187.4	191.7	191.1
Western Region	657.9	648.1	640.14	628.94	623.56	625.21	215.3	219.4	223.5	236.9	247.5	250.7
Goa	1926.1	1814.6	1739.71	1671.81	1774.72	2160.10	957.8	920.2	965.0	1011.7	953.6	1236.4
Gujarat	604.1	616.9	623.44	607.95	605.52	622.32	170.6	170.5	173.7	190.1	202.4	222.3
Maharashtra	666.2	645.2	629.70	622.23	613.25	606.03	226.2	233.0	236.7	247.9	258.5	250.8
Southern Region	690.2	660.9	652.17	654.22	652.23	670.67	243.9	249.8	253.4	263.5	273.7	283.6
Andhra Pradesh	532.4	532.5	536.29	545.24	549.36	570.30	159.3	165.1	169.7	183.0	197.5	205.6
Karnataka	724.3	689.6	671 .39	665.85	655.42	682.37	257.9	265.7	264.7	274.7	287.2	296.8
Kerala	885.0	854.2	862.37	856.89	844.20	842.99	367.4	381.0	389.3	402.4	406.8	410.5
Tamil Nadu	752.1	692.4	667.50	672.17	674.35	694.66	268.3	268.1	271.7	277.3	282.6	298.4
Pondicherry	888.4	842.3	843.93	807.84	784.03	906.09	262.5	294.0	309.6	286.5	330.4	400.3
All-India	598.3	591.8	584.01	580.81	569.71	574.96	191.8	195.1	199.2	205.0	212.8	215.6

Source: RBI, Basic Statistical Returns, 1996 to 2001.

end of year 2001. On the other hand, the number of deposit accounts per thousand females is increasing over the years. In the year 1996, there were only 192 deposit accounts per 1,000 females, which gradually increased to 205 in the year 1999 and went up to 216 accounts per 1,000 females by the end of year 2001. Though in absolute terms the deposit accounts per thousand males is much higher than it is for females, it is quite interesting to see that the deposit accounts per thousand males is decreasing while that for females is increasing over the years. What is the reason for this trend?

The trend of increasing number of deposit accounts per 1,000 population observed overall is on account of the increase in the trend of deposit accounts per 1,000females. Since in India almost all SHG members under the micro-credit programmes are females, could it be attributed to them? Is there any relation between micro-credit and this observed trend? Before testing the relationship we shall briefly discuss its emergence and the Indian experience with micro-credit programmes.

V. Growth of SHGs in India

Given the background of incapacity or disinterest of the formal banking sector to serve the needs of low income clientele, and the increased demand for credit from rural households, how can the gap between demand and supply of funds in the rural economy be bridged? What mechanisms could be used for this? Interestingly, the formal sector took the initiative to develop a supplementary credit delivery mechanism by encouraging institutional arrangements outside the financial system like SHGs with non-governmental organisations acting as facilitators or intermediaries. The beginning was made with NABARD's pilot project in Karnataka (1986-87) of linking SHGs with formal banks, mediating through NGOs (Tara 1999). This project known as the SHG-bank linkage project was expected to be advantageous to the banking sector from both angles of fulfilment of social goals (like reaching out the poor) and achieving operational efficiency (by externalising part of their transaction cost). The improvement in the SHG-Bank linkage programme is seen in Table 3. In the initial period in 1992-93, just 255 SHGs were linked to banks with Rs.2.89 million as refinance from NAB ARD. In a span of couple of years, in 2000-01, it rapidly expanded, linking 2,34,843 SHGs and refinancing of Rs.4007.46 million. If we see the statewise outreach, then the SHG-bank linkage programme covered 412 districts in 25 states and two union territories.

In Table 3, the growth of SHGs over the years was discussed. In Table 4 we can observe the growth rates of SHGs and SHGs per 1,000 females across the states during the period 1998-99 to 2000-01. This table reveals that though all listed states have a positive growth rate of SHGs, there is a wide variation among states. States such as Andaman and Nicobar, Gujarat, Karnataka, Kerala, Orissa and Uttar Pradesh have comparatively lower growth rates (below 100) whereas other states excel and have a SHG growth rate of above 100. However, it is not necessary that the states, that have a lower growth rate will have a lower number of SHGs. The states with lower growth rates might have begun their SHG-bank linkage programme at an earlier stage, so that it may already have sufficient linkages and further linking is quite difficult. Most of the states with lower growth rates will have a lower number of SHGs linked in the recent years compared to states that have ahigh growth rate. For example, we can observe from the table that, by the end of 2001 Kerala had 1,826 SHGs linked to banks but its growth rate was just 19. Goa has a comparatively lower number of SHGs linked to banks (27) in the same period, but its growth rate is as high as 160. Thus, one has to be careful in deriving inferences from this table. In the same table the growth rate of SHGs per 1,000 females, a co-variate of growth rate of SHGs, is also given. We can observe a trend similar to that of the growth rate of SHGs level.

Table 3: Growth of SHG-Bank Linkage Programme (1992-2001)

Year	Cumulative	
	No. of Groups	Amount of Loan (Rs. in Million)
1992-93	255	2.89
1993-94	620	6.53
1994-95	2122	24.45
1995-96	4757	60.58
1996-97	8598	118.36
1997-98	14317	237.95
1998-99	32995	520.60
1999-00	114775	1501.26
2000-01	234843	4007.46

Source: NABARD 2002.

By linking SHGs with formal banks, both banks as well as SHGs will be benefited. The involvement of SHGs with banks could help in overcoming the problem of high transaction costs in providing credit to the poor by passing on some banking responsibilities regarding loan appraisal, follow-up, recovery, etc, to the poor themselves. In addition to that, the character of SHGs and the relationship between members offers a way to overcome the problem of collateral, excessive documentation and physical access. By this, banks gain from the new risk-free credit market and a potential surplus sector (SHGs) and at the same time SHGs enjoy the advantage of larger and cheaper resources (Dasgupta 2001). However, SHGs have to open a deposit account in the bank to get cheaper loans under the micro-credit programme.

With this knowledge on formal banking habits and micro-credit SHGs at a national level, let us examine whether there exists any relationship between the number of SHGs per 1,000 females and the number of deposit accounts per 1,000 females. This provides the incentive to proceed further in testing the impact of micro-credit SHGs on banking habits of individuals and households.

VI. Relationship between Growth of SHGs and Bank Deposit Accounts

By close observation we can see that the growth rate of accounts per 1,000 females and SHG per 1,000 females are moving together. So, there might be a close relationship between the growth of SHGs and the number of bank accounts held by the females. It is necessary to support this argument empirically, but a bias might creep in if we are taking the growth rate of SHGs per thousand females as such, to associate with growth rate of bank deposit accounts per thousand females in each state. This is because those states that started the SHG-bank linkage programme earlier would have an overall low growth rate, and those states which started the programme at a later stage would have a high growth rate (Table 4). To minimise this bias, the initial period (1998-99), for which statewise data on the SHG-bank linkage programme is available, is taken and split into two categories on the basis of the median of the series. It takes only those states which had considerable numbers of SHGs per 1,000 females to be associated with growth rate of number of bank accounts per 1,000 females. The median of the series happens to be 0.018 and therefore, those states which had SHGs per 1,000 female greater than 0.018

Table 4: Growth Rates of SHGs and SHGs per 1,000 Females across the States (1998-2001)

States	Growth of SHGs over the Years				Growth of SHG/1,000 Female over the Years			
	1998-99	1999-00	2000-01	Growth Rate	1998-99	1999-00	2000-01	Growth Rate
Andaman and Nicobar	3	9	10	82.57	0.018	0.051	0.061	86.84
Andhra Pradesh	6579	29242	84939	259.31	0.179	0.786	2.258	255.39
Assam	10	46	156	294.97	0.001	0.004	0.012	288.79
Bihar	121	857	1846	290.59	0.003	0.018	0.046	324.17
Goa	4	14	27	159.81	0.005	0.018	0.041	180.97
Gujarat	879	1345	1375	25.07	0.038	0.057	0.059	24.70
Haryana	4	107	334	813.78	0.000	0.012	0.034	783.19
Himachal Pradesh	133	48	1166	196.09	0.041	0.014	0.390	210.24
Jammu and Kashmir	2	53	137	727.65	0.000	0.011	0.029	725.62
Karnataka	2002	3167	5627	67.65	0.079	0.124	0.217	65.51
Kerala	1291	1709	1826	18.93	0.079	0.104	0.112	18.59
Madhya Pradesh	461	1533	3174	162.39	0.012	0.040	0.110	200.29
Maharashtra	1058	3029	5509	128.19	0.024	0.069	0.119	121.14
Orissa	975	2021	3850	98.71	0.056	0.114	0.213	95.49
Pondicherry	15	144	150	216.23	0.028	0.257	0.308	233.26
Punjab	1	18	71	742.61	0.000	0.002	0.006	728.69
Rajasthan	465	526	2513	132.47	0.019	0.021	0.093	123.84
Tamil Nadu	2618	7671	16676	152.38	0.087	0.251	0.541	149.99
Uttar Pradesh	1464	7744	5457	93.07	0.019	0.097	0.069	92.59
West Bengal	554	2317	5351	210.79	0.015	0.061	0.138	205.40
All-India	**18639**	**61600**	**140194**	**173.97**	**0.039**	**0.128**	**0.283**	**167.91**

Source: NABARD (2002).

have been taken into analysis. And for these states the association between the per capita number of SHGs in the year 1998-99 and the growth rate of per capita accounts held by females (1996-2001) statewise[5] is positive (Figure 2). The states which have a lower number of SHGs per thousand females in the initial stages, such as Rajasthan, Meghalaya, UP and Maharashtra also had a lower growth rate of number of bank accounts per thousand females. On the other hand, those states which had a higher per capita number of SHGs per thousand females in the initial stages such as Tamil Nadu, Karnataka, Kerala, Orissa, etc, had a higher growth rate of number of bank accounts per thousand females.

Figure 2: Cluster Analysis Showing the Association between Growth Rate of SHGs and Growth of Female Bank Deposit Accounts in India

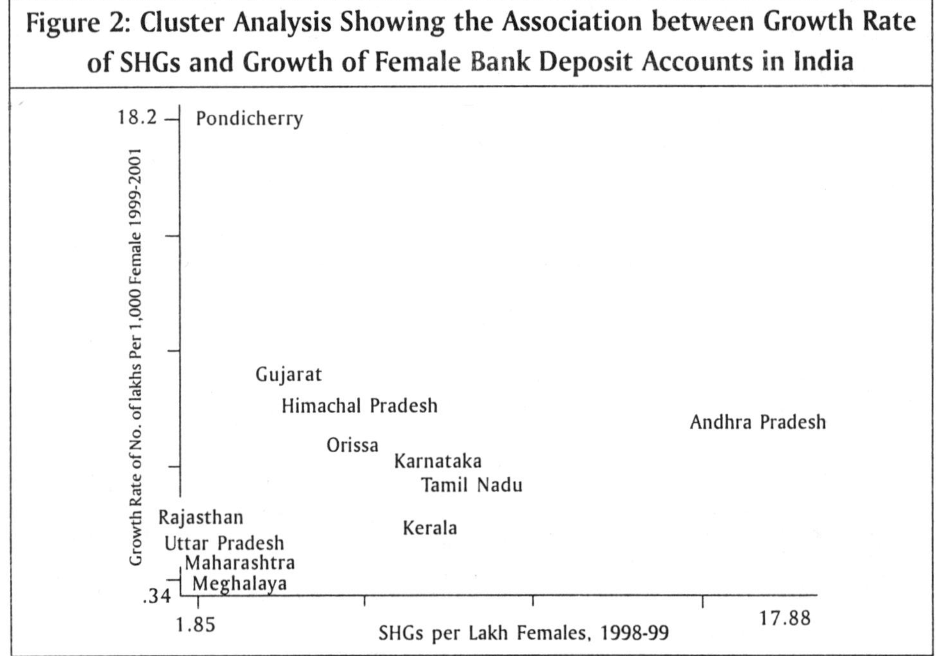

With this association at a macro level, it is necessary for us to test the relationship between SHG membership and bank account holdings of females with the help of micro-level data. As we have found that, on an average, per 1,000 population there are only around 400 deposit accounts with wide disparities among states. What determines per capita account holdings? What percentage of the population has a relationship with banks? Which segment of the population are they? Who are the excluded ones? Does the micro-credit programme reduce this exclusions? If so in what way?

[5] The statewise data for number of SHGs linked with banks is available only from 1998-99 onwards in the NABARD publication, NABARD and Microfinance.

Since the available secondary data is not sufficient for answering these questions, it is necessary to analyse banking habits and its determinants at a micro-level through an appropriate primary survey. Further, the other impacts of micro-credit programmes have to be analysed to answer some of the questions that arose in this discussion and to know the impact of micro-credit programmes on banking habits. In response to this, Section VII deals with the analysis of micro-level survey data.

VII. Determinants of Individual and Household Banking Habits

This section tries to test the observed positive association between the growth rate of SHGs and bank deposit accounts pertaining to females at a micro-level. We have taken two sample villages with a difference in the number of years of experience in operating SHGs. As it has been mentioned earlier, these two sample villages are Kavarayapatty, which is a less experienced village in terms of the number of years of operation of SHGs (two years) while the other village is Pottapatty with a comparatively higher number of years of experience (six years). In the course of the analysis, we also try to trace out the determinants of banking habits among individuals and households.

Summarising the characteristics of sample villages, there are some similarities between the villages such as the composition of religion (around 97 percent Hindus), dependent population (around 58 percent), agricultural orientation of the people (around 47 percent), etc. Apart from these similarities there are a few striking differences between the two villages in the composition of education, caste, employment status of the people, per capita landholding, per capita income/household income, etc. Though there is a larger proportion of SC population and landless households in Pottapatty, there is a higher proportion of educated and self-employed people there. At the same time, Kavarayapatty is better off in respect of landholding assets and type of houses owned. These striking differences might affect the distribution and composition of SHG membership and bank account holding status of individuals and households in each village, which we will be analysing in the forthcoming section.

Taking each of these dissimilar socio-economic variables that exist between the two sample villages and associating them with the bank account holding status (deposit/credit account) of individuals and households of the respective villages (using the simple method of cross tabulations), we can arrive at the factors that influence the bank account holding status of individuals and households. The cross tabulations indicate that variables such as sex, occupation, educational status of the individual/household head, household landholding, SHG membership of individuals and SHG leadership experience influence individual/household account holding status. The different variables that affect an individual and household credit and deposit account holdings are clear from Table 5.

But as Table 5 indicates that through cross tabulation there is a close correspondence between variables such as sex, occupation, education, family status,

Table 5: Covariates of Account Holding Status with Respect to Individuals and Households

Covariates of Individual's Deposit Account Holding Status	Covariates of Household's Deposit Account Holding Status	Covariates of Individual's Credit Account Holding Status	Covariates of Household's Credit Account Holding Status
Sex	–	Sex	–
Occupation	Occupation	Occupation	Occupation
Education	Education	Education	Education
Family Status	–	Family Status	–
Income	Per capita income	Income	Per capita income
SHG Membership	–	–	–
SHG Leadership	SHG Leadership	–	–
–	Total landholdings	–	Total landholdings

Notes:

1. For individual's account holding status the Covariates are with respect to the respective individuals. But for household's account holding status, the Covariates are with respect to the head of the household. For example, education implies the educational status of household head.
2. The codes are given in ascending order starting from zero for the first category.
   Sex: Male/female.
   Occupation: Unemployed/agricultural labour/wage labour/self-employed/regular salaried.
   Education: Uneducated/primary/secondary/higher secondary/above higher secondary.
   Family status: Other members of the family/head of household.
   Per capita income per month in Rs.100-350/351-750/above 750.
   Total household landholdings in acres: 0.01-0.05/0.06-2.50/above 2.50.
   SHG membership: Non-member/member.
   SHG Leadership: Never lead/lead at least once.

Source: Primary Survey Data.

income, SHG membership, SHG leadership and account holding status. It is not clear which variable affects it the most and what the magnitude of the influence of each variable is when all variables interact simultaneously. In this regard, cross tabulations have their limitations. Hence to confirm the magnitude of impact of each variable on account holding status, we use a binary logistic regression analysis (Logit model).

The binomial logistic regression model expresses a qualitative dependent variable as a function of several explanatory variables, both qualitative as well as quantitative (Hamilton 1992). If P is the probability of account holding, then

$$p = [1 + e^{\{-\beta X\}}]^{-1}$$

Where 'β' is a vector of the unknown coefficients and 'X' is a vector of covariates that affects the probability of holding an account. Thus, the general logistic model can further be expressed as

$$\text{Log}_e [P_i / \{1 - P_i\}] = \beta X = \sum_{j=0}^{k} \beta_j X_{ij}$$

which expresses the log odds of account holding status as a linear function of the explanatory variables. In this analysis, we have defined the binary dependent variable that is assigned the value of one if the individual/household possesses at least one bank account and zero for those who do not possess even one bank account. It shows the simultaneous effect of socio-economic variables on the likelihood of household/individual bank account holding status. The results suggest that not all the variables which had a significant association with account holding status independently, are significant predictors of account holding status. Some socio-economic variables such as occupation, which had significant association with the account holding status of both the households as well as individuals, were found to be insignificant when all variables are taken simultaneously.

However, the logistic regression analysis (Table 6) revealed that there is a positive relationship between the number of years of education and deposit account holdings both at individual as well as household level. The individuals and

Table 6: Results of Logistic Regression Indicating the Simultaneous Effect of Socio-Economic Variables on Household and Individual Account Holding Status

Account Holding Status	Individual Deposit Account Holding	Household Deposit Account Holding	Individual Credit Account Holding	Household Credit Account Holding
Variables		Coefficient(s) Based on Reference Category		
		Gender Exp(β)		
Males	1.5519	1.4049	0.8178	0.6682
		Family Status (Head/Other Members) Exp(β)		
Head of Household	10.2057***	–	24.2400***	–
		Educational Status Exp(β)		
Primary	0.9440	1.2565	0.6079	0.7457
Secondary	0.6706	0.824	0.5633	0.8414
Higher Secondary	4.3331**	7.4303**	1.5474	1.6726
Above Higher Secondary	15.6540***	7.4507*	1.4106	1.2808
		Occupational Status Exp(β)		
Agricultural Labour	0.3990	0.1142	0.3519	0.4808
Wage Labour	0.5019	0.1928	0.8548	1.1672
Self-Employed	2.3403	0.5910	1.6720	1.2404
Regular Salaried	1.7265	0.6458	1.1511	1.1335
		Landholding Status		
0.06 to 2.50 Acres	–	3.6687**	–	1.7525
Above 2.50 Acres		5.3336***	–	2.8670*
		Income Group Exp(β)		
Middle Income Gender	1.0682	2.7018	0.7008	0.8390
High Income Gender	4.8874*	9.8453*	4.2629	3.3820
		SHG Membership Exp(β)		
SHG Member	2.9976	15.8488	0.0062	0.0165
		SHG Leadership Exp(β)		
Lead At least Once	23.7217***	2.2813	239.9494	135.1558
		Model Fitness Measures		
-2 Log likelihood	308.060	154.176	174.556	139.0311
Model χ^2	232.278***	82.474***	94.008	23.816
Measure of Overall Predictability	94.42	86.18	96.95	88.02
N (No. of Cases)	985	217	985	217
Degrees of Freedom (df)	1	1	1	1

Notes: 1. Exp (β) Coefficients = Odd Ratios.

2. The reference category for 'Gender' is 'Female', 'Uneducated' for 'Educational Status', 'Unemployed' for 'Occupational Status', 'Low Income Group' for 'Income Group', 'Other Than Head' for 'Family Status', 'SHG Non-Member' for 'SHG Membership', 'Never Lead' for 'SHG Leadership Status'.

3. (***) Significant at all levels, (**) Significant at 5 per cent level, (*) Significant at 10 per cent level.

Source: Primary Survey Data.

households with education above higher secondary have 15 and seven times more likely to hold a bank account as compared to the uneducated. Similarly, the income of individuals and the per capita income of households does show a positive relationship with deposit account holding status of individuals and households. As income increases the likeliness of aperson/householdpossessing adeposit account increases. Apart from that, at an individual level the likeliness of an individual possessing a deposit account is more if he/she is the household head and/or if that person is or has been a leader of a micro-credit SHG atleast once. Family status also significantly influences the individual's deposit account holdings. If the person is the household head, then he/she is 10 times more likely to possess a bank credit account than other members of the family. At the same time, another factor, which affects household's deposit account holding status is the total land-holdings. It shows that an increase in the size of the landholding of a household will lead to an increase in the likeliness of that household possessing at least one deposit account.

Of all the predictors, an individual's leadership experience happens to be the most dominant factor in individual account-holding status, followed by education level. An individual who has been a leader of SHG is 23 times more likely to hold a bank account than a person who has not. The coefficient is very large and leadership experience makes a huge difference in deposit account holding status of an individual. With respect to household deposit account holding status, the per capita income of the household plays a dominant role. High-income groups are 9.8 times more likely to hold a bank account than a low-income household. On the other hand, with respect to bank credit account holding status of individuals and households, not many variables are significant. While individual credit account holding is influenced by family status, household credit account holding status is influenced significantly by its total landholding. Households with land above 2.5 acres are 2.8 times as likely to possess at least one bank credit account as persons who have land ranging from 0.01 to 0.06 acres. Similarly, at the individual level, if the person is the household head, he is 24 times more likely to possess a bank credit account than other members of the family.

VIII. Impact of Micro-Credit SHGs on Individual Banking Habits

The analysis of trends of banking habits at the macro level in Section IV revealed that per capita deposit accounts for females were increasing over the years, while this was not so for males. It was also observed that the overall number of deposit accounts was increasing, which gave the conclusion that the use in overall deposit accounts was due to the increase in deposit account holding of females. Since micro-credit SHGs in India are comprised of women, the analysis in Section VI exhibits a moderate association between the growth of per capita SHGs of females and the growth rate of per capitabank deposit accounts of females at a macro level. In order to test this observed association between the growth of SHGs and deposit account holding of females in recent years, this section tries to investigate the main objective of examining the impact of micro-financing SHGs on individual bank account holding status with respect to females.

To start with, we shall look at the percentage of the population who are members of SHGs. Table 7 shows that, on an average of both villages, 25.4 percentage of the total women folk are members of SHGs. Individually taken, Pottapatty village, which is more experienced in terms of the number of years of SHG operation, has higher proportion of its women involved in SHGs. Now we can see the association of SHG membership with bank account holding status.

It can be seen in Table 8 that 13.6 percent of SHG members have bank accounts. Out of these account holders 33 percent belong to Kavarayapatty the rest of the 67 percent belongs to Pottapatty. What leads to the variation in account holding status with respect to SHG members themselves? Let us try to trace, what determines the account holding of any SHG member.

The association between SHG members and bank deposit accounts holdings reveals that Kavarayapatty has only 11 percent of its members holding bank deposit accounts. On the other hand Pottapatty has a comparatively higher proportion of its SHGs members possessing bank deposit accounts (16 percent). Hence we can say that, as the number of years of SHGs existing in a particular place increases the likeliness of its members having bank deposit accounts becomes higher. But the above relationship may not hold good because many members might have opened their account before joining the group. Therefore, we cannot say that this is the

Table 7: Distribution of Female Population[6] on the Basis of SHG Membership and Bank Deposit Account Holding

Village	SHG Membership and Account Holding			
	Account Holding Status	Non-Member	Member	Total
Kavarayapatty	Without Account With Account	126 (79.2) 3 (42.9)	33 (20.8) 4 (57.1)	159 (100) 7 (100)
Total		129 (77.7)	37 (22.3)	166 (100)
Pottapatty	Without Account With Account	129 (75.0) 1(11.1)	43 (25.0) 8 (88.9)	172 (100) 9 (100)
Total		130 (71.8)	51 (28.2)	181 (100)

Note: Figures in parenthesis are percentages of respective counts to total account holders.

Source: Primary Survey Data.

Table 8: Distribution of Bank Deposit Account Holders among SHG Members According to Point of Time of Opening Account

Village	Bank Deposit Account Status				
	Without Account	With Account	Opened Before	Opened After	Total
Kavarayapatty	33 (89.2)	4 (10.8) {33.0}	1 (2.7) [25.0]	3 (8.1) [75.0] {30.0}	37 (100)
Pottapatty	43 (84.3)	8 (15.7) {67.0}	1 (2.0) [12.5]	7 (13.7) [87.5] {70.0}	51 (100)
Total	76 (86.4)	12 (13.6) {100}	2 (2.3) {100}	10 (11.4) {100}	88(100) {100}

Note: Figures in round brackets indicate percentages of respective counts to total SHG population in the respective village. Figures in square brackets indicate proportion to total account holders in the respective village only. Figures in flower brackets are proportion to total within each column variable.

Source: Primary Survey Data.

impact of SHGs on its members. If this claim has to be tested we need to see the point of time at which the member joined the SHG and the time she opened the account. If the individual's number of years as SHG member is greater than the number of the years of the existence of her bank account, we can claim that account opening by that member is an impact of the operation of the SHG.

6 For analysis of SHG members in comparison with the non-members, only the female population aged 15 years and above has been taken into consideration since the SHG members are exclusively adult females.

In Table 8, a considerable amount of the impact of higher exposure to SHGs can be seen. We can see the proportion of people who have opened their account before and after joining SHG to total account holding SHG members. Firstly, we observe that the operation of SHG itself has had much impact on bank account holding, irrespective of years of operation. In both the villages at least 75 percent of the SHG member account holders have opened their accounts only after joining the SHG. The impact of the duration of operation of the SHG is much clearer. Kavarayapatty, which is a less exposed village to SHG operation has 75 percent of its members opening accounts after joining the SHG, whereas in Pottapatty, which is a more experienced village in this regard, as many as 88 percent of SHG member account holders opened their accounts after joining the SHG.

By analysing the distribution of SHG members overall according to their leadership position and bank account holdings in Table 9, we can say that among SHG members 14 percent have their own individual bank accounts apart from their group account. But it is important to notice that out of those SHG members who have individual bank accounts, 83.3 percent of them have been in a position of leadership in the group. Leadership gives the members more insight into banking culture, as they are responsible for operating the group accounts. They are exposed fully to the operations of the bank and know how useful it is to have transactions with banks.

Table 9: Distribution of SHG Members According to Leadership and Bank Account Holdings

Leadership Status	Account Holding Status		
	Without Account	With Account	Total
Not Lead at all	55 (96.5) [72.4]	2 (3.5) [16.7]	57 (100)
Lead	21 (67.7) [27.6]	10 (32.3) [83.3]	31 (100)
Total	76 (86.4) [100]	12 (13.6) [100]	88 (100)

Note: Figures in round brackets are percentages of respective counts to total SHG in each group of leadership status. Figures in square brackets indicate proportions to total of each account holding status group.

Source: Primary Survey Data.

Being a leader in an SHG gives members incentives to have a relationship with banks directly. Regions more experienced with SHG operations will have more number of members with leadership experience, of SHG operation, as the leadership is given to each member in rotation. So more years of experience of SHG operation in an area, leads to more rotation and more SHG leaders and a higher increase in bank account holdings is higher. If the rotation of leadership is quicker, we can expect more number of bank accounts in that region. Since the rotation in Pottapatty village is very slow (once in a year and that too haphazard), the impact seems to be less than expected, though there is certainly some impact.

IX. Summary and Conclusion

In conclusion, the study has revealed that microfinance SHGs in India, which are classified under informal organisations, intentionally or unintentionally help formal banks by increasing the number of accounts by inculcating banking habits in rural people, especially the women. On the other hand, it has been found that banking habits are a positive function of the years of experience of microfinance programmes through SHGs in that particular area. The analysis also reveals that being a member in SHGs and, more importantly, having leadership experience in SHGs greatly influences the bank account holding. Leadership experience in SHGs would improve an individual's banking habits much more than simply membership. If the leadership position of each SHG is systematically rotated over appropriate time, such that each one in the group has a leadership experience, people will have more exposure to formal banking systems. This will inculate banking habits at a higher magnitude, thereby enhancing the advantage of banks in acquiring large numbers of deposit accounts.

(Mahendra Varman P, Lecturer Econometrics University of Madras, Chennai. He can be reached at eco_varman@hotmail.com).

References

Adams, D W and J D Von Pischke (1992): "Micro-Enterprise Credit Programmes: Deja vu", *World Development*, Vol. 20, No. 10.

Dasgupta, Rajaram (2001): "Working and Impact of Rural Self-Help Groups and Other Forms of Microfinancing: An Informal Journey through Self-Help Groups", *Indian Journal of Agricultural Economics*, Vol. 56, No. 3, July-September.

Hamilton, Lawrence C (1992): *Regression with Graphics: A Second Course in Applied Statistics*, California.

Hashemi, Syed M, Sidney Ruth Schuler and Ann P Riley (1996): "Rural Credit Programmes and Women's Empowerment in Bangladesh", *World Development*, Vol 24, No. 4, pp 635-53.

Kaladhar, K (1997): "Microfinance in India: Design, Structure and Governance", *Economic and Political Weekly*, October 18, pp 2687-2706.

Khandker R Shahidur (2000): "Savings, Informal Borrowings and Microfinance", *Bangladesh Development Studies*, Vol. 26, Nos. 2 and 3, June-September.

Kumaran, K P (2001): "Self-Help Groups of the Rural Poor in India: An Analysis", *National Bank News Review*, April-June, pp 31-37.

Madheswaran, S and Amita Dharmadhikary (2001): "Empowering Rural Women through SHGs Lessons from Maharashtra Rural Credit Project", *Indian Journal of Agricultural Economics*, Vol 56, No 3, July-September, pp 427-43.

Majumdar, N A (1997): "Overhauling the Somnolent Rural Credit System", *Economic and Political Weekly*, October 18, pp 2707-10.

Mark, M Pitt (2000): "The Effect of Non-Agricultural Self-Employment Credit on Contractual Relations and Employment in Agriculture: The Case of Micro-Credit Programmes in Bangladesh", *Bangladesh Development Studies*, Vol. 26, Nos. 2, 3, June-September.

Muhammad, Abdul Latif (2001): "Micro-Credit and Savings of Rural Households in Bangladesh", *Bangladesh Development Studies*, Vol. 27, March.

NABARD (2002): "Ten Years of SHG-bank Linkage: 1992-2002", NABARD and Microfinance.

Nair, S Tara (2000): "Rural Financial Intermediation and Commercial Banks: Review of Recent Trends" *Economic and Political Weekly*, January 29.

Namboodiri, N V and R L Shiyani (2001): "Working and Impact of Rural Self-Help Groups in Rural Financial Deepening", *Indian Journal of Agricultural Economics*, Vol. 56, No. 3, July-September.

Rose, S Peter (1998): *Commercial Bank Management*, McGraw Hill Publications, Chapters 12 and 13.

Rajasekhar, D (2000): "Microfinance Programmes and Women's Empowerment: A Study of Two NGOs, from Kerala", *Journal of Social and Economic Development*, Vol. 3, No.1, January-June, pp 76-94.

8

The Changing Role of Financial Sector in the Provision of Credit for Agricultural Growth: A Study with Reference to West Bengal

Subrata Kumar Roy

The paper is an empirical investigation into the extent of institutional credit delivery in rural West Bengal. It assumes that agricultural development bears a close relationship with credit and looks at the multi agency approach to provision of credit to agriculture. It then tries to evaluate its impact on agricultural growth by sample states. Then a district wise study is presented for West Bengal. It is shown that institutional credit has made an impact on agricultural production through change in the cropping pattern.

Agricultural development bears a close positive correlation with credit and finance. The relationship between credit and agricultural development is high but indirect. Agricultural credit is one of the most crucial inputs in all agricultural development programmes in India. At the time of independence,

Source: Artha Beekshan, Journal of Bengal Economic Association, Vol. 14, Nos. 3 & 4, December 2005 & March 2006.

the most important source of agricultural credit was the money lenders. The predominant position of the money lenders was due to the reason that there was no other source worth the name and the farmers were forced to borrow from them. This almost total dependence of farmers on the money lenders enabled the latter to dictate terms and exploit the former in a number of ways. On account of this reason, they can be termed antisocial elements. The government has, therefore, undertaken various steps to regulate the activities of the money lenders. The most important move to free the agriculturists from the clutches of the money lenders was the expansion of institutional credit to agriculture. As a result of the efforts undertaken by the government to expand the institutional sources of finance, the importance of moneylenders in rural credit has declined significantly while cooperatives and banks have increased their share in rural credit considerably.

It is to note that there exists several studies on IC/financial sector development in India (viz., Ootto Chowdhuri (2004), Sarkar and Ghosh (2004), Biswas and Rakshit (2004), Sinha (2004), Pal (2004), Mallick (2004), Upadhyay and Bosu Roy (2004), Bandyopadhyay (2004), Laha (2004), Basu (1979), Desai (1988), Bhattacharya (2003) etc.). From this brief review of existing literature it is evident that there is a scope to conduct a study on the changing role of financial sector in the provision of institutional credit (IC) for agricultural growth. In this context, the present paper makes an attempt to highlight the changing role of financial sector in the provision of IC for agricultural growth in India with special reference to West Bengal (WB) during the post-bank nationalisation period. Thus, the present paper is divided into four sections. In section I, we take a look at the evolution of multi-agency approach to provide IC to farmers. Section II is concerned with the trend direction/composition of flow of IC for farmers and also the impact of IC on agricultural growth in India by sample states. Section III examines the trend, direction/composition of flow of IC for farmers and also the impact of IC on agricultural growth in WB, by districts. Section IV makes the concluding observations.

I. Evolution of Multi-Agency Approach to the Provision of Institutional Credit to Agriculture in India

Since independence, a multi-agency approach consisting of cooperatives, commercial banks, and regional rural banks – known as IC – has been adopted to provide adequate and cheaper credit to farmers. The major policy in the sphere of agricultural credit has been its progressive institutionalisation for supplying agriculture and rural development programmes with timely and adequate flow of credit to assist weaker sections and less developed regions IC, as mentioned earlier, refers to the funds made available to the co-operative societies, commercial banks, and Regional Rural Banks (RRBs).

Faced with the serious problem of deteriorating agricultural production and the rapacious money lenders. The Government of India (GoI) set up cooperative credit societies and land mortgage banks. Cooperatives in India have a three-tier structure. At the lowest tier are the Primary Agricultural Credit Societies (PACs) organised at the village level. At the second tier are the District Central Cooperative Banks (DCCBs) organised at the district level. The DCCBs are of two types – cooperative banking union and mixed central cooperative banks. At the third and uppermost tier are the State Cooperative Banks (SCBs) organised at the state level. In the field of cooperation, the PACs provide mainly short and medium term loans and Land Development Banks (LDBs) provide long-term loans to agricultural sector. Initially, land mortgage banks were organised for the purpose of providing long-term credit to farmers. These banks were later called LDBs. In recent years, they have been renamed as Cooperative Agricultural and Rural Development Banks (CARDBs). The long-term credit structure consists of State Cooperative Agricultural Rural Development Banks (SCARDBs) and Primary Cooperative Agricultural Rural Development Banks (PCARDBs). A survey of rural credit in 1950-51 showed that the cooperatives could meet barely 3.3% of the total credit requirements of farmers, while the money lenders accounted for 93% of the credit needs of the farmers, On the recommendations of the All-India Rural Credit Survey Committee (AIRCSC) (1954), Reserve Bank of India (RBI) took a series of measures to strengthen the cooperative movement. The State Bank of India (SBI) was set up in 1955 to show, among others, a special concern for agricultural credit. It was AIRCSC (1969) which recommended the adoption of multi-agency approach to finance the rural sector. The GoI accepted that the rural credit could not be met by cooperative societies alone and that commercial banks should play an important role in the rural sector.

For a long period of time, the share of commercial banks in rural credit was meagre. The insignificant participation of commercial banks in rural credit in India is explained by the subsistence nature, dependence on monsoons of agriculture and its unorganised, individualistic functioning. Consequently, the commercial banks concentrated to meet the demand for credit of the industrial sector. It was partly to remedy this state of affairs that 14 major commercial banks were nationalised in 1969. This was followed by the nationalisation of 6 more banks in 1980. The rationale of priority sector lending was one of the causes of nationalisation of the top 14 commercial banks in 1969. The Working Group on Rural Banks (1975) recommended the establishment of RRBs to supplement the efforts of commercial banks and the cooperatives in extending credit to weaker sections of rural community. Consequent upon the recommendations of the Working Group, 5 RRBs were initially set up in 1975. Thus, the multi-agency approach of IC to agriculture was evolved over a number of years. While RBI was helping the cooperative sector directly, it was felt that multi-agency approach to rural finance required a special banking institution to coordinate and help ail the institutions specialising in rural finance. It was for this reason that National Bank for Agriculture and Rural Development (NABARD) was set up as the apex bank for rural finance in 1982. It took over from RBI all the functions that was latter performed in the field of rural credit. The Agricultural Refinance and Development Corporation (ARDC), which was set up in 1963 to meet the long-term credit needs of the rural areas, has also been merged with NABARD. Three main functions of NABARD are refinancing, institutional development and inspection of client banks.

The National Credit Council Study Group under the chairmanship of D R Gadgil first recommended the area approach to nationalised banks. The Committee on Bankers (known as the Nariman Committtee), appointed by the RBI in 1969, accepted the area approach to nationalised banks and gave a practical shape to it under the title Lead Bank Scheme (LBS). The basic aim of LBS is that one of the commercial banks performs as a lead bank in a district for coordinating credit deployment in a district. Public Sector Banks (PSBs) were advised to formulate Special Agriculture Credit Plans (SAPs) since 1994-95 to fix self-act targets for agricultural lending for each year. The PSBs adopted (since February 1988) Service Area Approach under which each semi-urban and rural branch of commercial banks was assigned a specific area comprising a cluster of villages within which it would operate, adopting a planned approach for its economic growth. The Narasimham Committee (1991) was primarily interested in improving the financial health of PSBs and Development Financial Institutions (DFIs), so as to make them viable and efficient and meet fully the emerging needs of the real economy. The basic approach of the committee was that greater market orientation would strengthen the financial system and thus improve its efficiency. The Narasimham Committee was against the continuance of the priority sector sending. The GoI did not accept this recommendation. Under the guise of social banking, the GoI has used the PSBs to finance many of its pet programmes on poverty reduction and poverty alleviation. The changes which have been taking place in India since 1969 have necessitated banking companies to give up their conservative and traditional system of banking and take to new and progressive functions. Banks have thus been diversifying their activities into a host of financial services by setting up subsidiaries/mutual funds or contributing to the equity of companies offering financial services. Despite stiff opposition from bank unions and political parties in the country, the GoI accepted all major recommendations of Narasimham Committee and started implementing them straightaway. The Finance Ministry of the GoI appointed Narasimham as chairman of one more committee to review the progress of banking sector reforms to date and chart a programme on financial sector reforms necessary to strengthen India's financial system and make it internationally competitive. In recent years, a number of microfinance initiatives have been introduced. Microfinance is a novel approach to banking with the poor. Another notable development in recent years is the introduction of Kisan Credit Cards (KCC) in 1998. The purpose of the KCC scheme is to facilitate short-term credit to farmers.

II. Institutional Credit for Agricultural Growth in India by States: Trend, Direction/Composition and Role

In this section, we shall examine the trend, direction/composition of flow of IC and also the role of IC in accelerating agricultural growth in all-India as well as 12 sample states, viz., Andhra Pradesh (AP), Gujarat, Haryana, Himachal Pradesh (HP), Madhya Pradesh (MP), Maharashtra, Orissa, Punjab, Rajasthan, Tamil Nadu,

Uttar Pradesh (UP), and West Bengal (WB). It is to note that IC means the credit provided by both commercial banks including RRBs and co-operatives. In this analysis the commercial bank credit includes credit of both commercial banks and RRBs. On the other hand, the cooperative credit is the sum of credit of different cooperative organisations, viz., Primary Agricultural Credit Societies (PACS), Farmers' Service Societies (FSS), Large Size Agricultural Multi-Purpose Society (LAMPS) and Land Development Banks (LDBs).

(i) Agricultural Credit in India by States

We shall analyse the trend, direction/composition of flow of agricultural credit in the following manner.

(A) Institutional Credit: Trend in Sample States *vis-à-vis* All India

Let us discuss first the trend of IC in the sample States as well as all-India. The IC comprises the commercial bank (including RRBs) credit and cooperative credit. So far as the trend of IC is concerned, it is observed that in all-India, the IC per hectare has increased over years from Rs.88,27 in June 1973 to Rs.5262.13 in March 2000 (Table 1), in case of AP, the IC per hectare has shown a rising trend during June 1973-June 1983 from Rs.155.31 to Rs.914.41 and declined to Rs.206 in June 1988, but increased again to Rs.5228.04 in March 2000, In case of Gujarat, the IC per hectare has increased from Rs.181.81 in June 1973 to Rs.2614.75 in March 2000. In case of Haryana, HP, Punjab, Maharashtra. Rajasthan, Tamil Nadu, WB and MP, the IC per hectare has a rising trend over years during June 1973 to March 2000. In Orissa, the IC per hectare has shown a rising trend during June 1973-June 1983 from Rs.69,53 to Rs.503.30. But it declined to Rs.376.01 in June 1988, but again it increased to Rs.3960.07 in March 2000. It is observed from Table 3(a) that the Compound Annual Growth Rates (CAGRs) of IC have been significant for all-India and sample states.

(B) Commercial Bank Credit – Trend in Sample States vis-à-vis All-India

Focusing on the trend of Commercial Bank Credit (CBC) it is observed that in India as a whole, the CBC, per hectare has risen from Rs.35.25 in June 1973 to Rs.1570.89 in March 2002 (Table 2). In case of AP the CBC per hectare has shown a rising trend during June 1973-June 1983 from Rs.36.76 to Rs.514.99. But it declined to Rs.134.89 in 1988. However, it again increased to

Rs.5652.62 during March 2002. The CBC per hectare has risen over years during June 1973-March 2002 for both Gujarat and Haryana. For other sample states the CBC per hectare has also shown a rising trend during the same period. It is observed from Table 3(a) that the CAGRs of CBC have been significant for All India and sample states.

(C) Co-operative Credit – Trend in Sample States *vis-à-vis* All India

Let us analyse the trend of Cooperative Credit (COC) per hectare in the sample states in all India perspective. In India, the COC per hectare has increased from Rs.53.02 in June 1973 to Rs.4459.35 in March 2000 (Table 3). In case of AP, the COC per hectare showed rising trend over years during June 1973 and June 1983 from Rs.118.55 to Rs.399.42 but has declined to Rs.71.11 in June 1988 and again increased to Rs.1119.20 in March 1994, but declined to Rs.984.52 in March 2000. The States like Gujarat, Haryana, HP, MP, Maharasrra, Orissa, Punjab, Tamil Nadu and WB have shown a rising trend of COC per hectare during June 1973 and March 2000. On the other hand, for the two states, viz., Rajasthan and UP, the COC per hectare has increased over years during June 1973-June 1988, but declined in March 1994 and again increased in March 2000. It is observed from Table 3(a) that the CAGRs of COC have been significant for All India and sample states,

(D) Commercial Bank Credit by Size Classes of Land Holdings in Sample States *vis-à-vis* All India – An Analysis of Direction/Composition

Let us highlight the direction/composition of CBC across the different size classes of land holdings. In AP it is observed that the percentage share of CBC in total CBC has shown slowly rising trend over years during 1980-95 for all the size classes of land holdings (Table 4). In Tamil Nadu, the percentage share of a size class CBC to total CBC (PCBC) has risen over years for all size classes of land holdings except the size class of upto 2.5 acre, in MP, the PCBC has shown a rising trend for size class of 'above 2.5 to 5 acres' and the declining trends for the size class of 'above 10 acres' and no discernible trend for the size class of upto 2.5 acres. In the case of UP, Gujarat, Maharashtra, Punjab and all-India, the PCBC has risen over years with some fluctuations for the size classes of 'upto 2.5 acres', 'above 2.5 to 5 acres' and 'above 5 acres'. In Orissa, the PCBC has shown a rising trend during 1980-95 for the size classes of 'above 2.5 acres', 'above 5 acres' and 'above 10 acres', but declining trend for the size class of 'upto 2.5 acres'. In Haryana, the PCBC has remained more or less constant for the size classes of 'upto 2.5 acres' and 'above 2.5 to 5 acres', has risen for the size classes of 'above 5 acres' and has fallen for the size class, 'above 10 acres'. In HP, the PCBC has shown fluctuation for the size classes of 'upto 2.5 acres' and 'above 5 acres", but declining trend for the size classes of '2.5 to 5 acres'. In WB, the PCBC has slowly risen over years during 1980-95 for all the size classes except the size class of 'above 2.5 to 5 acres'. In Rajasthan, the PCBC has remained almost constant for all the size classes, except for the size class of 'above 10 acres' where it has declined over years during 1980-95.

The analysis of data on the credit availability for India and WB. Tables 4(a) and 4(b) show that weaker sections (i.e., relatively smaller size classes of land holdings) has received considerable amount of loans per hectare in relation to the amount of loans received by the rich farmers (land holding size greater than 4 hectares). It is observed that the weaker sections have sometimes got larger amount of credit as compared to the rich farmers.

(E) PACS Credit and Cooperative Credit by Size Classes of Land Holdings in Sample States and India: An Analysis of Direction/Composition

Concentrating on the percentage of a size class PACS credit to total PACS credit (PPACC) it is observed that in all India, there exists no definite trend for any size class of land holdings during 1976-77 and 1997-98 (Table 5). In Gujarat, the PPACC has increased, though very slowly, over years for three size classes, namely, upto 1 hectare, 1-2 hectares and 2-4 hectares, but declined for other size classes of land holdings. In case of HP, the PPACC has decreased over years for all the size classes of land holdings. In Punjab, the PPACC has increased, though at a very slow rate, over years during 1976-77 and 1997-98 for the size classes 1 to 2 hectares, 2 to 4 hectares, and 4 to 8 hectares, but declined for other size classes. In Rajasthan, the PPACC has slowly declined over years during 1976-77 and 1997-98 for the size classes of 'up to 1 hectare', '4 to 8 hectares', and "above 8 hectares', but declined for other classes. In case of Tamil Nadu, the PPACC has shown fluctuations for all the size classes of land holdings during 1976-77 and 1997-98. In UP, the PPACC has no trend for all size classes.

In Haryana, the PPACC has shown fluctuations for the size classes of 'upto 1 hectare', '1 to 2 hectares' and '2 to 4 hectares' but rising and declining trends for the size classes of '4 to 8 hectares' and 'above 8 hectares' respectively. In the case of MP the PPACC, has fluctuated for all the size classes showing no discernible trend, except the size class of above 8 hectares for which it has declined over year during 1976-77 and 1997-98. In both Maharastra and Orissa, the PPACC has fluctuated for all size classes of land holdings during 1976-77 and 1997-98. In both AP and WB, almost similar trends are observed for all the size classes of land holdings except the size class of 1-2 hectares.

The analysis of data on the credit availability for India and WB (Tables 5(a) and 5(b)) show that the weaker sections (smaller size class of land holdings) have received considerable amount of loans per hectare in relation to the amount of loans received by rich farmers (land holding size greater than 4 hectares). It is observed that the weaker sections have sometimes got larger amount of credit as compared to the rich farmers.

Focusing on the percentage of COC of a size class in the total COC (PCOC) in all-India, it is observed that it has fluctuated over years for all size of classes of land holdings during 1976-77 and 1994-95 (Table 6): The PCOC has increased over years for smaller land holdings viz., upto 1 hectare, 1-2 hectares, and 2-4 hectares and decreased over years for larger land holdings like 4-8 hectares, and above 8 hectares.

(F) Trend of Cropwise PACS Credit in Sample States *vis-à-vis* All India

Let us have a look at the trend of cropwise PACS credit for different size classes of land holdings in India as well as sample states (Table 7). In the case of both foodgrains and wheat, the PACS credit has increased over years in all the sample states and India. In case of paddy, the PACS credit has shown a rising trend for the sample states, other than Orissa. The PACS credit for other crops, like pulses, cotton, oilseeds and sugarcane, has shown a rising trend in most of the sample states and all India.

(ii) Role of Institutional Credit in Agricultural Growth in India by States

Agricultural growth is influenced by change in area, change in yield, change in Cropping Pattern (CP), etc. In this study, we have selected change in CP as a dependent variable for examining the role of IC in agricultural growth across the sample states in India.

Using the percentage of area under non-foodgrains to gross cropped area (NFA) as a measure of CP change in the sample states a cross section analysis using simple regression model have been made for several years to study the impact of IC on CP change influencing agricultural growth. The estimated regression equations are as follows:

1974-75: $NFA = 16.27 + \underset{(1.98)}{0.032^{**}} IC$; $R^2 = 0.28$; $F = 3.95$

1975-76: $NFA = 10.84 + \underset{(2.18)}{0.0006^{**}} IC$; $R^2 = 0.32$; $F = 4.74$

1976-77: $NFA = 11.79 + \underset{(2.21)}{0.06^{**}} IC$; $R^2 = 0.33$; $F = 4.86$

In the above equations, ** indicates that coefficients are significant at 5% level and figures in brackets indicate t-ratios. The regression results show that IC has statistically significant impact on the change in CP influencing agricultural growth and the IC can explain 28 to 33% variation in CP across the sample states.

III. Institutional Credit for Agricultural Growth in the Districts of West Bengal: Trend, Direction/Composition and Role

In this section, we shall examine the trend, direction/composition of flow of IC and also the role of IC in accelerating agricultural growth in the districts of WB.

(i) Agricultural Credit in WB by Districts

We shall highlight the trend, direction/composition of flow of agricultural credit in the following manner.

(A) Trend of IC in the Districts of WB

Let us examine the trend of IC in different districts of WB. It is observed that there exists a rising trend of IC during June 1981 and March 2001 in seven districts in the state, namely, Bankura. Birbhum, Burdwan, Hooghly, Nadia, Purulia and West Dinajpur (Table 8). On the other hand, the IC per hectare has fluctuated over years during June 1981 and March 2001 in the other districts of WB For example, in case of Cooch Behar the IC per hectare has increased over years during June 1981 and June 1985 from Rs.249.57 to Rs.329.71, but declined to Rs.275.07 in June 1988 and increased over years since June 1988. It is observed from Table 10(a) that the CAGRs of IC have been significant for WB and its districts.

(B) Trend of Commercial Bank Credit in the Districts of WB

As far as trend of CBC per hectare is concerned, it is observed that it has increased over years during June 1973 and March 2002 in the 13 districts, viz., Bankura. Birbhum, Burdwan, Cooch Behar, Hooghly, Howrah, Malda, Murshidabad, Purulia, 24-Parganas, West Dinajpur, Darjeeling and Midnapore but fluctuated in other districts, viz., Jalpaiguri, Nadia during the same period (Table 9). It is observed from Table 10(a) that the CAGRs of CBC have been significant for WB and its districts.

(C) Trend of Co-operative Credit in the Districts of WB

Highlighting on the trend of COC per hectare it is found that for most of the districts (i.e., 13 districts) the COC, per hectare has fluctuated during 1980-81 and 2000-01 (Table 10). However, despite the fluctuations the COC per hectare has shown rising trends in all these 13 districts, namely, Bankura, Birbhum, Burdwan, Cooch Behar, Hooghly, Howrah, Jalpaiguri, Malda, Murshidabad, 24-Parganas, Purulia, West Dinajpur and Midnapore. In the other two districts, namely, Nadia and Darjeeling the COC per hectare has increased over years during the same period. It is observed from Table 10(a) that the CAGRs of COC, have been significant for WB and its districts.

(D) PACS Credit by Size classes of Land Holdings in the districts of WB: An Analysis of Direction/Composition

Focusing on the PPACC in the districts of WB it is observed that in Birbhum. Bankura and Midnapore, there exists a slow rising trend for the size classes of 'upto 1 hectare', '1 to 2 hectares', but a declining trend for the size class of 4 to 8 hectares. The PPACC, has not shown any definite trend during 1976-77 and 1986-87 for different size classes of land holdings in Malda, Jalpaiguri, 24 Parganas, Howrah, Nadia, Murshidabad, Hooghly, Burdwan, Cooch Behar, Purulia and Darjeeling (Table 11), It has declined over years during I982-83 and 1984-85 in West Dinajpur.

(E) LDB Credit by Size Classes of Land holdings in the Districts of WB: An Analysis of Direction/Composition

Let us consider the trend of the percentage share of different land holdings size classes in LDB credit in the total LDB credit (PLDBC) in the different districts of WB. It is observed that the PLDBC has shown different trends for different size classes of land holdings in the different districts of WB (Table 12). In case of Birbhum, the PLDBC has shown a rising trend for two size classes – 1 to 2 hectares and 'upto 1 hectare', but a declining trend for other size classes. In Bankura, the PLDBC has shown an increasing trend for the size classes of 1-2 hectares and 2-4 hectares and an opposite trend for other size classes. In Nadia, Murshidabad and Darjeeling, the PLDBC has revealed the similar trend across the different size classes of land holdings. In Midnapore, the PLDBC has shown a slowly rising trend over years for all the size classes except the size class of 'upto 1 hectare'. In Malda, the PLDBC has decreased over years for all the size classes except the size class of 1-2 hectares. In West Dinajpur, the PLDBC. has declined with some fluctuations for the size classes of 1-2 hectares, 2-4 hectares, 4-8 hectares, but has increased with some fluctuations for the size class of above 8 hectares' and increased sharply over years for the size class of 'upto 1 hectare'. In Jalpaiguri, the PLDBC, has shown a declining trend for the size classes of 'upto 1 hectare' and '2-4 hectares'. In case of 24-Parganas, the PLDBC has increased sharply over years for the size classes of 'upto 1 hectare' and '4-8 hectares'. In case of Howrah, PLDBC has risen over years for the size classes of '1-2 hectares', and '2-4 hectares'. In case of Hooghly, the PLDBC has increased over years for the size classes of '2-4 hectares' and '4-8 hectares'. In Burdwan, the PLDBC has fluctuated over years for the size classes of '1-2 hectares', '2-4 hectares' and 'above 8 hectics', while it has increased sharply for the size class of 'upto I hectare'. In case of Cooch Behar, the PLDBC has declined over time for the size class of 'above 8 hectares', while for other size classes it exhibits no trend.

(ii) Role of IC in Agricultural Growth in the Districts of WB

Agricultural growth is influenced by change in area, change in yield, change in CP, etc. In this study we have selected change in CP (measured by the NFA) as a dependent variable for examining the role of IC in agricultural growth across the districts in WB. A regression analysis has also been made by using cross section data districts in WB for some years on the variables of our concern to verify the above results. The regression results are given below:

1973-74: NFA = 12.41 + 0.04** IC; (3.92) R^2 = 0.54; F = 15.36

1976-77: NFA = 12.67 + 0.03** IC; (5.44) R^2 = 0.69; F = 29.57

1979-60: NFA = 7.38 + 0 04** IC; (3-79) R^2 = 0,52; F= 14.36

1980-81: NFA = 11.83 + 0.02** IC; (2-51) R^2 = 0.33; F = 6.29

1986-87: NFA = 7.06 + 0.026* IC; (2.25) R^2 = 0.28; F = 5.06

In the above equations, * and ** indicate coefficients significant at 5% and 1% level, respectively and figures in brackets indicate t-ratios. The estimates of the regression coefficients and their levels of significance show that IC has made significant contribution to the agricultural growth through change in CP in quite a good number of districts in the state through its significant impact upon the growth of non-foodgrains production in the districts of the state.

Conclusions

Agricultural credit is one of the most crucial inputs in all agricultural development programmes in India. Since independence, a multi-agency approach has been adopted to provide adequate and cheaper credit, viz., IC to farmers in India. There has been a massive flow of IC to agriculture in both the sample states of India and districts of WB side by side, the flow of credit is more favourable to smaller size of land holdings i.e., the percentage share of different type of IC has increased over years for the smaller size of land holdings and sometimes they have received larger amount of agricultural credit as compared to the larger size of land holdings. Again, the IC has made a positive impact on agricultural growth through change in CP. From the above observations, the following policy prescriptions may be made: First, since the IC plays a substantial role in accelerating agricultural growth through change in CP in favour of commercial crops, so the government must put greater emphasis on increasing the availability of IC to farmers, particularly poorer ones to accelerate agricultural growth of a country like India. Second, since most of the farmers in India are very poor and also need external source of finance, viz., IC, for the adoption of modern technology in agriculture, so the provision of substantial amount of credit, particularly IC is essential. Thus, the IC should be made in required amount and in time. Transaction cost of IC should be reduced so that it can adequately compete with non-IC. The provision of larger amount of IC to poorer section of farmers is also necessary to rescue them from the perpetual debt condition prevailing in the rural areas. Third, an appropriate cropwise credit policy is necessary to ensure the food security of the country.

Acknowledgement

This paper is based on author's Ph D research work. The author also expresses his thanks to Prof. Raj Kumar Sen, Department of Economics, Rabindra Bharati University, West Bengal. Prof. S N Sau, Department of Economics with Rural Development, Vidyasagar University, West Bengal, and Prof. R S Das, IIT, Kharagpur, West Bengal for their valuable suggestions.

(Subrata Kumar Roy belongs to the Department of Economics, Sabang S K Mahavidyalaya, West Bengal.)

References

1. Biswas J, and S.K.Rakshit (2004), "Financial Liberalisation and Stock Market Development: Experiences of India and Select Asian Markets" Artha Beekshan. Vol. 13, No. 3, December.
2. Bhattacharya. S. (2003), *Rural Credit and Class Differentiation: West Bengal under Left interventionist Regime*, K. P Bagchi and Company. Kolkata.

3. Bandyopadhyay. D, K. (2004), "Pattern of Corporate Finance and Implication of Corporate Governance in India". *Artha Beekshan*. Vol.13. No. 3, December.

4. Basu. S.K. (1979). *Commercial Banks and Agricultural Credit: A Study in Regional Disparity in India*. Bombay.

5. Desai. D.K. (1988), "Institutional Credit Requirements for Agricultural Production–2000 A.D." *Indian Journal of Agricultural Economics* (IJAE). Vol.43. No. 3. July-September.

6. Datta Chowdhuri, T. (2004), "Financial Sector Development in India", *Artha Beekshan*, Vol. 13, No. 3, December.

7. Dasgupta. R. (2002), "Priority Sector Lending: Yesterday, Today and Tomorrow". *Economic and Political Weekly*. Vol. XXXVIL No. 41, October 12.

8. Laha. P (2004), "Growth of Financial Sector in Independent India: A Historical Sketch", *Artha Beekshan*, Vol.13, No. 3. December.

9. Mallick. M. (2004). "Role of Public Sector Banks in Rural Development of India since 1970s", *Artha Beekshan*, Vol. 13. No. 3, December.

10. Pal, G.K.(2004). "Foreign Banks in India: Profitability and Social Responsibility", *Artha Beekshan*. Vol.13. No. 3. December.

11. Ray, S.K. (2000). "Impact of Credit Availability on Change in Cropping Pattern in India with special reference to West Bengal", An Unpublished Ph D Dissertation, Vidyasagar University, West Bengal.

12. Sarkar, D. and B.K. Ghosh (2004). "A Study of Market Efficiency and Volatility in the Indian Stock Market, FOREX Market and Bullion Market", *Artha Beekshan*, Vol.13, No. 3, December.

13. Sinha, R.R (2004), "The Life Insurance Sector in India". *Artha Beekshan*, Vol. 13, No. 3, December.

14. Upadhyay, S and H Basu Roy (2004). "Recent Trends in NPA and Recovery Management Policy Techniques of the Indian Commercial Banks", *Artha Beekshan*. Vol.13, No. 3. December.

Table 1: Institutional Credit/hectare in India by States

(in Rs.)

	June 1973	June 1978	June 1983	June 1988	March 1994	March 1997	March 2000
Andhra Pradesh	155.31	299.55	914.41	206	3271.3	3677.14	5228.04
Gujarat	181.81	305.68	850.5	1491.04	2370.16	7220.93	2614.75
Haryana	125.32	386.32	953.79	2853.82	3489.81	4099.71	23472.31
Himachal Pradesh	107.29	212.48	557.28	1224.41	2006.82	2806.52	6067.05
Madhya Pradesh	72.8	133.18	307.95	762.95	1679.51	2379.62	1506.36
Maharashtra	150.72	267.85	703.03	961.99	2089.62	3589.72	11594.14
Orissa	69.5 3	146.43	503.3	376.07	1 200.58	1923.1	3960.07
Punjab	229.4	429.81	1134.48	2334.36	3499.02	4999.15	28357.38
Rajasthan	35.51	109.76	295.25	994.14	1058.77	1960.78	3409.88
Tamil Nadu	332.3	657.13	1465.65	2623.11	5735.24	7756.36	23052.33
Uttar Pradesh	29.29	159.81	575.3	819.85	1415.15	1965.26	4373.22
West Bengal	107.69	265.64	491.33	887.58	1032.98	1692.09	3897.05
All India	**88.27**	**148.22**	**320.73**	**603.63**	**837.44**	**2206.45**	**5262.13**

Source: (i) Banking Statistics, RBI; (ii) Statistical Statements Relating to Co-operative Movement in India. NABARD; (iii) Area and Production of Principal Crops in India, Government of India.

Table 2: All Scheduled Commercial Bank's Agricultural Credit Per Hectare in India by States

(in Rs.)

	June 1973	June 1978	June 1983	June 1988	March 1994	March 1997	March 2000
Andhra Pradesh	36.76	176.85	514.99	134.89	2152.1	3485.61	5652.62
Gujarat	44.28	95.62	256.66	798.68	1253.12	4573.49	2883.27
Haryana	15.71	142.91	405.08	1251.48	1802.55	1854.7	7365.82
Himachal Pradesh	6.25	67.95	323.84	716.54	1 122.1	1206.77	9401.6
Madhya Pradesh	6.52	38.13	123.82	340.9	556.75	264.75	1487.25
Maharashtra	48.35	119.35	314.19	430.87	865.15	1370.93	2993.11
Orissa	3.43	43.53	199.1	208.87	872.5	1177.36	1439.43
Punjab	21.98	205.81	640.39	1200.93	2110.7	2488.47	1080.78
Rajasthan	8.6	39.33	146.53	462.49	676.63	682.54	1979.6
Tamil Nadu	83.98	94.48	853.1	1898.29	3341.4	4573.49	7681.85
Uttar Pradesh	24.54	77.61	260.6	480.77	1078.8	1212.91	2714.46
West Bengal	73.19	142.77	284.06	570.59	969.44	1224.9	2153.11
All India	**35.25**	**113.86**	**162.77**	**332.61**	**253.65**	**1767.68**	**1570.89**

Source: (i) Banking Statistics, RBI; (ii) Area and Production of Principal Crops in India. Government of India.

Table 3: Co-operative Agricultural Credit/Hectare in India by States

(in Rs.)

	June 1973	June 1978	June 1983	June 1988	March 1994	March 1997	March 2000
Andhra Pradesh	118.55	122.7	399.42	71.11	1119.2	191.53	984.52
Gujarat	137.53	210.06	593.9	692.36	1117.04	2647.44	790.01
Haryana	109.61	243.41	548.71	1602.34	1687.26	2245.01	18823.77
Himachal Pradesh	101.04	144.53	233.44	7.87	884.72	1599.75	20968.56
Madhya Pradesh	86.28	85.05	184.13	422.05	1122.76	2114.87	2564.86
Maharashtra	102.37	148.5	388.84	531.12	1224.47	2218.79	9415.48
Orissa	66.1	102.9	304.2	167.2	328.08	745.75	2875.04
Punjab	207.42	224	94.09	1133.43	1368.32	2510.68	20037.1
Rajasthan	26.91	70.43	148.72	531.65	382.14	1278.24	2100.31
Tamil Nadu	248.32	562.65	612.54	727.82	1793.84	3183.07	16479.31
Uttar Pradesh	4.75	82.2	314.7	339.08	336.57	752.35	2406.3
West Bengal	34.5	122.67	207.27	316.99	463.54	467.19	2639.53
All India	**53.02**	**34.36**	**157.96**	**271.02**	**583.79**	**438.77**	**4459.35**

Sources: (i) Statistical Statements Relating to Co-operative Movement in India. RBI/NABARD; (ii) Area and Production of Principal Crops in India, Government of India.

Table 3(a): Compound Annual Growth Rates (CAGRs) of Credit Per Hectare in India by States

Sl. No.	States	Institutional Credit/Ha	Commercial Bank Credit/Ha	Co-operative Credit/Ha
1.	All India	16.98*	18.93*	19.21*
2.	Punjab	18.35*	22.92*	21.61*
3.	Haryana	18.87*	24.91*	21.32*
4.	Rajasthan	19.92*	27.86*	25.31*
5.	Maharashtra	13.98*	18.18*	20.31*
6.	Gujarat	18.88*	21.92*	19.32*
7.	Tamil Nadu	15.63*	23.92*	21.61*
8.	Andhra Pradesh	16.72*	19.53*	15.23*
9.	Madhya Pradesh	21.92*	23.77*	19.95*
10.	Uttar Pradesh	16.98*	19.92*	16.98*
11.	Himachal Pradesh	19.92*	29.99*	19.32*
12.	Orissa	16.78*	23.77*	18.53*
13.	West Bengal	10.72*	13.89*	15.31*

Note: * indicates value significant at 1% level.

Table 4: Percentage Share of Disbursed Credit from Scheduled Commercial Banks of a Size Class of Land Holding in India by States

	Year	Upto 2.5 Acres	Above 2.5-5 Acres	Above 5 Acres	Above 10 Acres
Andhra Pradesh	1980	29.18	26.57	21.8	21.44
	1981	26.42	26.59	32.61	23.38
	1986	31.1	40.43	28.47	–
	1991	31.39	32.61	36.07	–
	1995	32.2	30.73	37.07	–
Gujarat	1980	9.02	11.19	20.94	58.85
	1981	9.85	10.1	19.04	61
	1986	8.29	14.5	77.21	
	1991	8.32	16.59	75.09	
	1995	12.39	17.26	70.42	
Haryana	1980	3.94	3.94	12.82	79.29
	1981	4.83	4.91	14,42	75.84
	1986	39.42	60.58		
	1991	6.51	13.75	79.74	
	1995	5.85	11.14	83.01	
Himachal Pradesh	1980	36.66	27.76	17.48	18.1
	1981	42.98	26.3	12.9	17.83
	1986	53.45	15.6	30.94	
	1991	31.26	16.83	57.9	
	1995	33.69	20.66	45.65	
Madhya Pradesh	1980	9.98	5.39	31.72	52
	1981	11.22	17.57	25.47	43
	1986	12.77	23.79	63.91	
	1991	26.63	30	43.39	
	1995	11.02	20.02	68.96	–
Maharashtra	1980	10.01	12.57	25.1	52.3
	1981	8.7	13.11	24.61	53.5
	1986	11.83	19.68	68.44	
	1991	16.1	22.67	61.21	
	1995	19.29	22.61	58.1	
Orissa	1980	53.58	21.82	14.78	9.81
	1981	44.15	22	17.24	16.59

Contd...

Contd...					
	1986	42.9	34.19	22.9	
	1991	37.25	30.74	32	–
	1995	35.21	33.17	31.6	–
Punjab	1980	4.8	5.73	19.9	69.57
	1981	3.83	6.46	17.67	72.04
	1986	20.15	15.27	64.59	
	1991	5.88	15.21	78.93	
	1995	6.14	15.49	78.37	
Rajasthan	1980	8.16	11.37	16.47	63.55
	1981	7.9	12	17.11	62.98
	1986	8.87	13.64	77.49	
	1991	10.98	17.41	71.6	–
	1995	11.92	13.39	74.7	–
Tamil Nadu	1980	47.32	19.6	12.83	20.25
	1981	44.77	21.03	12.93	21.27
	1986	38.9	29.85	31.25	–
	1991	40.58	24.61	34.82	
	1995	37.86	29.02	33.12	–
Uttar Pradesh	1980	13.44	16.51	10.19	61.83
	1981	11.53	17.2	16.58	54.69
	1986	18.44	22.32	59.24	–
	1991	20.44	23.75	56.01	
	1995	19.57	22.74	57.75	–
West Bengal	1980	31.16	29.67	13.45	26.8
	1981	32.67	25.75	8.39	33.05
	1986	27.16	16.91	55.93	
	1991	36.44	19.32	44.24	–
	1995	43.46	19.04	37.5	–
All India	1980	21.44	16.84	16.97	44.74
	1981	21.41	13.28	18.57	46.74
	1986	22.82	22.18	55	
	1991	12.76	33.59	53.66	
	1995	39.25	36.93	23.82	
	2000	22.61	23.56	53.81	

Source: Report on Currency and Finance, RBI.

Table 4(a): Commercial Bank's Agricultural Credit Per Hectare by Size Classes of Land Holdings (LHs) in India

	Agricultural Credit Per Hectare (in Rs.)		
LHs (in Hectare)	**1980-81**	**1985-86**	**1990-91**
Below 1 Hectare	208.58	565.99	512.63
1.0-4.0 Hectare	117.18	511	1255.25
Above 4 Hectare	170.07	460.88	573.24

Source: (1) Report on Currency and Finance; (2) Agricultural Census, Government of India

Table 4(b): Commercial Bank's Agricultural Credit per Hectare by Size Classes of Land Holdings (LHs) in West Bengal

LHs (in Hectare)	Agricultural Credit Per Hectare (in Rs.)		
	1980-81	**1985-86**	**1990-91**
Below 1 Hectare	211.91	463.24	625.24
1.0-4.0 Hectare	156.7	300	404.14
Above 4 Hectare	199.27	868.1	823.16

Source: (1) Report on Currency and Finance, RBI; (2) Agricultural Census, Government of India.

Table 5: Percentage Share of PACS Credit of a Size Class of Land Holding in India by States

State/Year	Total	Upto 1 ha	1-2 ha	2-4 ha	4-8 ha	Above 8 ha
Gujarat						
1976-77	100	4.58	9.67	17.43	34.34	33.85
1983-84	100	7.51	13.42	21.76	26.59	30.52
1991-92	100	4.48	12.72	21.05	25.62	38.7
1994-95	100	9.31	16.6	26.15	28.99	18.94
1997-98	100	12.56	14.53	20.29	25.8	26.82
Himachal Pradesh						
1977-78	100	17.94	39.06	25.8	14.12	3.05
1983-84	100	27.33	44.15	3.1	15.89	9.51
1989-90	100	33.67	37.01	15.73	6.61	6.96
1993-94	110	14.8	17.66	11.85	5.52	0.39
1997-98	100	54.36	20.18	10.47	7.99	2.99
Punjab						
1976-77	100	19.02	15.43	25.16	17.93	22.45
1983-84	100	9.83	25.21	27.09	21.04	16.81

Contd...

Contd...						
1989-90	100	22.19	13.23	37.37	14.7	12.48
1993-94	100	10.53	26.73	36.39	24	2.32
1997-98	100	10.74	26.08	43.59	16.57	3.02
Rajasthan						
1977-78	100	6.48	13.86	21.66	31.62	25.94
1983-84	100	13.22	20.01	23.41	24.1	19.25
1991-92	100	11.09	37.6	20.56	20.26	10.4
1994-95	100	7.07	17.67	27.23	27.45	20.55
1997-99	100	7.01	17.01	25.05	26.97	23.96
Tamil Nadu						
1976-77	100	31.15	18.9	23.41	18.63	7.89
1980-81	100	14.1	31.26	27.93	20.74	10.59
1988-89	100	19.65	20.44	42.63	9.72	7.54
1994-95	100	44.27	18.13	24.79	8.51	4.36
1997-98	100	25	20.37	18.67	22.26	13.7
Uttar Pradesh						
1976-77	100	19.32	27.64	23.21	15.37	19.46
1980-81	100	27.39	27.8	23.56	17.56	3.68
1988-89	100	56.72	17.22	12.3	10.68	3.03
1997-98	100	18.08		–	14.42	4.11
Haryana						
1976-77	100	10.36	27.08	29.59	19.06	13.88
1983-84	100	9.6	22.56	29.7	28.91	9.21
1989-90	100	4.91	18.16	29.9	40.56	6.43
1994-95	100	3.03	21.14	29.82	40.72	
Madhya Pradesh						
1976-77	100	4.77	11.67	20.62	29.95	32.97
1983-84	100	12.1	17.83	27.6	24.05	18.43
1989-90	100	11.39	17.91	26.25	26.79	17.69
1997-98	100	18.86	24.45	20.66	19.26	16.77
Maharashtra						
1976-77	100	7.34	12.28	20.7	30.02	29.65
1983-84	100	10.38	17.9	24.71	24.14	22.84
1991-92	100	7.16	13.4	21.55	25.35	32.16
1994-95	100	7.68	14.87	19.27	23.87	34.29
1997-98	100	13.56	18.13	24.11	21.28	22.92
Orissa						
1976-77	100	19.9	28.01	26.47	16.58	19.03
1983-84	100	30.2	34.75	23.64	9.75	1.65
						Contd...

Contd...						
1989-90	100	21.03	24.6	46.82	26.3	1.55
1994-95	100	10.01	27.1	32.12	11.45	19.21
1997-98	100	24.9	34.17	21.82	8.11	1
West Bengal						
1980-81	100	32.81	35.55	17.08	10.83	3.71
1983-84	100	38.58	37.24	19,29	3.55	1.31
1987-88	100	41.43	34.93	18.55	4.07	1
1997-98	100	34.95	29.47	15.65	9.44	10.49
Andhra Pradesh						
1976-77	100	21.16	21.45	21.1	19.35	16.91
1978-79	100	21.28	22.91	22.85	18.46	14.49
1987-88	100	30.61	24.35	23.77	12.94	8.38
All India						
1976-77	100	15.05	18.31	22.1	23.73	20.81
1983-84	100	24.12	2.92	31.23	24.56	17.71
1989-90	100	20.43	20.38	26.05	19.6	13.04
1994-95	100	18.76	20.4	23.43	20.89	16.51
1997-98	100	20.32	21.33	22.19	10.36	17.8

Source: Statistical Statements Relating to Co-operative Movements in India, NABARD/RBI.

Table 5(a): PACS Credit by Size Classes of Land Holdings (LHs) in India

(in Rs.)

Size of LHs	1980-81	1985-86	1990-91
Upto 2.0 Hectare	203.75	135.55	270.03
2.0-4.0 Hectare	166.54	219.89	254.6
Above 4.0 Hectare	512.49	154.46	186.7

Source: Statistical Statements Relating to Co-operative Movements in India. NABARD and Agricultural Census, Government of India.

Table 5(b): PACS Credit by Size Classes of Land Holdings (LHs) in West Bengal (in Rs.)

Size of LHs	1985-86	1990-91
Up to 2.0 Hectare	182.67	126.99
2.0-4.0 Hectare	119.01	129.41
Above 4.0 Hectare	77.65	119.39

Source: Statistical Statements Relating to Co-operative Movements in India. NABARD and Agricultural Census, Government of India.

Table 6: Percentage Share of Co-operative Credit of a Size Class of Land Holding in India

State/Year	Total	Upto 1 ha	1-2 ha	2-4 ha	4-8 ha	Above 8 ha
1976-77	100	15.89	18.11	21.75	23.14	21.58
1980-81	100	18.55	21.18	24.28	21.6	14.39
1989-90	100	21,08	21.85	24.67	19.1	13.29
1994-95	100	19.41	19.56	22.95	20.37	17.7

Source: Statistical Statements Relating to Co-operative Movements in India, NABARD/RBI.

Table 7: Cropwise PACS Short-Term Credit Per Hectare in India by States

(in Rs.)

State/ Year	Food Grains	Wheat	Paddy	Pulses	Cotton	Oil Seeds	Sugarcane	Jute
Himachal Pradesh								
1980-81	15.84	15.34	–	–	–	–	86.77	–
1983-84	33.53	28.71	–	–	–	–	227.02	–
1989-90	39.04	31.16	–	–	–	–	236	–
1992-93	46.08	43.8						
West Bengal								
1980-81	63.02	44.16	–	–	–	–	704.07	71.08
1982-83	71.27	49.95	–	–	–	–	294.65	76.68
Uttar Pradesh								
1980-81	78.4	86.55	–	–	160.14	–	154.12	–
1983-84	97.58	107.42	–	–	248.16		147.95	–
1987-88	104.06	118.78	–	–	124.98	–	159.93	–
1988-89	100.18	115.82	–	–	119	–	163.62	–
Tamil Nadu								
1980-81	52.51		–	–	36.54	–	319.32	–
1983-84	160.06		–	–	473.33	–	1010.25	–
1989-90	538.27				728.33	–	950.4	–
1992-93	360.45		–	–	477.37	–	–	–
Madhya Pradesh								
1980-81	64.26	112.34	52.49	12.94	187.87	–	1513.38	–
1983-84	77.63	128.66	66.2	12.5	241.52	–	2441.57	
1989-90	156.11	256.3	137.6	30.26	268.03	79.43	3958.7	–

Contd...

Contd...								
Haryana								
1980-81	282.1	134.17	462.98	19.22	270.46	–	796.97	–
1983-84	351.01	385.48	594.29	49.1	318.45	–	1059.76	–
1989-90	575.97	510.51	758.87	43.64	317.93	140.83	2979.88	–
1992-93	659.09	583.93	717.27	31.75	371.21	256.71	3233.9	–
Andhra Pradesh								
1980-81	108.16		143.94	9.52	110.52	–	1379.06	35.82
1983-84	185.22		265.66	12.99	96.06	–	–	3006.65
1989-90	412.47		463.91	9.21	–	–	–	–
1992-93	478.43		460.78	8.29	450.44	34.77	4415.86	4.18
1993-94	31898.03	20142.54	11083.85	–	–	–	–	
Gujarat								
1980-81	263.19	302.72	194.32	21.04	252.44	–	1122.16	–
1983-84	326.49	453.53	167.54	34.13	327	–	1266.99	–
1988-89	573.6	577.64	359.45	58.61	45.45	284.52	10694.73	–
1993-94	1355.81	1447.98	571.78	108.81	91.73	675.9	4853.04	–
1994-95	1310.23	988.11	641	108.95	92.73	78.81	1549.98	–
Punjab								
1980-81	397.73	328.18	473.07	–	207.47	–	450.53	–
1983-84	540.84	430.74	624.46	–	299.62	–	189.41	–
1988-89	551.2	1475.48	574.79	–	217.33	–	504.73	–
1992-93	1000.34	842.57	1276.78	10.88	137.47	–	1382.36	–
1994-95	1428.06	1266.75	1668.04	12.67	19.81	–	577.05	–
Rajasthan								
1980-81	59.49	134.6	–	7.43	190.54	–	279.26	–
1983-84	85.03	178.54	–	7.39	202.53	–	337.35	–
1988-89	103.28	195.64	–	11.6	271.36	–	1341.5	–
Maharashtra								
1980-81	153.43	55.13	279.29	4.29	172.36	–	2132.22	2.2
1983-84	184.33	55.44	119.83	8.35	165.42	–	3553.06	108.53
1988-89	461.88	127.21	154.5	28.47	480.82	–	7290.55	–
1992-93	217.81	63.64	52.14	12.29	145.74	88.91	3154.4	66.57
1994-95	868.74	208.22	354.52	29.64	628.62	260.61	9523 96	–
								Contd...

Contd...								
Orissa								
1980-81	78.39	–	100.22	2.15	–	–	1231.24	25.8
1983-84	102.42	–	125.6	3	–	–	1989.57	36.1
1988-89	87.77	–	107.05	477	–	–	1538.34	47.04
1992-93	65.66	135.01	80.15	106	286.11	20.98	954.35	21.58
1994-95	174.07	2643.33	172.03	12.77	221.06	132.69	5964.38	360.08
All India	968.56	154.03	–	–	177.59	–	676.23	54.72
1980-81	151.25	172.93	–	–	237.42	–	775.75	89.72
1983-84	244.11	270.89	–	–	441.92	–	1443.56	174.07
1992-93	1270.63	226.62	–	–	323.29	–	1076.94	4153 04
1993-94	363.56	323.39	–	–	542.48	–	2187.0	6541.12

Source: Statistical Statements Relating to Co-operative Movements in India, NABARD/RBI.

Table 8: Institutional Credit per Hectare in West Bengal by Districts

(In Rs.)

Districts	June 1973	June 1978	June 1983	June 1988	March 1994	March 1997	March 2002
Bankura	240.18	313.66	339.26	456.16	793.87	932.66	1392.42
Birbhurn	342.46	403.65	435.26	11112	1239.86	1582.34	1859.64
Burdwan	403.32	522.66	591.79	1243.65	1486.52	1842.73	2682.45
Cooch Behar	249.57	329.71	275.07	337.02	528.75	742.16	889.75
Darjeeling	1157.06	938.24	2021.04	2752.82	4242.05	3689.07	1746.37
Hooghly	548.75	915.97	729.7	1107.24	1608.04	2342.55	4212.06
Howrah	781.7	947.4	1575.04	1652.08	1631.38	1426.68	2629.24
Jalpaiguri	552.83	224.48	289.9	689.18	1099.39	1266.44	766.16
Malda	279.5	911.68	S5S.2I	587.54	1020.15	1198.82	108999
Midnapore	402	892.11	830.35	1249.52	1578.05	1529.48	2797.87
Nadia	443.15	562.96	595.96	795.9	816	1185.69	1572.63
24-Parganas	571.62	577.25	750.91	1451.05	1538	1265.58	2575.47
Purulia	165.72	179.21	296.86	425.69	673.44	685.07	741.6
West Dinajpur	150.72	215.6	375.1	464.42	585	873.44	1095.96
Murshidabad	442.85	375.66	556.27	449.87	802.89	879.46	1572.63

Source: (i) *Banking Statistics, RBI.*
(ii) *Statistical Statements Relating to Co-operative Movement in India, RBI/NABARD.*
(iii) *Statistical Abstract, Government of West Bengal.*
(iv) *Co-operative Statistical Cell, Government of West Bengal.*

Table 9: Commercial Bank's Agricultural Credit per Hectare in West Bengal

(in Rs.)

Districts	June 1981	June 1985	June 1988	June 1991	March 1994	March 1997	March 2001
Bankura	4.85	42	137.33	231.38	536	736	910.15
Birbhum	12.17	54.46	210.4	352.8	996	1196	1177.7
Burdwan	19.34	117.05	267.49	376.65	1143.25	1343	2114.71
Cooch Behar	1.39	38.45	142.8	173.06	463	663	644.56
Darjeeling	752.25	764.07	820.58	1531.94	2655	2481.49	2845.56
Hooghly	46.76	293.39	579.26	587.38	1300.56	1500.56	2675.83
Howrah	77.91	111.44	286.39	1075.92	1086	1286	1117.33
Jalpaiguri	272.34	343.41	366.61	227.71	984	1184	1020.67
Malda	7.04	55.47	208.52	443.98	730	930	84942
Midnapore	9.79	41.8	98.85	519.5	941.46	1141	1310.75
Nadia	27.46	121.06	298.11	297.5	501.55	781.55	891.12
24-Parganas	50.06	144.4	315.9	575.56	1202.05	1402	1449.6
Purulia	13.17	36.29	62.39	173.81	427.53	627.53	472.33
West Dinajpur	1.41	36.75	107.24	183.7	294.05	496.85	753.23
Murshidabad	7.49	62.66	176.62	370.37	516	717	760.66

Source: (i) *Banking Statistics, RBI.*
(ii) *Statistical Abstract, Government of West Bengal.*

Table 10: Cooperative Credit per Hectare in West Bengal by Districts

(in Rs.)

Districts	1980-81	1984-85	1997-88	1990-91	1993-94	1996-97	2000-01
Bankura	169.44	138	107.88	123.57	257.87	196.66	574.57
Birbhum	134.61	163	82.46	178.87	243.12	386.34	717.74
Burdwan	206.55	260	215.14	276.52	343.27	499.73	922.81
Cooch Behar	182.07	179	102.01	97.32	135.75	79.16	230.7
Darjeeling	152.73	295.65	489.1	1249.52	1587.05	1207.58	660.02
Hooghly	102.64	248	142.32	101.25	307.48	841.99	738.72
Howrah	547	640	499.12	690.35	545.38	140.68	584.09
Jalpaiguri	93	79.49	62,11	45.73	115.39	82.44	3663.15
Malda	110.23	116	111.23	259.02	290.15	268.62	343.36

Contd...

Contd...

Midnapore	337	338	310.76	604.31	645.59	388.48	1770.03
Nadia	284.86	279.01	283.76	298.38	234.45	404.14	812.71
24-Parganas	351.41	147.21	175.35	255.32	335.95	638.05	1343.54
Purulia	104.01	115.61	123.05	105.5	345.91	57.54	228.74
West Dinajpur	150.62	175.21	191.31	190.57	290.15	376.59	561.77
Murshidabad	179	186.89	185.9	312.06	286.89	162.46	768.38

Source: (i) Statistical Abstract, Government of West Bengal.
(ii) Co-operative Statistical Cell, Government of West Bengal.

Table 10 (a): Compound Annual Growth Rates (CAGRs) of Credit Per Hectare in West Bengal by Districts

SI. No.	Districts	Institutional Credit/ Hectare	Commercial Bank Credit/Hectare	Cooperative Credit/Hectare
1.	West Bengal	19.88*	19.85*	13.05*
2.	Burdwan	19.72*	19.53*	12.29*
3.	Birbhum	23.37*	19.31*	12,02*
4.	Bankura	25.86*	17.36*	21.92*
5.	Cooch Behar	22.54*	19.72*	16.18*
6,	Hooghly	19.58*	18.65*	23.66*
7.	Howrah	19.72*	12.64*	16.18*
8.	Jalpaiguri	15.55*	19.84*	16.18*
9.	Malda	25.86*	13.77*	16.39*
10.	Midnapore	28.45*	11.29*	11.21*
11.	Murshidabad	22.14*	10.41*	12.33*
12.	Nadia	16.18*	10.74*	13.04*
13.	24-Parganas	19.72*	17.47*	14.08*
14.	Purulia	19.72*	15.83*	16.18*
15.	West Dinajpur	29.69*	19.35*	18.33*
16.	Darjeeling	16.72*	18.41*	11.10*

Note: (i) * indicates value significant at 1% level.

Table 11: Percentage Share of PACS – Credit of a Size Class of Land Holding

Districts/Year	Upto 1 ha	1-2 ha	2-4 ha	4-8 ha	Above 8 ha year
24-Parganas					
1980-81	30.31	45.29	22.62	.76	–
1982-83	33.42	42.18	23.56	0.84	–
1984-85	39.67	37.78	20.29	2.26	–
1985-86	44.05	36.32	17.31	2.32	–
1986-87	33.89	24.34	36.98	9.78	–
Howrah					
1982-83	53.15	33.71	13.14	–	–
1984-85	55.34	27.83	16.84	–	–
1985-86	55.32	30.06	14.62	–	–
Nadia					
1980-81	36.88	18.82	21.74	22.56	–
1982-83	48.94	48.7	2.36	–	–
1984-85	46.43	46.14	7.42		
1985-86	47.64	46.72	5.64	–	–
1986-87	30.42	69.58	–	–	–
Murshidabad					
1982-83	36.72	32.88	28.4	2	–
1984-85	33.64	30.53	33.55	2.28	–
1985-86	33.56	31.48	32.96	2	–
Hooghly					
1980-81	23.01	31.31	15.11	19.61	10.42
1982-83	58.59	24.79	12.92	3.7	–
1984-85	74.09	20.2	5.71	–	–
Burdwan					
1980-81	55.52	19.8	23.23	14.1	7.75
1982-83	22.91	34.85	25.12	12.8	4.32
1984-85	24.58	36.06	24.72	11.6	3.08
1985-86	14.61	38.6	37.92	5.14	3.72
1986-87	19.69	31.25	35.79	12.54	0.74
Bankura					
1980-81	11.3	31.48	27.25	20.73	9.23
1982-83	54.52	29.5	14.46	1.52	–
1984-85	57.01	30.88	14.99	0.002	–
1985-86	48.81	25.55	13.18	12.45	–
1986-87	43.66	38.65	15.58	2.11	–

Contd...

Contd...					
Birbhum					
1980-81	23.21	20.11	21.95	21.69	13.04
1982-83	22.99	33.5	15.69	3.26	24.31
1984-85	23.47	23.88	25.72	12.43	14.51
1985-86	26.78	25.89	30.56	–	16.71
Purulia					
1982-83	39.84	24.56	35.61	–	–
1984-85	10.69	81.41	6.98	0.93	–
1985-86	37.84	29.19	6.38	26.58	–
Midnapore					
1980-81	40.33	25.34	22.73	10.63	0.98
1982-83	45.91	32.17	15.08	6.59	0.25
1984-85	56.2	32.29	10.11	1.39	–
1985-86	51.3	34.7	13.39	0.61	–
1986-87	50.63	34.36	11.6	3.41	–
Malda					
1980-81	52.91	12.86	29.11	5.12	–
1982-83	32.67	31.37	31.31	4.65	–
1984-85	40.78	36.05	19.08	4.09	–
1985-86	38.62	34.68	20.94	5.56	–
Jalpaiguri					
1980-81	13.57	65.78	11.85	8.8	–
1982-83	35.05	18.31	29.66	16.97	–
1984-65	36.46	30.43	20.33	12.78	–
1985-86	42.72	34.61	9.16	13.51	–
1986-87	68.69	19.33	11.99		
Cooch Behar					
1982-83	33.72	42.75	21.46	2.07	–
1984-85	42.8	31.23	24.87	1.1	–
1985-86	34.19	42.8	20.77	2.23	–
1986-87	29.32	42.64	21.07	6.98	
Darjeeling					
1980-81	0.85	98.42	0.54	0.19	–
1982-83	15.63	62.36	12.8	9.23	–
1984-85	3.98	62.8	20.01	13.21	–
1985-86		14.65	8.92	76.22	–
1986-87	65.79	34.21			

Source: Co-operative Statistical Cell, Government of West Bengal.

Table 12: Percentage Share of Land Development Bank's Outstanding Credit of a Size Class of Land Holding in West Bengal by Districts

Districts	Year	Upto 1 ha	1-2 ha	2-4 ha	4-8 ha	Above 8 ha
Bankura	1980-81	23.21	20.4	21.95	21.69	13.04
	1985-86	5.25	18.77	62.45	13.57	–
	1987-88	10.88	25.72	55.67	7.81	–
Birbhum	1980-81		16.45	59.2	23.56	–
	1985-86	23.94	47.84	24.58	3.58	0.04
	1988-89	26.99	54.42	7.86	10.93	–
Burdwan	1980-81	16.73	17.51	28.37	25.33	12.06
	1985-86	26.13	42.72	19.11	11.37	0.66
	1987-88	34.52	26.77	19.83	22.17	1.69
Cooch Behar	1980-81	5.81	89.2	3.7	1.28	–
	1985-86	38.43	42.07	10.24	4.18	5.08
	1987-88	32.28	54.29	11.71	1.42	0.29
Darjeeling	1980-81	35.29	30.32	22.49	7.79	
	1985-86	55.13	33.12	11.73	–	–
	1986-87	43.24	39.01	11.73	6	–
Hooghly	1985-86	46.79	39.88	12.91	0.4	–
	1988-89	29.64	37.7	20.3	12.33	0.33
Howrah	1985-86	60.48	26.4	12.63	–	–
	1988-89	35.01	41.89	12.06	11.64	4.42
Jalpaiguri	1980-81	27.94	4.01	24.74	6.89	0.42
	1985-86	22.95	45.93	31.12	–	
	1988-89	26	62.76	11.24	–	–
Malda	1980-81	30.19	23.85	26.37	19.58	
	1985-86	27.01	57.13	15.85	–	–
	1986-87	21.02	63.09	–	15.9	–
Midnapore	1980-81	46.92	33.84	14.84	3.67	0.73
	1985-86	49.6	37.72	10.39	2.18	0.86
	1988-89	15.21	40.37	33.58	9.39	1.44
Nadia	1985-86	33.66	33.37	26.66	6.29	–
	1987-88	34.99	42.04	11.3	1.03	1.25

Contd...

Contd...						
24-Parganas	1980-81	30.31	45.29	22.02	1.78	–
	1985-86	50.99	32.58	11.11	53	–
	1988-89	63.08	34.5	2.41	–	–
Purulia	1985-86	37.84	29.19	6.38	26.58	
West Dinajpur	1980-81	4.37	36.84	32.77	26.02	–
	1985-86	25.89	44.57	26.6	2.76	0.17
	1988-89	67.94	13.76	8.84	7.56	1.95
Murshidabad	1980-81	34.78	17.74	20.5	26.96	–
	1985-86	50.31	38.09	7.73	3.71	0.16
	1987-88	56.6	41.85	0.18	1.35	–

Source: Co-operative Statistical Cell, Government of West Bengal.

9

Kisan Credit Card – An Engine of Growth

S D Mishra

This paper evaluates the Kisan Credit Card scheme which is a dominant feature of government initiatives in the rural areas. It evaluates the scheme with help of a sample study. The differences in productivity of card holders and non-card holders are highlighted. It is shown that card holders have opted for better technology and hence, their productivity has been higher.

Kisan Credit Card scheme is a dominant feature of government initiatives in the rural areas. Improving the access of low strata of farmers (small, marginal and tenant farmers) to the financial services is one of the effective tools to bring broad basing the economic growth. It is a means to increase the asset base as also providing opportunities to gainfully employee themselves and enhance their contributions to the development of the economy. Their economic activities particularly farm activity whereever existing need to be financed by the formal financial system in a big way. There are also more than 7 crores of agricultural labourers, some of them tenant farmers, whose plight is worse than that of poor

Source: Compendium of BANCON 2005.

farmers. So, if families of these farmers and the landless labourers are taken into account, it may be said that they eke out their existence and are almost untouched by the National endeavor of modernising agriculture. A more sensible strategy of bringing millions of small, marginal farmers and tenant farmers who are in possession of land, be adopted into the process of modern production. In fact, if these farmers become producers in the sence of rich farmers, the imbalance of growth in the Indian economy could be removed and the problem of abject poverty could be tackled. If they know that the farm can yield more and if they know that they need not helplessly look at the sky or the money lender, the tenant farmers supported by credit, by commercial bank, in terms of vital inputs can become the engines of their own growth.

A noteworthy aspect of increasing the productivity of these small, marginal and tenant farmers is that it would not only increase the per capita availability of food grains but also help increase the availability for those persons who need it the most.

Small/marginal farmers and tenant farmers is one of the components of the weaker sections. On account of strong policy environment associated with direct lending rate and further setting a target of 25% of priority sector advances or 10% of net bank credit to the weaker section, a large network of banking infrastructure provide finance services in the rural area in a big way. Culmination of such schemes is Kisan Credit Card (KCC) which was introduced in the year 1998.

Kisan Credit Card (KCC) scheme is to designed meet urgent agricultural credit requirements for agricultural operations as also working capital requirements for allied activities like diary, poultry etc. of farmers. KCC enables a farmer to avail a loan sanctioned to him as and when he needs to purchase inputs like seed, fertilizer and pesticides or get cash resources to increase crop production and to meet working capital or term loan requirement for activities allied to agriculture. Besides for non-farm credit needs of the borrowers i.e., consumption. Component upto 25% of the sanctioned limit maximum to Rs.25000. Besides cardholders can also avail of agricultural term loan to fulfill their requirement so that their farm productivity could be increased to the maximum extent.

The beneficiaries under the scheme are issued a credit card cum passbook incorporating the name, address, particulars of land holding, borrowing limit, validity period, which will serve both as an identity card as well as facilitate recording of the transactions on an ongoing basis. The card among others provide for a passport size photograph of the holder. The borrower is required to produce this card cum passbook whenever he operates the account.

The credit extended is in nature of a revolving cash credit and to provide for any number of drawls and repayments within the limit. The credit limit is fixed on the basis of the operational land holding, cropping pattern and scale of finance as recommended by the District Level Technical Committee for fixation of credit card limit, operational land holding is considered on the basis of inclusion of the leased in land minus leased out land in owned area of the borrower.

A personal Accident Insurance Scheme for card holders covering them against death and disability introduced from October 10, 2001 also provides personal accident insurance cover against accidental or permanent death this disability for a capital sum insured of Rs.50.000, while for partial disability, the compensation is Rs.25.000. The Policy covers KCC holders up to the age of 70 years. The premium is Rs.17.85 per person per annum while for three years policy, the premium is Rs.451 per person. The premium is shared by the KCC holders and the issueing bank in the ratio of 2:1.

The low strata of farming community i.e., small, marginal and tenant farmers generally have deficit household budget and they need credit even of small quantum to tide over their emerging consumption and production needs. Thus, KCC scheme has come to their rescue and recognized as one of the tools for their increasing farm productivity and well being.

In this context, one of the branches of a leading nationalized banks which had issued largest number of KCC in comparision to their other branches all over India was purposely selected for the convenience of the author. The branch issued 1500 KCC involving total cash credit limit of Rs.3.75 crore since the launching of the scheme. These card holders are scattered over in 14 villages i.e., Barbalia, Bhondari, Bhadewa, Bhilampur, Debaria Bhateswa, Dharwasand, Gautam Khera, Govindpur, Kondara Raipur, Miranpur, Mirapur, Sulsamau, Sysendi and Uttargaon of Mohanlal Ganj Block of Lucknow District.

Sampling

A list of card holders from the above villages falling in the category of small, marginal and tenant farmers have been prepared and 20% are selected at random with probability proportional to the total number of beneficiaries in each of three categories. Thus, small farmers cover 49 beneficiaries, marginal 24 and tenant farmers 17, making a total of 90 beneficiaries under the study. Further, an equal number of 90 sample families (comprising of 50 small farmers, 21 marginal farmers and 90 tenant farmers) in each of the above categories who are non-cardholders from the above villages are also randomly selected and a comparison of them are made. Thus, the study relates to 90 card holders and 90 non-cardholders, making a total of 180 sample family under the study.

In the present paper an attempt has been made to study.

1. The extent of limit sanctioned and credit availed by the identified families;
2. Utilization of loan;
3. Impact of finances made under KCC on:
   A. farm practices such as adoption of improved technology viz., improved method of cultivation, improved seeds, fertilizers, improved implements and insecticides;
   B. Intensity of cropping; and
   C. Yields of major crops and farm earnings and income.
4. To find out productivity of credit availed under the KCC scheme with the help of multivariate production function that is COBB DOUGLAS Production Function; and
5. Finally to suggest ways and means to make credit more productive.

The study yields useful results which are discussed below:

Details of Kisan Credit Cards Issued, Limit Sanctioned and their Disbursement

The study was carried out in Mohan Lal Ganj Block of Lucknow District where small/marginal and also tenant farmers, dominate in the area. The branch has made good performance in issuing of KCC for such weaker section in the area.

Table 1: Details of Kisan Credit Card, Seasonwise Limit Sanctioned and their Availment of Finance on the Sample Farms

Farmers	No. of issued KCC		Area in acres		Total Sanctioned Limit			Total disbursements			Share of each class of farmers ers in total disburse-ments
	No.	% to Total	Cultivated Area	Gross Area sown	Kharif	Rabi	Annual	Kharif	Rabi	Annual	
Small	49	54.45	22050 (4.50)	367.50 (7.50)	95.06.00 (19.400)	14.50.400 (29600)	24.01.000 (49000)	76.02.00 (15514)	1302100 (26573)	20.62300 (42087)	76.35
Marginal	24	26.66	54.00 (2.25)	102.00 (4.25)	304800 (12700)	283200 (11800)	588000 (24500)	240000 (10000)	240200 (10008)	480200 (20008)	17.78
Tenant	17	18.89	17.00 (1.00)	25.50 (1.50)	102.000 (6000)	61200 (3600)	163200 (9600)	100000 (5882)	58500 (3441)	158500 (9323)	5.87
All farms	90	100.00	291.50 (3.24)	495.00 (5.50)	1357400 (15082)	17.94.800 (19942)	3152200 (35024)	1100200 (12224)	1600800 (17786)	2701000 (30,010)	100.00

Figures in Parenthesis give average per KCC.

As already narrated, the study relates to 49 small, 24 marginal and 17 tenant farmers making a total of 90 farmers who have been enjoying the credit limit under the scheme of the last 4 years.

It is observed that the bank sanctioned limit of Rs.15082 for Kharif season crops and Rs.19942 for Rabi season crops making an annual limit of Rs.35024 per card holder for all farms, ranging from Rs.49000 to a small farmer to Rs.9600 to a tenant farmers depending upon their adoptibility of cropping pattern. Tenant farmers is not diversified in growing different crops on his farm as land leased in taken from the big farmers is not more fertile.

It is also pertinent to mention that bank has not fully followed the scale of finance while sanctioning limit for the different seasons to the farmers.

Borrowers are also not found enjoying full limit as sanctioned by the bank. As against sanctioned limit of Rs.15000 they have availed only 12000 for Kharif season, and as against Rs.20000 they have availed Rs.18,000 for Rabi seasons making less availment annual limit by Rs.5000 per card holder. The sample borrowers have availed limit as per their requirements. The same is found true for all the three types of borrowers. The details can be seen from the subsequent tables.

Scale of Finance and Limit Sanctioned by the Bank for Major Crops

While fixing limit by the bank acreage of different crops is taken into consideration. The bank has not sanctioned limit considering full scale of finance as approved by DLRC. It is found less by 31% for paddy, 36% maize, 25% for wheat, 24% for potato, 28% for gram and 69% less for growing of vegetables. It is good that bank has adopted uniform scale of finance irrespective of category of the farmers whether it is small or tenant farmers. Farmerwise details can be seen from the following Table 2.

Table 2: Breakup of Crop-Wise Limit Sanctioned and their Approved Scale of Finance Per Acre on the Sample Farms

	Paddy		Maize for cobs		Wheat		Potato		Gram		Vegetables	
Farmers	Scale of Finance	Cash credit limit Sanctioned by the Bank	Scale of Finance	Cash Credit limit Sanctioned by the Bank	Scale of Finance	Cash credit limit Sanctioned by the Bank	Scale of Finance	Cash credit limit Sanctioned by the Bank	Scale of Finance	Cash credit limit Sanctioned by the Bank	Scale of Finance	Cash credit limit Sanctioned by the Bank
All farms	8800	6000 (31.81)	4400	2800 (36.37)	9600	21200 (25.00)	7200	16000 (24.53)	2600	2000 (28.58)	5200	1600 (69.24)

Intensity of Cropping

The intensity of cropping for card holders and non-cardholders for different categories of farmers can be seen from Table 3.

Table 3: Details of Average Cultivated Area, Gross Area Sown and Intensity of Cropping Per Farm on Sample Farm

Farmers	Cultivated Area	Gross Area Sown	Intensity of Cropping
Small			
CH	4.50	7.50	166.66
NCH	3.90	6.25	160.25
Marginal			
CH	2.25	4.25	188.88
NCH	2.00	3.00	150.00
Tenant			
CH	1.00	1.50	150.00
NCH	0.50	0.75	150.00
All Farmers			
CH	3.24	5.50	169.75
NCH	2.90	4.80	165.51

CH = Card Holder NCH = Non Card Holder

Intensity of cropping for card holders and non-cardholders is observed more or less the same, except that of marginal farms. It varies from 150 in case of tenant farmers to 188 to marginal farmers for card holders while from 150 to 160 for non-card holders.

Productivity of Credit Availed under Kisan Credit Card Scheme

The main purpose of this study is to examine the impact of credit *vis-à-vis* other inputs involved in the production of crops on its output. A multivariate production function represents the relationship between these inputs and output. The COBB DOUGLAS production function of the form.

$$Y = a X1^{b1} \; X2^{b2} \; X3^{b3} \dots\dots\dots Xn^{bn}$$

has been fitted, where Y is the output, a is constant, and X1, X2 .... Xn denote the various inputs and b1, b2 .... bn are the elasticities of production with respect to the inputs X1, X2, ... Xn respectively. The sum of elasticities i.e.,

$$\sum_{i=1}^{n} bi$$

is called the elasticity of production and if

$$\sum_{i=1}^{n} bi > 1, \quad \sum_{i=1}^{n} bi = 1, \quad \sum_{i=1}^{n} bi < 1$$

indicates that the production is increasing, constant and decreasing returns to scale respectively. The variables X1, X2, ... Xn are the factors used in the production process and will explain the variations in the total production.

The data from 90 sample farms who had availed the finance under kisan credit card and utilized full or some of loan for raising the crops have been used for deriving the production function.

Total output of different crops has been taken as the dependent variables (Y). The independent variables chosen are given below.

X1 = Credit availed and utilized for production of crops in Rs.

X2 = Total working capital other than credit availed and utilised for production of crops.

X3 = Land in acres.

The following COBB-DOUGLAS multiple regression equation has been worked out between the above dependent and independent variable.

$$Y = 36.14\ X1^{0.24934}\quad X2^{0.47764}\quad X3^{0.17364}$$

The coefficient of multiple correlation (R) is 0.90757 which is significant at 5% and 1% level of significance. R^2 the coefficient of multiple determination is 0.82368 showing thereby that about 82% of the variation in output is explained by the independent variables factors selected in the equation. Inspite of the fact that all the factors are included in the equation, 18% of the variation remain unexplained.

Table 4 gives the various statistical estimate as derived from the fitted equation.

Table 4: Elasticities of Production (bi), their Standard Error (SE), EP and R^2

Sl. No.	Factors		bi	SE
1.	Crops Production Credit		0.24934 **	0.08679
2.	Total Working Capital other than Crop Production Credit		0.47764 **	0.07935
3.	Land		0.17364**	
		EP	0.90062	0.03949
		R^2	0.82368	
		R	0.90757	

** Significant at 1% level of Significance.

Elasticities of Production for various input factors are positive and significant at 1% probability level. Thus, the output could be increased by using more of these inputs. The sum of elasticities is less than one and hence indicates diminishing returns to scale. Table 5 gives Marginal Value Productivity (MVP) for different inputs.

Table 5: Marginal Value Products (MVP) and Geometric Mean (GM) of Input Variables			
Sl. No.	Factors	GM	MVP (Rs.)
1.	Crops Production Credit Availed under KCC	113.24	3.50714
2.	Total Working Capital other than Crop Production Credit Availed under KCC	290.25	2.62113
3.	Land	0.55	497.91846
	Y	1592.80	

A perusal of the foregoing table reveals that the land has a predominant effect on output. However, crop production credit under KCC and other working capital other than crop production credit also have good potentialities to enhance the output.

Adoption of Improved Technology

Under improved technology, use of improved seeds, fertilizers, implements and insecticides has been included. Credit availed under KCC scheme are likely to show a better impact of improved technology for differences between card holders than that for non-cardholders. It is in view of this fact that the card holders, non-cardholders with regard to the adoption of improved technology have been worked out in the Table 6.

Table 6: Card Holders and Non-Card Holders Differences in the Adoption of Improved Technology

Farmers	Proportion of Farmers Adopting (Percent)					Proportion of Gross Area Sown covered by (Percent)				
	Improved Method	Improved Implements	Improved Seeds	Fertilizers	Insecticides	Improved Method	Improved Implements	Improved Seeds	Fertilizers	Insecticides
Small										
CH	81.60	85.68	87.72	100.00	40.80	87.70	78.60	70.00	90.00	11.09
NCH	50.00	60.00	60.00	100.00	30.00	61.11	62.61	50.70	65.55	08.04
Marginal										
CH	70.56	76.44	58.80	100.00	35.28	68.61	70.58	51.19	68.90	6.70
NCH	52.60	6312	52.68	84.48	26.30	60.12	50.12	39,90	56.66	3.78
Tenant										
CH	74.88	49.92	33.28	49.92	-	40.11	46.26	31.04	51.85	-
NCH	33.32	23.80	14.28	23.80	-	20.00	25.56	11.91	20.23	-
All farms										
CH	72.16	69.20	57.24	78.69	22.11	64.72	62,22	48.68	68.11	5.26
NCH	45.10	4777	37.70	67.81	18.32	45.52	43.32	30.00	46.60	3.50

When the proportion of farmers and proportion of area under improved technology for card holders and non-cardholders for all farms is compared, it is observed that these proportions are higher among card holders than non-cardholders. Kisan Credit Card scheme can thus, be said to have a favourable impact on the card holder with regards to the adoption of improved technology. The statistical significance of this difference is tasted with the help of 't' test only in case of improved seeds and fertilizers. Table 7 gives the 't' value of percentage of gross area sown covered by improved seeds for card holders and non-card holders on the sample farms.

Table 7: 't' Test for the Differences in the Means of Percentage of Gross Area Sown Covered by Improved Seeds for Card Holders and Non-Cardholders on the Sample Farms.

Farmers	DF	SE	't' value
Small	71	2.374	3.308**
Marginal	18	3.213	2.535*
Tenant	9	3.566	3.182**

* Significant at 5% level of significance. ** Significant at 1% level of significance.

It will be seen from the Table 7 that the differences in the means of percentage of gross area sown covered by improved seeds for all the three type of farmers separately is significant. For small and tenant farmers, it is found significant at 1% probability level while for marginal farmers, it is significant at 5% level. Thus, the impact of KCC on card holders has been statistically significant.

Table 8 gives the 't' value of the percentage of gross area sown covered by fertilizers for card and non-cardholders.

Table 8: 't' Test for the Differences in the Means of Percentage of Gross Area Sown Covered by Fertilizers for Card Holders and Non-Cardholders on the Sample Farms.

Farmers	DF	SE	't' value
Small	97	2.433	3.958**
Marginal	31	4.134	2.215*
Tenant	15	3.446	2,206*

* Significant at 5% level of significance. ** Significant at 1% level of significance.

Table 8 reveals that the differences in the means of percentage of gross area sown covered by fertilizers for small farmers is significant at 1% probability level while remaining farmers are found significant at 5% probability level. The impact of KCC on the card holders has been found statistically significant.

Card Holders and Non-Cardholders Differences with Regard to Average Yield of Major Crops

The card and non-card holders differences with regard to the adoption of improved technology is likely to contribute to differences in the average yield of major crops. The same is set out in the Table 9.

Table 9: Yield Per Acre of Major Crops for Card Holders and Non Card Holders on the Sample Farms *(Quantity in Qts.)*

Farmers	Major Crops			
	Paddy		Wheat	
	CH	NCH	CH	NCH
Small	14.89 (+33.15)	11.44	13.60 (+33.85)	10.16
Marginal	12.62 (+20.30)	10.49	12.04 (33.62)	9.01
Tenant	8.68 (+9.80)	7.90	9.26 (+32.28)	7.00
All Farms	11.98 (+22.24)	9.80	11.63 (+22.24)	9.50

CH = Cardholders NCH = Non-Cardholders

It will be seen that the yield per acre for all the major crops are higher for card holders than that for non-cardholders. Further, the average yields for all the major crops increase with the increase in size of farms.

The statistical significance of the differences in the average yields of major crops grown by the card holders an non-cardholders is tested with the help of the 't' test. Table 10 shows the 't' value of average yield major crops.

Table 10: 't' Test for the Differences in Means of Average Yield of Major Crops for Card Holders and Non-Cardholders on Sample Farms.						
	Paddy			**Wheat**		
Farmers	**DF**	**SE**	**'t' value**	**DF**	**SE**	**'t' value**
Small	97	0.421	5.547**	97	0.464	5.695**
Marginal	34	0.656	1.739	34	0.727	5.888**
Tenant	43	0.483	2.104*	43	0.705	2.514*

* Significant at 5% level of significance. ** Significant at 1% level of significance.

As can be seen from the Table 10, the difference in the means of average yield of paddy between card and non-cardholders for small and tenant farmers is significant at 1% and 5% level respectively while for marginal farms it is insignificant. The difference between means of average yield of wheat between card and non-cardholders for small and marginal farmers is significant at 1% level while for tenant farmers it is significant at 5% level of significance.

Cost of Cultivation, Output and Net Income for the Major Crops

Cost of cultivation, output and net income per acre for the major crops for card holders and non-card holders can be seen from Table 11.

Table 11: Average Cost of Cultivation, Output and Net Income Per Acre for Major Crop on the Sample Farms						
Farmers	**Cost of Cultivation**		**Output**		**Net Income**	
	Paddy	**Wheat**	**Paddy**	**Wheat**	**Paddy**	**Wheat**
Small						
CH	5000	7000	7585	10,360	2585 (+27.33)	3360 (+68.33)
NCH	3800	5500	5830	7496	2030	1996
Marginal						
CH	4500	6300	6430	9024	1930 (+4.60)	2724 (+ 50.83)

Contd....

Contd...						
NCH	3500	4900	5345	6706	1845	1806
Tenant						
CH	3000	5000	4420	6856	1420 (+7.57)	1856 (+54.66)
NCH	2700	4000	4020	5200	1320	1200
All farms						
CH	4000	6000	6100	8676	2100 (+17.31)	2676 (+21.63)
NCH	3200	4700	4990	6900	1790	2200

Output includes total value of product and by product. It will be seen from Table 11 that output and net income per acre for all the major crops is higher for card holders than for non-cardholders. For the total sample farms, paddy shows a percentage increase of 17.31, wheat 21.63 over the net income of non-cardholders. This shows that credit limit for major crops in the area has adequately been fixed by the bank to fulfill their requirement of financial assistance for raising crops. This enables them to adopt improved technology significantly on their farms which creates significant impact in increasing of yields thereby getting higher net income in comparision to non-cardholders in the area.

Utilization of Credit Availed Under KCC Scheme

The impact of availed credit under KCC scheme is determined by the extent to which it is productively used. In the study, data regarding the utilization of loan were collected and the same are given in Table 12.

Table 12: Utilization of Credit Availed Under KCC Scheme

Farmers	Credit Availed Under KCC Scheme (Rs.)	Proportion of Borrowing Utilized for (Percent)			
		Current/Capital Expenditure in Agriculture	Consumption	Social/ Obligation	Non-farm Capital Expenditure
Small	20,62,300	70.53	14.53	7.58	7.36
Marginal	4,80,200	59.88	25.78	8.32	6.02
Tenant	1,58,500	49.75	34.12	10.82	5.31
All farms	**27,01,000**	**58.62**	**26.02**	**9.23**	**6.13**

It will be observed from the Table 12 that the actual utilization of loan as reported by the sample farmers indicates diversion to the extent of about 41 percent. Only 59 percent of the borrowings from KCC scheme are utilized for the stipulated purpose that is for expenditure in agriculture, 26% for consumption, 9% to meet social obligation and 6% for non-farm capital expenditure. Further, proportion of borrowings utilized for consumption and social obligation purposes are found increasing with decrease in size of farms.

Conclusion and Suggestions

The bank has made good performance in issuing of KCC for weaker section of the society. They have favoured small, marginal and even tenant farmers in solving their financial crisis faced in growing of crops by fixing limit for Kharif and Rabi season separately under Kisan Credit Card Scheme. The bank sanctioned the limit of Rs.15000 for Kharif season and Rs.20000 for Rabi season making an annual limit of Rs.35000 per card holder for all farms, ranging from Rs.49000 in case of small farmers to Rs.9600 to tenant farmers depending upon adoptibility of cropping pattern. It has also been observed that bank has not fully followed the scale of finance while fixing limit of a farmer. On the other side, borrower has also not enjoyed full limit as sanctioned by the bank. This shows that whatever limit is given by the bank, the borrower finds it adequate in raising of crops.

It is further observed that only 59 percent of the borrowings under KCC are utilized for the farming and diversion is also seen to the extent of 41 percent.

The average size of land holding for card and non-cardholder is observed as 3.24 acres and 2.90 acres respectively and intensity of cropping is more or less the same for card and non-cardholders and for all farms it is 170.

Productivity of credit availed under KCC scheme is worked out. The COBB-DOUGLAS production function has been used to find the relationship between the inputs and outputs i.e., impact of credit *vis-à-vis* other inputs involved in the production of crops on its output. It has been concluded that output could be increased by using more inputs i.e., crop production credit under KCC and other working capital other than crop production credit also have good potentialities to enhance the output.

Card holders and non-cardholders differences with regard to the adoption of improved technology has been worked out. When the proportion of farmers and proportion of area under improved technology for card and non-cardholders is compared, it is observed that these proportion are higher among card holders than non-cardholders. The statistical significance of the difference is tested with the help of the 't' test only in case of improved seeds and fertilizers. For improved seeds it is significant at 1% probability level for small and tenant farmers and at 5% level for marginal farmers. The differences in the means of percentage of gross area sown covered by fertilizers for small farmers is significant at 1% probability level while remaining farmers are found significant at 5% probability level.

The yields per acre for all the major crops are higher for card holders than that of non-cardholder. Differences in the means of average yield of paddy between the card and non-cardholder for small and tenant farmers is significant at 1% and 5% level respectively. The differences between means of average yield of wheat between card and non-cardholders for small and marginal farmers is significant at 1% level while for tenant farmers it is significant at 5% level of significance. Output and net income per acre for all the major crops is found higher for card holders and non-cardholders. For the total sample farms, paddy shows a percentage increase of 17.3, wheat 21.63, over the net income of non-cardholders.

It is thus, concluded that credit limit for major crops in the area has adequately been fixed by the bank to fulfill their requirements of financial assistance for raising crops. This enables them to adopt improved technology significantly over their farms which creates significant impact in increasing of yields thereby getting higher net income in comparison to non-cardholders in the area.

There is a scope for further increasing of output if diversion of credit for other purposes is reduced or scale of finance is fully adopted while fixing of the limit.

(S D Mishra, Senior Manager, Central Bank of India, Lucknow.)

Section II

Strategies for Improved Performance

10

A Design for Efficient Financial Intermediation and Deepening of Rural Financial Markets

Tamal Datta Chaudhuri

The literature has extensively deliberated on the relationship between financial sector growth and real sector growth. To extend the logic, rural financial growth should drive rural sector growth and should also be driven by it. However, the paper highlights that there are major realistic hurdles for financial sector growth in the rural sector. On one hand, they range from high transaction costs, small requirements, abject poverty, and lack of collateral and on the other, there are various perceptions regarding rural development and required need of institutions. While the competitive market model may fail, state driven rural development schemes have not performed better either. This paper takes a look at the existing literature and the data and shows that a combination of market forces and social support systems might work. The paper also highlights the fact that besides social concern for upliftment of the poor, in the current state of the Indian market, opportunities at the bottom of the pyramid do provide sufficient incentives to the financial intermediaries to move to the rural sector for business growth.

1. Introduction

Providing finance to the rural sector, in particular to the rural poor, is not an easy proposition as the rural folk do not have any assured source of income, they do not have sufficient savings or any assets to offer as collateral, they are not educated and at times live in remote areas where communication is not that easy. They do not have access to the formal banking system and more often than not are indebted to the local money lender. There also exists heterogeneity in terms of ethnicity, culture, and language.

The above characteristics immediately throw up certain constraints for availing financial resources from formal sources like banks. These include limited information on each individual that can be observed and monitored, absence of any collateral/security for the loan, no recorded evidence of their abilities and loan repayment capabilities, small credit requirements leading to high monitoring costs, absence of any permanent residence or location in remote areas which are far away from any financial center making monitoring difficult. Seasonality of operations and dependence on nature also acts as a discouragement for formal sector lenders. The risks involved in lending to the rural sector thus stem from high transaction costs, volatility in income flows, limited information for loan monitoring and high default risk.

In spite of all the difficulties, any strategy for economic development has to carry the rural population along. Strategies have to be designed such that the rural sector gets benefited, in particular, development of the rural financial sector. There are four ways of looking at rural financial sector development and accordingly there can be four different strategies. The first strategy builds on the observation that the poor are generally concentrated in the rural areas of any underdeveloped, developing or emerging economy. Poverty reduction would thus require making available financial resources to the rural poor such that they can adopt alternative income generating schemes. In this strategy, poverty is perceived as a public good and it requires governmental intervention. It is presumed that farmers do not get credit from formal sources, farmers are too poor to save, farmers need credit to adopt new technology; and agriculture is undercapitalized. For poverty reduction, the government will either have to use its own administrative machinery and financial resources to help the poor, or direct the formal financial system to provide the necessary financial resources. Poverty reduction is the responsibility of the state, and thus either the state will make funds available directly through various welfare-oriented schemes, or have directed credit programs through banks and financial institutions.

In this strategy, it is felt that if the poor do not get benefited from economic growth, then necessary focused efforts need to be made. Thus, besides budgetary allocation, targets need to be fixed for the financial sector players in terms of priority sector lending. This model thus subscribes to subsidies and other forms of financial support for the rural poor.

The second strategy is based on the hypothesis that the rural sector is as good a business-generating sector as the urban sector, and thus financial resources should automatically flow there. However, the problem in the rural sector is with credit delivery. Credit from the formal sector does not flow due to lack of appropriate institutions. The strategy thus is to have appropriate institutions in place for credit delivery.

The third strategy also looks at rural sector finance as a business opportunity, but this originates from the possibility that income from the urban financial sector could stagnate due to the presence of many players and intense competition leading to lower margins. In this context, the vast rural sector of India provides ample scope for increase in growth in income and profits. According to this line of thought, formal financial sector players, for their own motive of income and profit generation will move to the rural sector which in turn would take care of the poverty issue. This may be characterized by the phrase – "Opportunities at the Bottom of the Pyramid." The strategy would thus be to have the right institutions in place in the rural sector for proper play of market forces and allow level playing field for these players.

The fourth strategy draws on the relationship between financial sector growth and real sector growth. Growth in agriculture is an income-generating proposition, which will generate savings and lead to rural financial sector growth. This is important as otherwise rural savings will move out of the rural sector for use in the urban sector. On the other hand, rural financial sector growth will facilitate growth in the rural real sector by making available finance at rates much lower than informal sources. Lower cost of funds will encourage productivity growth and related development.

The concern in India on rural financial sector development (as reflected in the literature, in various issues of Economic Survey, Speeches by Finance Ministers and in various Reports of Reserve Bank of India) and the strategies adopted, encompasses all the above four approaches. There are subsidy-driven welfare-oriented schemes for the poor, there are specific schemes for rural women, there are directed credit schemes for banks and institutions and there are institutions like NABARD and Regional Rural Banks. There are other papers in this volume, which deal in detail on specific programmes. However, whatever be the approach and the corresponding strategy, the basic concern is to make financial resources available to the rural sector.

2. Data on the Indian Economy

The various formal agencies that are involved in providing finance to the rural sector include Scheduled Commercial Banks (SCBs), Regional Rural Banks (RRBs), Co-operative Banks, Self-Help Groups (SHGs), Micro Finance Institutions (MFIs), and Local Area Banks (LABs). The following provides some data for the Indian economy with regard to funding of the rural sector.

Table 1 shows that share of agriculture, forestry and fishing, mining and quarrying in GDP at factor cost has been decreasing over time. It must then be true that the other growing and emerging sectors of the economy are drawing away financial resources from agriculture. This is reflected in Table 2. The percentage share of advances to agriculture has not shown any growth in recent years which tends to say that the public sector banks are advancing money to the rural sector to satisfy the lending requirements and not as a

Table 1: Share of Agriculture, Forestry and Fishing, Mining and Quarrying in GDP at Factor Cost

Year	%
1950-51	59.19
1960-61	54.75
1970-71	48.12
1980-81	41.82
1990-91	34.92
2000-01	26.24
2001-02	26.28
2002-03	23.86
2003-04	23.93
2004-05	22.42
2005-06	21.74

Source: Economic Survey, 2006-07.

business proposition. The other figures are still quite insignificant to make any big impact.

Table 2: Percentage of Total Advances (Amount Outstanding) to Agriculture and other Priority Sectors by Public Sector Banks

	June 1999	March 2000	March 2001	March 2002	March 2003	March 2004	March 2005	March 2006
Agriculture	5.36	14.3	15.7	22.36	14.52	15.05	15.32	15.25
Funds Provided to RRBs	–	1.4	0.1	0.2	Neg	Neg	Neg	Neg
Advances to Self-Help Groups	–	.02	.04	0.1	0.22	.22	.26	.40
Advances to Food and Agro-processing Sector	–	0.93	1.7	1.12	0.83	.71	.21	.32

Neg: Negligible.

Source: Economic Survey, 2006-07.

On the other hand, as shown in Table 3, the government, through plan allocation has been consistently trying to improve the lot of the rural people. The difference between Tables 2 and 3 is that while Table 3 is driven by social welfare and other considerations of increasing agricultural productivity, Table 2 represents market forces.

Table 3: Percentage Distribution of Plan Outlay by Heads of Development

	Third Plan	Fourth Plan	Fifth Plan	Sixth Plan	Seventh Plan	Eighth Plan	Ninth Plan	Tenth Plan	Annual Plan 05-06	Annual Plan 06-07
Agriculture and Allied Sectors	12.7	14.7	12.3	6.1	5.8	5.16	4.9	3.9	3.8	3.7
Rural Development	–	–	–	6.4	7	7.9	8.7	8.0	7.7	7.0
Irrigation and Flood Control	7.8	8.6	9.8	10	7.6	7.5	6.5	6.8	7.1	7.5

Source: Economic Survey, 2006-07.

Table 4: Loans and Advance of PACS, SCARDBS and PCARDBS

(Rs.crore)

	PACS		SCARDBS		PCARDBS	
	Amount Advanced	Amount Outstanding	Amount Advanced	Amount Outstanding	Amount Advanced	Amount Outstanding
1980-81	1769	2621	–	–	362	1609
1986-87	3304	4732	203	301	354	1657
1987-88	3688	5242	190	8	356	1574
1990-91	4311	6486	384	1348	376	2014
2000-01	25698	34522	2586	12596	1866	8276
2001-02	30770	40779	2746	14110	2045	10005
2002-03	33996	42411	2959	15365	2177	10814
2003-04	35119	43873	2837	16263	2164	11311
2004-05	39212	48785	3292	17425	2569	12763
2005-06	na	na	2819	17895	2184	12792

PACS: Primary Agricultural Credit Societies.

SCARDBs: State Cooperative Agricultural Rural Development Banks.

PCARDBs: Primary Cooperative Agricultural Rural Development Banks.

Source: Handbook of Statistics of the Indian Economy, September 18, 2006
Report on Trend and Progress in Banking, RBI, 2005-06.

Although Table 4 gives the indication that there has been an overall increase in absolute volume of funds lent to the rural sector, the Credit/Deposit Ratio by Regional Rural Banks (RRBs) has gone below unity as shown in Table 5. This immediately implies that resources raised from the rural sector has moved out of this sector, most probably due to lack of profitable deployment opportunities.

Table 5: Credit – Deposit (C/D) Ratio of RRBs

	Aggregate Bank		C/D Ratio
	Deposits (Rs. Crore)	Credit (Rs. Crore)	
1980-81	232	285	1.23
1990-91	4560	3497	0.8
2000-01	35995	15211	0.42
2001-02	42494	18033	0.42
2002-03	47644	21359	0.45
2003-04	53390	25057	0.47
2004-05	58286	31651	0.54
2005-06	64195	36050	0.56

Source: Handbook of Statistics of the Indian Economy, RBI, September 18, 2006

With respect to credit delivery, Table 6 indicates that Scheduled Commercial Banks (SCBs) have moved towards non-rural areas for new business. Even RRBs have moved to semi-urban and urban areas for business growth as shown in Tables 7 and 8.

Table 6: Distribution of Scheduled Commercial Banks' Offices

Year	Rural	Total	R/T
1981	17656	35707	0.49
1991	35206	60220	0.58
2001	32562	65919	0.49
2002	32380	66190	0.49
2003	32303	66535	0.48
2004	32121	67188	0.48
2005	32082	68355	0.47
2006	30750	69118	0.44

Source: Handbook of Statistics of the Indian Economy, RBI, September 18, 2006.

Table 7: Nature of Credit Flow of RRBs

	2002-03	2003-04	2004-05	2005-06	2006-07
Flow of Credit to Agriculture From RRBs as % of Total credit to Agriculture	8.72	8.71	9.90	8.43	10.15
Credit/Total Investments	64.0	59.0	61.0	65.0	na

Source: Economic Survey 2006-07 & Handbook of Statistics of the Indian Economy, RBI, September 18, 2006.

Table 8: Distribution of RRB Offices

	1996	2003	2005	2006
Rural	12448	11989	11525	11509
Semi-urban	1844	2183	2414	2422
Urban	373	477	493	506
Metropolitan	7	22	49	51
Total	**14672**	**14671**	**14481**	**14488**

Source: Report on Trend and Progress in Banking, RBI, 2005-06.

Data from NSSO 2003 survey shows that of the 147.90 million rural households, there are 89.35 million cultivator households, i.e., 60.41%. Of this 49% are indebted to some sources and 51% are not indebted at all. Of this 51%,

88% are those belonging to the small farmer/middle farmer category with less than 2 hectares. Further, of the total cultivator household population, only 27% are indebted with formal sources. Of this 27%, the bias in the banking system is towards households with large land holding. There is also a state-wise dispersion in the level of indebtedness.

The above data indicates that there is enormous scope in terms of financial inclusion. There is a large untapped source of funds and also for funds advancement. So instead of looking at "trying to do good for the betterment of the poor", it is an "opportunity" that needs to be seized. It is obvious that the current environment is not doing what it was supposed to do. There is a conflict among the thinkers as to which of the four approaches are optimal. In this context, the following provides the essential ingredients for an optimal architecture.

3. The Design

The financial sector in India has been experimenting with ways to use Self-Help Groups (SHGs) for making available financial resources to the rural sector. These are groups formed by the rural households themselves who collect deposits and make advances to the members of the groups. The banks also treat the SHGs as an entity and lend to them for lending to the rural households. The structure of the SHGs is informal. As stated in Thorat (2005), the innovative methods that have been adopted for credit delivery include SHG Bank linkage, SHG Micro Finance linkage, SHGs forming co-operatives, OBC Grameen Project, Kisan Credit Card, Grameen Credit Card, Bhumiheen Credit Card, Grain Banks and Homestead Finance. It is suggested by him that the following delivery channels can also be used, namely Micro Finance Institutions, Post Offices, Farmers' Clubs and Village Development Boards. According to Thorat (2005), the way forward for rural financial development should include internet kiosk for credit delivery, credit franchisee arrangement for risk sharing with banks, financing marketing co-operatives, presence of ATMs and use Smart Card. There should also be a data base for pooling and dissemination of information on clients and their repayment record. For this it is necessary to set up a Credit Information Bureau.

In order to make rural financing effective, the need for support services and an enabling environment is essential. For this agricultural extension services, market linkages, comprehensive agri centers, non-traditional markets for auctioning of horticulture products, Apni Mandi, forward markets for final products and inputs and insurance products like crop insurance and weather insurance would be extremely helpful.

To sharpen the credit delivery mechanism in the rural sector in India, we can draw upon the experiences of other countries in designing instruments, institutions, regulatory bodies and legal environment for credit delivery. Further, besides exclusive focus on credit, the system should also look at the entire gamut of financial services like deposits, remittances, insurance, instruments, factoring, stores of value. We feel that to be effective and efficient, rural financial institutions should:

- Have fully autonomous management that can be held accountable for the bank's financial performance;
- Be insulated from local pressures for staffing;
- Be free to fix lending and borrowing rates so that there is a spread;
- Adopt best practices for prudential norms, accounting etc;
- Have a system of staff accountability;
- Have a strong MIS with on-site and off-site supervision;
- Use technology for reducing transaction costs;
- Operate on a hard budget constraint;
- Have specific non-renewable initial capital and subsidies;
- Adopt an assessment criteria in terms of subsidy dependence index and outreach index;
- Have the freedom to choose salary structure and performance related incentive;
- Provide incentives for timely payment in terms of rebate; and
- Have a sense of permanence.

Given the above ingredients for an optimal design of the rural financial sector, the linkages among the various components are shown in Diagram 1. The rural financial architecture has been developed in four layers. The first tier consists of Scheduled Commercial Banks (SCBs); in the second tier there are RRBs, LABs, Co-operative Banks and MFIs; in the third tier are SHGs and correspondent bankers; and the fourth tier is made up of support/advisory institutions.

One may observe that provision of direct credit by first and second tier institutions to the rural sector has not been drawn. Instead, they are operating through the third tier. The first two tiers are leveraging on the third tier. Currently, all the three tiers are involved in providing credit. The role of the support level institutions have been highlighted and also the role of the state in providing physical infrastructure.

Diagram 1

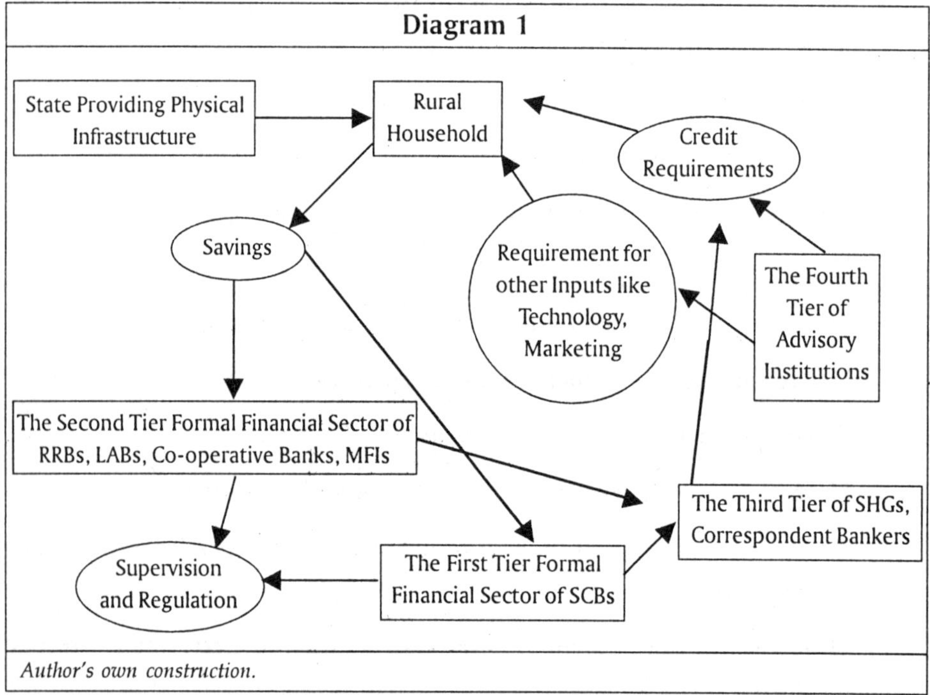

Author's own construction.

To get a better understanding of the design, the following schematic presentation is made which brings out the various aspects of rural development in detail. While Sequence 1 gives an overview of the various steps involved, Sequences 2, 3 & 4 give the details of each sequenc.

Identifying the sources of poverty, its spatial distribution, opportunities for income generation and the constraints for rural growth constitute the first step in the design. Given this, the three broad approaches include areas and forms of social intervention, the role of the market and mix of market and social forces.

The following three sequences deal with the approaches in detail.

Sequence 1

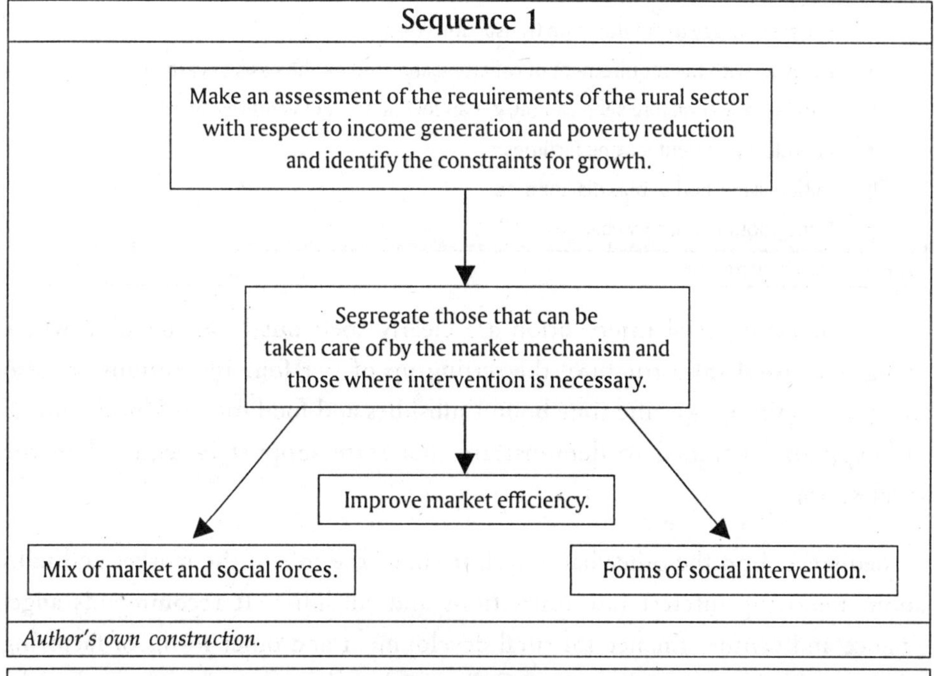

Author's own construction.

Sequence 2

Forms of Social Intervention

- Subsidised credit;
- Focused agro based centres in the public sector;
- Training;
- Matching grants for community based funds;
- Start-up capital from government sources;
- Subsidy for early innovators;
- Marketing tie-ups;
- Lines of credit at market rates;
- Targeted food support;
- Investment in rural infrastructure;
- Employment generation via food for work programmes.

Author's own construction.

Sequence 3
Improve Market Efficiency
• Remove interest rate restrictions; • Remove subsidy; • Provide banking and insurance under one roof; • Use technology to cut down on transaction costs; • Do away with the requirement of collateral and lend on the basis of cash flow; • Provide collateral free seed capital, get angel finance, get venture capital; • Provide equipment leasing facilities; • Initiate a method of bills discounting; • Bring about regulatory changes.
Author's own construction.

The areas of social intervention are clearly spelt out in Sequence 2 where along with rural infrastructure, the setting up of tier four institutions are also included. Training, specific time bound subsidies and food for work programmes are explicitly included to demonstrate that state support is required in the rural sector.

Sequence 3 on the other hand is clear about the role of the market and talks about removing interest rate restrictions and subsidies. It recommends angel finance and venture finance for rural development and other forms of factoring services to bring about liquidity. Collateral-based lending is proposed to be replaced by cash flow based lending to get around a major deficiency of the existing formal system of lending. The information system in the rural sector is imperfect and for the market mechanism to work, a strong information system is recommended.

Certain areas still remain where the state and the market has to exist side by side as it does not exclusively fall in either's domain. This is shown in Sequence 4. The basic theme is to use institutions to fill the information gap for efficient functioning of the market.

Sequence 4
Mix of Market and Social Forces • Organise rural people into Self-Help Groups (SHGs); • SHGs to be the economic agent for collection of deposits for deposit in a bank; • The bank will lend to a SHG who will on-lend to rural people; • Interest rate would be free; • The loans would be collateral free and the bank would have charge on the receivables; • The SHGs will be collection agents; and • Banking correspondents to be appointed.
Author's own construction

The above discussion and the suggested design have been drawn from other country experience and the literature and also the extent of progress that India has made in this regard. A clear distinction has been made between the role of state and the role of the market. In the introduction to this book, a brief description has been given about the policy reforms and the current thought process in India.

(Tamal Datta Chaudhuri is a Faculty at Icfai Business School, Kolkata. He can be reached at tamal5302@yahoo.com).

References

1. Claudio Gonzalez-Vega, (2003), "Deepening Rural Financial Markets: Macroeconomic, Policy and Political Dimensions", International Conference on *Best Practises in Rural Finance.*
2. Hans DieterSiebel, (2001), "SHG Banking: A Financial Technology for Marginal Areas and reaching the very poor", IFAD Rural Finance Working Paper No.167910.
3. Jacob Yaron, Mc Donald Benjamin, Stafanie Charitonenko, (1998), "Promoting efficient financial rural intermediation", World Bank Research Observer.
4. Manfred Zeller, (2003), "Models of Rural Financial Institutions", International Conference on *Best Practises in Rural Finance.*
5. "Report of the Review Group on the Working of the Local Area Bank Scheme", RBI, September 2002.
6. "Report of the Working Group on Flow of Credit to the SSI Sector", RBI, 2004.
7. "Report of the Advisory Committee on Flow of Credit to Agriculture and Related Activities from the Banking System", RBI, June 2004.

8. "Report of the Task Force on Revival of Co-operative Credit Institutions", RBI, December 2004.

9. "Report of the Internal Group to Review Guidelines on Credit Flow to SME Sector", RBI, 2005.

10. Report of the Internal Working Group on RRBs, RBI.

11. Report of the Internal Group to Examine Issues Relating to Rural Credit and Microfinance", RBI, 2005.

12. Ulrich Hess, (2003), "Innovative Financial Services for Rural India, Monsoon Indexed Lending and Insurance for Small Holders, Agriculture and Rural Development", Working Paper No. 9.

13. Y S P Thorat, (2005), "Innovation in Product Design, Credit Delivery, and Technology to Reach Small Farmers", Paper presented in Bancon 2005.

11

Paradigm Shift in Rural Banking: A Case of Microfinance Movement in India through SHG-Bank Linkage Program

A Ramanathan

NABARD is trying to free the small rural borrowers from the clutches of local moneylenders by providing loans to them at affordable rates through 750 NGOs and 3,64,000 client managed Self-Help Groups (SHG). Average loan size provided by these SHG is less than $22. Recovery performance is considered good. These savings led Self-Help Group Program of NABARD, really an innovative one.

Behold what is rapidly becoming the largest self-help undertaking in human history, bringing hope, dignity, and empowerment to tens of millions of low-income families worldwide. Behold a movement with global outreach, which has penetrated beyond city slums and market towns to even the most isolated villages. Behold an industry that embraces thousands of NGOs, credit unions, public and private banks, and hundreds of thousands of community-based

Source: Professional Banker, September 2005. This article earlier appeared in the book titled, "Innovations in Banks", published by the Icfai University Press.

Self-Help Groups, which are enabling many of the planet's poorest households to generate the additional income and savings they need to keep their children alive, nourished, healthy, and able to attend school. Behold a profession, which appears simple in concept but is extremely difficult in practice, because it involves myriad adjustments to highly different cultural settings, methodologies, and institutional structures, while simultaneously facing complex challenges involving client outreach, financing, evaluation, governance, training, government regulation, economic instability, civil disturbances, and natural disasters.

NABARD/India: Of all the innovations reported in this paper, the one which has achieved the largest scale to the world's poorest families is clearly the savings-led, Self-Help Group Program of the National Bank for Agriculture and Rural Development (NABARD). Building on an infrastructure of 1,42,000 rural and semi-urban branches whom NABARD refinances (one for every four villages in India), NABARD has enrolled the participation of 750 NGOs as facilitators of 3,64,000 client-managed Self-Help Groups (SHGs), averaging 16 members each, to serve 5.8 million rural saver-borrowers of whom 85% are women. These SHGs mobilize their own savings, transforming them into loans to members (average loan size less than $22), and plow their earnings from interest income back into equity. After a year or so, the experienced SHG is allowed to supplement their member loan portfolio by borrowing from their nearest NABARD-supported bank branch office. The program's on-time repayment rate is 95%. NABARD is currently negotiating with international donors for loan funding in excess of $1bn to further expand its hybrid public-private-SHG methodology to tens of millions of additional rural clients both within India as well as throughout the Asian region.

– 'Innovations From The Field:
A Daringly Brief Summary of a Huge Phenomenon'
by John K Hatch with Sara R Levine and Amanda Penn (June 2002).

Ever since the first bout of nationalization of commercial banks in July 1969, credit planning has become an integral part of overall national development planning. Since India lives in its villages and agriculture is the mainstay for majority of its populace, credit planning for agricultural and rural development received a priority status. The features of a typical loan product evolved as a sequel to that were: (i) a large per unit cost with or without state subsidy; (ii) concessional or market rate of interest; (iii) a longer repayment period; and (iv) backed by physical collateral as security.

With the above loan products, the credit needs of poorest of poor – those surviving on a day-to-day basis without ensured food, shelter, healthcare, education, and so on – requiring small sums with shorter repayment periods and not able to provide physical collaterals but are quite prepared to pay an interest rate somewhat higher than the one prevailing in formal sector, could not be institutionalized and in a typical third-world country like ours, they constitute one-third of population. Financial products are considered as the building blocks of a country's economy. With one-third lacking these building blocks, can we usher in an all-inclusive nation building process? Definitely not. Then what is the way out?

Further, IT and e-mass communication means have contributed to an all-round rising consciousness about what a good life is, and the triumph of democracy over all other forms of governance has given the people a forum to express themselves more assertively in voicing their needs and concerns. They have been increasingly holding their elected representatives accountable for their performance towards these. Their impatience for development is almost on the verge of flaring up into a state of social emergency. In this backdrop, the banks, like any other business organizations, cannot afford – rather the people's representatives of the country cannot afford them to allow – to ignore the demands of the people who are in need of their products and services and at the same time carry on business and grow.

In case, they want to thrive in their business and are interested in their long-term growth and sustainability, they must seek integration with the society. And this is not possible unless they become sensitive enough in accommodating the needs of the socially and economically deprived from their functioning and meaningfully contributing in the development tryst of the latter. In other words, only economic performance, i.e., how much internal wealth they generated through their business is not enough for banks in this new-age economy to thrive in a nation. They have to give equal importance to their social performance objectives as well. But social performance is not at the cost of economic performance, as the former cannot be sustained over a long run. The compelling question, therefore, before them was, how could they meet the demands of the society while being in profit?

During the same time, the country was witnessing another development. Some of the NGOs (Non-Governmental Organizations) providing MicroFinancial services to the most downtrodden as an add-on activity primarily aimed at increasing the delivery, impact and sustainability efficiency of their social sector (mainstream) services, were found to be converting themselves into full-fledged Micro Finance Institutions (MFIs) and making business out of it. The studies conducted in the field brought out the following sequence, which led to the above development:

- NGO's intervention was through group building (Promoting Self-Help Groups (SHGs) among the project participants so as to ensure their informed and active participation in the project implementation).
- Along with pursuing their main social agenda items, they also facilitated the SHGs to build a group fund through regular contribution of thrifts.
- The groups used the money in meeting the emergent, small and frequent credit needs of the members for all purposes with almost nil paper works.
- They worked on a democratic basis. Whom to give, for what to give, how much to give, at what rate of interest and for what repayment period; all got decided in a democratic framework.
- Appraisal, monitoring, rescheduling and recovery of loans were done through the operation of peer dynamics/pressure.
- It worked on 'it pays for itself' basis and therefore it is market-driven; not policy driven. In other words, it didn't require any outside subsidy to make the credit operations viable and sustainable.

Encouraged by this experience, the NGOs concerned lent money supplementing the group funds and there was near 100% repayment by the groups. This made them slowly to convert themselves into full-time Micro finance operators.

After nationalization, banks might have gone to many unbanked areas but they could not make appreciable progress in banking with all those who were not in a position to provide valid physical security and/or whose loan amount was so small that it failed to cover the cost of transaction. Whereas NGO-MFIs could do banking with these 'unbankable' with profit!

It opened the eyes of the formal sector financial institutions. Based on the studies conducted by NABARD during 1985-87, the following decisions were taken:

- To accept the NGO-promoted groups as they are; that is their amorphous legal character should not be tampered with.
- To facilitate the NGOs, banks and other statal/para-statal bodies to form such groups.
- There is no need to have another set of institutions catering specially to the needs of the hitherto financially unserved since we have already one retail rural credit delivery outlet for every four villages.
- Accordingly, to adopt supplementary credit route by linking them with the formal sector and SHGs being treated as the social collaterals or collateral substitutes.
- To develop policy response so that SHG organizations are used as foundation to formalize credit.

Concerns to Reach the Unreached based on Existing Paradigms	Shifts in Paradigm and Solutions
1. Macrofinance Products (The products are built on macro sums and factors e.g., Rs.10,000 loan as a product of Rs.2000 as annual installment, five annual installments, and interest on the reducing balances at quarterly rests.)	Micro-finance Products (The products are built on micro sums and factors. The choices and options of poorest of the poor in a society are built into in the design features of these products. For example, the same loan of Rs.10,000 can be a product of Rs.5, 2000 daily installments, and interest on the reducing balances at monthly rests. The poorest of the poor can then conveniently relate this loan product in their livelihood pattern).
2. Small loans; high transaction costs.	Enlist community participation; externalize a major portion of transaction costs.
	Contd...

Contd...	
3. Defaults with physical collaterals and less impact efficiency of the legal and administrative modes of contract enforcement in the event of repayment failures.	Substitution by social collaterals in the form of SHGs and contract enforcement through operation of peer dynamics/pressure which has high impact efficiency.
4. SHG being an informal entity lacks firm legal character. With this amorphous legal character, whom to sue in the event of default.	Joint and Several Liability Group. Each member can be sued to the extent of what a group has defaulted.
5. Asset-oriented. This could give a financier at least the benefit of seeing a tangible primary security.	Person-oriented. Irrespective of the capacity to manage the financial amount involved in acquiring an asset, if the loans are given based on what the assets in question to be acquired demand, there is a chance of it becoming a bad debt. Rather, loan should be considered to the extent one's financial management capability deserves.
6. Loans given for production purpose only because one can be assured of repayment from the future enhanced incomes.	Can be for consumption since quantum of credit is determined mostly by the existing surplus generating capacity of the family.
7. Group Activity Loan. Traditionally bankers favored extending loan for a single activity to be pursued by all the members of a group as a partnership firm/cooperative society/company.	Success rate is poor in group activity loan since group economic activity among the poor is a good appreciation of ideal but bad appreciation of human behavior. An act of prudence should be on individual micro enterprises with SHG serving as the hub.
8. Poverty alleviation is through asset accretion.	Poverty reduction through asset protection.
9. Saving = Income – Expenditure (Saving is a dependent function).	Expenditure = Income – Thrift. (In this equation, thrift is a comparatively independent function, and therefore, can be resorted to by any person. As such, even the poorest of the poor can save and form SHGs.)
	Contd...

Contd...	
10. Loan to users.	Loans can even be through members to users.
11. Reliance on walk-in business.	Adopt 'Outreach' approach.
12. Depended on the external bodies of the society to supply good clients and banks used them.	Client development through investment in relationship and capacity building (Credit Plus Approach).
13. Will these small loans make business sense?	As a portfolio, an emphatic 'Yes'. Additionally, its general impact on the overall business growth of the bank is also tremendous. This is on account of the thorough sanitization of socio-political milieu of the operating environment of credit in the area.

This historic decision heralded the following major paradigm shifts in rural banking, leading to a huge innovation unparallel in the history of evolution of Rural Financial Technology:

After what John K Hatch, Sara R Levine and Amanda Penn wrote on the movement in June 2002, the progress during the following three years (2002-05) has only further added to the hugeness of this huge phenomenon. Starting with a pilot project in 1992, as on March 31, 2005, through 14.26 lakh SHGs, credit needs of around two crore households hitherto unbanked could be formalized with a cumulative credit flow from the banks recording a figure of Rs.5,674 cr! Indeed, SHG-Bank Linkage Program facilitated by NABARD is by far the largest and fastest growing initiative in the world and the 'Queen' of all innovations in rural banking in India and elsewhere in the world. It is, therefore, no wonder that, to commemorate UN General Assembly's Resolution to designate 2005 as the 'Year of Micro Credit', on 19 November 2004, the micro entrepreneur groups were chosen to ring the opening bell of 11 stock exchanges across the world including NASDAQ, Karachi, Jakarta, Milan, Amsterdam, Zurich and Manila. In India, it was the members of SHGs who rang the opening bell in the Bombay Stock Exchange.

(A Ramanathan, is the Chief General Manager at National Bank for Agriculture and Rural Development, Punjab & Haryana Regional Office, Chandigarh.)

Microfinance Movement in India

– Tamal Datta Chaudhuri

Providing finance to the rural poor on commercial terms for productive deployment has many arguments in its favour. They range from income generation, empowerment of women, promotion of the rural artisans and traditional art, to freedom from the local money lenders. Overall, it is seen as a means of reduction in poverty through income generation on a self sustaining basis, without resorting to grants or subsidies. The linkages down the line are growth in education, better awareness, etc. The arguments against are lack of collateral, high transaction costs, lack of education, remote location etc.

One way of getting around the negative points has been growth in Micro Finance and the SHG Bank linkage program. Banks have started partnering with Micro Finance Institutions (MFIs) to lower transaction costs and also effectively deliver credit to the right users. For example ICICI Bank's rural portfolio has grown to around Rs.16,000 crore and is more than 6 per cent of the bank's assets. ABN AMRO Bank is targeting to work with and nurture 50 micro finance institutions in the current year. SBI has set a target of linking with 1 million SHGs by March 2008.

According to "Microfinance in India: A State of the Sector Report 2006" by CARE foundation, there are two models of micro finance. One is the SHG Bank linkage program and the other is direct credit by banks to the MFIs. The former has covered around 143 million poor and the latter has helped 7.3 million households of which 3.2 million are poor. The banks have also found lending to MFIs convenient as this helps them to cover their 40 per cent credit target to the priority sector. The requirement of Venture Funds is being met through funds like Lok Capital, Aavishkar and Bell Weather who are interacting continuously with new entrepreneurs. ICICI Bank has set up Center for Microfinance Research at the Institute of Financial Management and Research for training and strategy building to enable better access of the rural poor to funds. It has been observed till date that the rural poor are not bad borrowers and their repayment track record is good.

Table 1 shows the growth in SHG Bank Linkage in Priority States. This has been possible due to the efforts of NABARD which has led to seven times increase in the number of credit linked SHGs during 2002 to 2006. The initiatives undertaken include widening the spatial distribution of its programme, training of NGOs, banks, farmers clubs, governmental agencies etc., bringing the Panchayati Raj Institutions into this expansion programme and encouraging co-operative banks to lend to SHGs. NABARD has also supported partner agencies like Individual Rural Volunteers, Indira Gandhi National Open University, New Delhi and Yashwantrao Chavan Maharastra Open University, Nasik which run various programmes on women empowerment. NABARD has started a pilot project for development of Micro Enterprises (MEs) by members of matured SHGs and this will follow the 3-M approach. This is reproduced below from NABARD Annual Report 2006. (Box 1)

Table 1: Cumulative Growth in SHG-Bank Linkage in Priority States (As on March 31)

State	2002	2003	2004	2005	2006
Assam	1,024	3,477	10,706	31,234	56,449
Bihar	3,957	8,161	16,246	28,015	46,221
Chhattisgarh	3,763	6,763	9,796	18,569	31,291
Gujarat	9,496	13,875	15,974	24,712	34,160
Himachal Pradesh	5,069	8,875	13,228	17,978	22,920

Contd...

Contd...					
Jharkhand	4,198	7,765	12,647	21,531	30,819
Maharashtra	19,619	28,065	38,535	71,146	1,31,470
Madhya Pradesh	7,981	15,271	27,095	45,105	57,125
Orissa	20,553	42,272	77,588	1,23,256	1,80,896
Rajasthan	12,564	22,742	33,846	60,006	98,171
Uttar Pradesh	33,114	53,696	79,210	1,19,648	1,61,911
Uttaranchal	3,323	5,853	10,908	14,043	17,588
West Bengal	17,143	32,647	51,685	92,698	1,36,251
Total Priority States	**1,41,804** (31)	**2,49,462** (35)	**3,97,464** (37)	**6,67,761** (41)	**10,05,272** (45)

Figures in parentheses indicate percentage share of priority State in total number of SHGs credit linked.

Source: NABARD Annual Report 2006.

Box 1: 3M-Micro-Enterprise Model

The 3M Model uses micro-finance, micro-markets and a micro-planning methodology to help the poor start Micro Enterprises based on their potential for self-help and means of local sustainability. Being a generic approach to micro-enterprise development. it (i) can be conveniently applied to any rural area in the country; (ii) is self-substaining relying on local resources, existing skills and local markets and not on any external agency for support; (iii) follows a micro-planning approach based on grassroots level information from villages where SHGs are located and focuses on location specific solutions; and (iv) focuses on intervention at both village and project levels through a detailed micro-enterprise plan. The grounding of 3M approach requires, survey of the project area, analysis of the data collected from the survey, preparation of Micro Enterprise plans and their implementation. The model has been illustrated below.

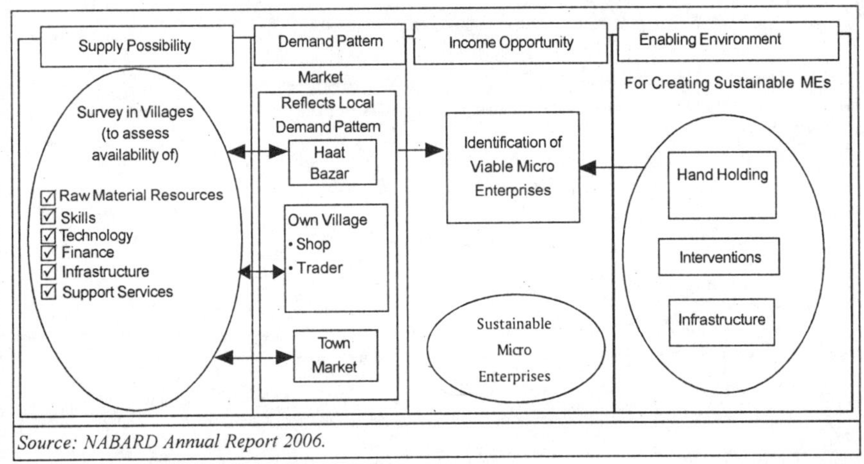

Source: NABARD Annual Report 2006.

Contd...

Contd...

Currently, according to Economic Survey 2006-07, 547 banks including scheduled commercial banks, RRBs and co-operative banks are actively involved in the Self-Help Group (SHG)-Bank Linkage Program. As on March 31, 2006, Rs.11,398 crore loan has been availed by 2,238,565 SHGs from the banking system and the average size of a loan is around Rs.50,000. This has enabled 329 lakh poor families in the country to obtain finance from the banking system.

(Tamal Datta Chaudhuri is a Faculty at Icfai Business School, Kolkata. He can be reached at tamal5302@yahoo.com).

References

1. NABARD Annual Report 2006.
2. Gargi Banerjee (December 4, 2006), "The Way Ahead", *Business World.*
3. Manas Chakraborty (December 4, 2006), "Taking Banking to the Poor", *Business World.*

12

Financing Rural Poor: Performance of Micro-Finance Sector in India

Paramita Raut

Micro-finance system in India has opened up numerous opportunities for the rural population to gain access to formal finance. The largest component of micro finance has been the SHG-Bank linkage model. Micro financing in rural India is mainly organized through Self-Help Groups formed by the rural people though collective savings and investments in income generating activities. The paper shows that the SHG-Bank linkage model has grown in a skewed fashion in India with some states like Andhra Pradesh being ahead of others. Further, scheduled commercial banks have done a better job than co-operative banks.

An effective system for provision of financial services to the poor households as well as underprivileged sections of society has always been in the focus of various policy programs[1] initiated by the Government of India during the reforms years of the nineties. With the relatively matured mainstream financial intermediation and a vast branch-network, the Scheduled Commercial Banks in India, have been working towards improving access to formal finance to rural poor.

Source: Artha Beekshan, Journal of Bengal Economic Association, Vol. 14, Nos. 3 & 4, December 2005 & March 2006.

In this context, the emergence of Micro-finance system in the Indian financial scenario has unveiled several opportunities for the rural population to scale up their access to formal finance and to meet their diverse financial needs.

'Micro-finance' has been defined by the task-force on Micro-finance constituted by the National Bank for Agriculture and Rural Development (NABARD) as "provision of thrift, credit and other financial services and products of very small amounts to the poor to enable them to raise their income and improve their living standards". By far the largest component of Micro-finance in India, in terms of scale of operation, geographical coverage and outreach, is the SHG-Bank

Table 1: Micro-finance Models in India

Operational Features	**Grameen**	**SHG**	**Individual Banking/ Sector Cooperative**
Client Type	Primarily Women Groups (usually 5 members)	Primarily Women Groups (10 to 20 members)	Primarily Men Individual Clients
Service Focus	Credit – Regular cycle	Savings and Credit	Credit
Role of MFI Staff	Organise (groups dependent on staff)	Guide and Facilitate (groups may develop autonomy)	Organise
Mechanism (Meeting Schedules)	Weekly Meetings	Monthly Meetings	Variable-Often Daily*
Interests on Savings	6-9%	Bank rate (4.25 % + profit share)	Above 6%
Savings Products	Rs.5-25/week	Rs.20-100/month	Variable
Insurance	–	In early stages	Links to National Companies
Credit Products	Rs.2-5,000	Rs.5-10,000 Internal loans Facilities from Group Funds	Rs.15-35.000
Effective Interest Rate	29-41%	14-36%	18-24%
Developmental Services	Usually None	Through Associated NGOs/Banks/MFIs	Enterprise Support

* Individual transactions linked to production cycle.

Source: EDA Rural. 2004.

linkage model. In recent years, the micro-finance industry has also witnessed the emergence of two institutional structures viz, the Grameen-model[2] and the Individual Banking or Cooperative Micro-finance Institutions. These specialized Micro-finance Institution (MFIs) models are, however, relatively minuscule in comparison.

The broad objectives of the Micro-finance system are:

- To foster savings and micro-credit among rural population, particularly empowering women by their participation in productive services (farm/ non-farm), building capacity, leadership building and involving them in decision-making and planning in households and group activities;
- To ensure sustainable livelihood of the community by promoting income generation through micro-enterprises and bringing in improvement in agricultural practices (diversification of crops, marketing, asset building, etc.);
- To build-up effective liaison between village based organizations and training institutions, resource agencies and government, departments which can assist them in development initiatives; and
- To strengthen and empower the Self-Help Groups or community groups so that they can articulate and address their strategic interests including issues relating to Panchayati Raj, literacy, environmental concerns, community health, etc.

The present paper attempts to showcase the experiences of the Micro-finance sector in India, which have evolved different financial products and services, institutional models and outreach channels to meet the above-said objectives of 'inclusion with impact'. The central theme of the paper is to assess the potential of Micro-finance in the country to ensure active poverty-targeting among rural population. In this connection, the paper focuses on the performance of credit delivery mechanisms of different Micro-finance agencies (particularly, the Scheduled Commercial Banks) for improving rural financial health in the recent years. It also explores the scope of outreach of the Self-Help Groups in terms of access to micro-credit and other financial services.

The SHG-Bank Linkage Program: How widespread and effective is Micro-finance in rural India?

In India, financial policies have attempted to involve the institutional network of commercial banking in the provision of Micro-finance to the rural economy and the poor through Self-Help Groups (SHGs). Starting with a pilot project, early back in 1992, NABARD developed SHG-Bank linkage approach as the core strategy that could be used by the banking system in india for increasing their outreach to the poor. The strategy involves forming SHGs of the poor, encouraging them to pool their thrift regularly and using the pooled thrift to make small interest bearing loans to members, and in the process, learning the nuances of financial discipline. The modes of linkage[3] between the bank and borrowers are- (i) Bank acting as a SHG promoter (SHPI) i.e., "takes initiatives in forming the groups, nurtures them over a period of time and then providing credit to them after satisfying itself about their maturity to absorb credit"; (ii) banks and SHGs are linked through facilitating agencies (NGOs or government agency) to whom direct loans are provided; and (iii) NGOs acting as the facilitating and intermediating agents and banks providing direct credit to them. This linkage approach has been observed not merely as a credit program but as part of an overall arrangement for providing financial services to the poor in a sustainable manner leading to social and economic empowerment of the members of these SHGs.

NABARD (1997) captures this by defining SHGs as "small, economically homogenous affinity groups of rural poor, voluntarily formed to save and mutually contribute to a common fund to be lent to its members as per the group members' decision".

Empirical evidences show that Micro-financing in rural India is mainly organized through Self-Help Groups formed by the rural people with the objective of improving their livelihoods through collective savings and investments in income-generating activities. This model comprises largely rural womenfolk who are able to participate in various income earning opportunities in situ and hence improve their employment status. In the later half of the nineties, there has been a proliferation of women SHGs across India, particularly in the Southern states (Narayana, 2002). These groups are designed not only as a strategy for poverty alleviation, but also to increase women's access to resources and their power in household decision-making (Sundaram, 2001). Several literatures have shown that credit needs of the poor are determined in a complex socio-economic milieu, where the dividing line between credit for 'consumption' and 'productive' purposes is rather blurred. Hence, it is difficult to adopt the traditional banking approach to lending and to insist that loans are not used for consumption. In this situation, the SHG-Bank linkage program has been observed as a modest performer in the micro-finance sector in the recent years. Moreover, most development initiatives working through SHGs are specifically targeting the poorest people. For example, the World Bank funded Andhra Pradesh District Poverty initiatives Project aims, amongst others, at supporting investment in sub-projects proposed by grass-root institutions of the poor to accelerate their entry and expand their involvement in social and economic activities. In order to reach the poor, this project used a three-fold system of targeting: geographic targeting (selection of the poorest districts, and within these the poorest mandals); group targeting (through formation of group-based activities for the poor); and self-targeting (through a focus on small, technologically manageable investments that are attractive primarily to the poor organising themselves into common interest groups) (World Bank, 2000).

To ensure active poverty targeting, micro-finance programs are often designed to open up realistic investment opportunities for the poorest households in the country and the SHGs are considered to be an effective channel to carry out this purpose (Nair, 2005). Micro-finance policy framework rests on the fact that "micro credit serves best those who have identified an economic opportunity and who are in a position to capitalise on that opportunity if they are provided with a small amount of ready cash. Thus, those poor who work in stable or growing economies, who have demonstrated an ability to undertake the proposed activities in an entrepreneurial manner, and who have demonstrated a commitment to repay their debts (instead of feeling that the credit represents some form of social revindication), are the best candidates for micro credit" (Satyamurti *et al.* 2002). Data on SHGs (Table 2) show that the number of SHGs formed and nurtured through credit-linkage programs have grown steadily in the recent years both in absolute and relative terms. Of the total SHGs formed, more than 1.6 million have been linked with 35,294 bank branches of 560 banks in 563 districts across 30 states in India. Cumulatively, they have so far accessed credit of Rs.6.89 billion.

About 24 million poor households have gained access to the formal banking system through the linkage program (NABARD, 2005).

Table 2: Cumulative Nos. of SHGs and Bank Loans Across Regions (2003 & 2005)

(amount in Rs. million)

Regions	Cumulative No. of SHGs Provided with Bank Loan upto 31.3.03	Cumulative Bank Loan upto 31.3.03	Cumulative No. of SHGs Provided with Bank Loan upto 31.3.05	Cumulative Bank Loan upto 31.3.05
North	34,923	771	86,018	2.395.18
N-E	4,069	60	34,238	1,019.61
East	90,893	1,204	2,65,628	5.183.06
Central	81,583	1,447	1,97,365	5.014.56
West	42,180	869	96,266	2.950.77
Southern	4,63,172	16,134	938,941	52,421.42
Total	**253.648**	**20,485**	**16,18,456**	**68.984.60**

Source: Annual Report. NABARD, 2003 & 2005.

Among three modes of linkages (Table 3), nearly 12 percent of the SHGs are of type I while the type III link "is likely to be found more convenient by banks for credit linkage" (80.3 percent). However, the skewed distribution of SHGs across regions poses a threat to the qualitative development of the micro-finance industry as a whole. Figures show that about 86 percent of the total SHG credit linkages (explained by the amount of outstanding loans) in the country is concentrated in the southern states, particularly Andhra Pradesh. The states of Manipur, Jharkhand, Chattisgarh, Bihar, Assam, Punjab and many Union Territories have comparatively low coverage of SHGs though they have larger shares of the poor. This skewed distribution may be attributed to the over zealous support extended by the state governments to the program and also some issues related to region-specific formation and growth of non-statal agencies (NGOs) in carrying out the Micro-finance activities. Considering the SHG activities across bank-groups (Table 4), the growing number of SHGs sponsored by the commercial banks and the rural banks points out that the mainstream financial institutions do find their SHG portfolios 'safe and performing' and they are much willing to reach out to the poor in developing 'relationship banking' through the micro credit deployment programs. However, the sluggish response of the Cooperative banks is a matter of concern in this regard. The banks' lending to SHGs or micro credit has not shown impressive progress in terms of accounts and amount.

Table 3: Regional Spread of SHGs and Bank Loans According to 3 Models

(figures in percent/shares to total)

Regions	Type I Model		Type II Model		Type III Model	
	No. of SHGs	Bank Loans	No. of SHGs	Bank Loans	No. of SHGs	Bank Loans
North	11.2	10.1	88.8	89,9	0.0	0.0
N-E	77.9	87.6	15.2	10.1	6.9	2.3
East	42.5	35.3	45.2	54.6	12.3	10.1
Central	23,4	23,7	74.1	74.5	2.6	1.9
West	35.2	35.8	58.6	56. 1	6.2	8.1
Southern	12.2	9.4	80.3	85.5	7.5	5.1

Source: Annual Report. NABARD, 2003 & 2005.

Table 4: Agency-wise Distribution of SHGs and Bank Loans among Regions

(as on 31.03.05)

Regions	Cumulative No. of SHGs (% shares)				Cumulative Bank Loan to SHGs (% shares)			
	CBs	RRBs	Cooperative Banks	Total	CBs	RRBs	Cooperative Banks	Total
Northern	4.33(42.48)	5.62(36.85)	8.42(20.66)	5.31(100)	2.42(42.07)	4.01 (35.15)	8.53(22.78)	3.47(/00)
N-E	1.64(40.15)	3.36(55.11)	0.67(4.14)	2.12(100)	1.71(69.77)	1.30(26.85)	0.54(3.37)	1.48(100)
Eastern	11.69(37.12)	19.84(42.12)	26.12(20.76)	16.41(100)	5.65(45.36)	9.91(40.16)	11.73(14.48)	7.51(100)
Central	9.66(41.28)	17.92(51.20)	7.03(7.52)	12.19(100)	5.31 (44.02)	11.96(50.06)	4.64(5.93)	7.27(100)
Western	6.35(55.63)	4.23(24.77)	8.94(19.61)	5.95(100)	4.50(63.39)	3.17(22.53)	6.49(14.08)	4.28(100)
Southern	66.33(59.59)	49.02(29.24)	48.82(10.98)	58.01(100)	80.11(63.80)	69.65(27.90)	68.07(8.31)	75.99(100)
Total	100	100	100	100	100	100	100	100

Source: NABARD, 2005.

The commercial banking system, mainly the Public Sector Banks, has also gained much importance in the recent years (since latter half of the nineties) in deploying institutional credit to rural poor. Considering the SHG activities across the Public Sector Banks (Table 5), however, we observe a mixed trend in credit disbursement per SHG. Some banks have shown negative growth in number of SHGs followed by negative growth in loans lent out to the self-help groups during the years 2001-03. However, Bank of India, Bank of Maharashtra, State Bank of Hyderabad and Andhra Bank have been able to increase their credit figures in spite of having negative growth in the number of SHGs. The average amount of loan disbursed has increased from Rs.22,690 to Rs.49,306 over three years. The relative variation in loan disbursement across the banks has been also reduced by 20 basis points at the same time. The Micro-finance activities through SHG linkage have further expanded by the participation of new-age private sector banks like ICICI Bank, UTI Bank, HDFC Bank, etc.

Table 5: Growth Rates in Loan Disbursed to SHGs by the Public Sector Banks (2001–2003)

(Amt in Rs.'000 rate in percent)

Banks	Bank Loan Disbursed per SHG (2001-02)	Bank Loan Disbursed per SHG (2002-03)	Annual Growth in Loan Disbursed Per SHG (2001-03)	Annual Growth in Number of SHGs in model II (2001-2003)
ALB	9.85	25.76	249	64.4
ANB	19.68	80.25	79.7	-17,9
BOB	16.38	43.21	84.6	1
SOI	2.97	41.37	33.3	-3.7
BOM	17.09	63.72	94.1	-11.3
CAN	28.09	46.22	174.5	86.4
CBI	26.84	53.03	110.6	28.3
COR	23.93	56.26	89.9	• 7
DENA	6.00	51.62	63.4	-36.8
INB	23.43	82.44	II 5.7	-2.9
IOB	19.52	59.65	107.9	1.7
OBC	26.22	34.81	-18.07	-26.4
PSB	48.37	43.54	209.6	230.4
PNB	17.9	41.95	336	14.7
SYN	20.75	76.05	154.4	5.8
UCO	17.8	30.2	93.6	34.6

Contd...

Contd...				
UNB	17.7	54.16	141.7	12.6
UBI	2.62	19.26	354.2	5.2
VB	25.53	30,37	349.9	286.1
SBJ	13.23	22.52	58.1	13.5
SBH	16.28	62.04	113.1	-7.2
SBI	18.57	SS.2	151.2	17.7
SBIN	52.28	32.23	218.5	385.5
SBM	31.91	38.87	164.6	126.2
SBP	53.88	52.16	99	103.9
SBS	6.6	79.33	-40.1	-49.2
SBT	29.17	55.05	71.2	14.2

Source: Progress in SHG-Bank Linkages. NABARD, 2003.

However, strong empirical evidences of high administrative costs and growing dependence on subsidies are being observed in the functioning of almost all microcredit programs, which in turn, are believed to hinder the expansion in scale of operation of such organizations[4]. Some economists have also observed that the erosion of profits in the banking system on account of micro credit has a bearing on the defaults on loans taken by the bigger borrowers (Shetty, 1997) and

SHG-Bank Linkage Programs: Merits and Demerits

Merits	Demerits
For SHGs and Members	
– locations advantage;	– savings may not be insured;
– community participation;	– psychological barriers;
– own fund controlled by members;	– predominance of male members;
– on-lending activities among members;	– low financial strength;
– savings mobilization and capacity building;	– high repayment structure;
– diversification of non-farm activities/livelihood;	– political interference and manipulations;
– access to subsidized finance under development program;	– loans often used for consumption rather than productive purposes.
– increased women participation, enhancing their contribution to household income;	
– reduced dependence on informal money lenders and non-institutional sources.	

Contd...

Contd...

For Banks/MFIs/Cooperatives	
– promoting banking habits among poor;	– credit indiscipline among borrowers;
– outreach among rural poor;	– no standardized legal and supervisory provisions;
– deposit mobilization through savings;	
– enhancing rural economic productivity through easy finance;	– improper identification of target groups;
– focus on target groups – marginal farmers, women, rural artisans;	– dependence on NGOs for credit disbursement;
– asset-building and economizing cost of lending;	– high transaction costs;
– enhancing credit abso(ption capacity of rural households;	– operational restrictions hindering 'up-scaling';
– diversification of risk through diversification of loan portfolios;	– regional imbalances;
– building up support system through nonfinancial assistance (technical support, skill development, training etc.);	– no comprehensive records of recovery status, loan-appraisal.
– developing non-farm productive activities and services.	

often leaves the poor unbanked (Yunus, 1999). Moreover, regional disparities in disbursement of credit across the country indicate a perpetuation of inequitable distribution of development benefits among the poor. This disturbing trend, further, highlights the need to identify the pros and cons of bank-linkage programs in order to ensure the long-run financial viability of the micro-finance policies and development strategies in rural India. Who has access to what financial services? This kind of information is crucial in helping the financial service providers to design better ways of delivering better services profitably on a significantly larger scale, assessing effectiveness of their interventions and achieving wider public policy goals.

Emergence of Micro-Finance Institutions

The SHG-Bank Linkage program has evolved as the largest micro-finance working model in India. However, the recent trend on micro-finance development identifies another group of organizations which acts as MFIs. They are basically extremely heterogeneous group comprising NBFCs, societies, trusts and cooperatives. They are provided financial support from external donors and apex institutions including the Rashtriya Mahila Kosh (RMK), SIDBI Foundation for micro-credit and NABARD and employ a variety of ways for credit delivery. Since 2000, commercial banks including Regional Rural Banks have been providing funds to MFIs for on-lending to poor clients. While there is no published data on private MFIs operating in the country, the number of MFIs is estimated to be around 800. A large majority of them operate on much smaller scale with clients ranging between 500 and 1500 per MFI, It is estimated that the MFIs' share of the total institution-based microcredit portfolio is about 8 percent (Thorat 2005). According to the CGAP's Guiding Principles on Regulation and Supervision on Micro-finance (2003), the goal of supporting Micro-finance programs is to expand outreach and create sustainable institutional framework in the country to deliver financial services to the poor. The competitive selection[5] criteria for MFIs constitute:

- consolidation of partners/NGOs;
- provision of legal and technical guidelines to monitor partner MFIs; and
- customizing methodology of outreach and operations according to local circumstances.

Outreach of MFIs is explored in terms of their geographical location, the gender of clients, their social group, poverty level and access to formal sector finance. At present, around 45 SFMC partner MFIs are operating mainly in rural areas (78 percent of members are rural) but are concentrated in the south and western regions of the country (90 percent of total members).

The basic developmental objectives of these MFIs are to attain financial self-sufficiency rather than depending on the donor funding and govt. subsidies for sustainability. However, in absence of a policy framework and regulatory norms for MFIs to access public funds, these institutions are facing critical challenges in bridging the gap between demand and supply of financial services among rural poor. Often these MFIs pass on the higher cost of credit to their clients who are 'interest insensitive' for small loans but may not be so as loan sizes increase. It is, therefore necessary for MFIs to develop strategies for increasing the range and volume of their financial services.

Conclusion

The present study reveals that the Micro-finance industry in India has inculcated strong banking habits among rural poor through the extensive credit delivery mechanism of SHG-Bank linkage programs. The models also show that the financial resources are being sourced from existing banking infrastructure of the country following various development strategies. However, we observe growing regional disparities in the distribution of micro-credit and direct investments under this program. Further, the new MFIs with their organizational diversity and complex working strategies are yet to maximize the potential benefits that the rural poor can enjoy.

(Paramita Raut is Guest Lecturer in the Department of Economics in Ravindra Bharati University, Kolkata.)

Endnotes

1 Swarnjayanti Gram Swarozgar Yojana (SGSY) is one of such self-employment programs for the rural poor, officially launched on April 1, 1999 by the Government of India. The scheme aims to cover 30% of the rural poor in each block through a credit-cum-subsidy linkage programs. At least 50% of the beneficiaries of this scheme would be Scheduled Castes and Scheduled Tribes, 40% women and 3% disabled. All beneficiaries are to be drawn from families who are Below-The-Poverty-Line (BPL), identified through a BPL census, and the percentages referred to above are based on this BPL population. The quotas seek to ensure that the scheme benefits less advantaged members within the BPL community, if not the poorest of the poor.

2 Modern micro-finance was born in Bangladesh in the 1970s, in the aftermath of the country's war of independence, when Muhammad Yunus, Professor of Economics at the University of Chittagong, began an experimental research project providing credit to the rural poor of Bangladesh. That experiment, driven by *a strong sense of developmental idealism developed into what is now the world's most famous micro-finance institution, the Grameen Bank, and institutions that replicate its pioneering methodology worldwide.*

3 A paper on Microcredit-SHG-link Banks; *http://www.nabard.org/roles/mcid.htm*

4 Zaman, H (2000), "Assessing the Poverty and Vulnerability Impact of Micro-credit in Bangladesh, A case Study", Background Paper for WOR, 2000/2001. World Bank, Washington.

5 From the outset, MFIs are to be instilled with the concept that they should be looking towards commercial sources of fund.

References

Chavan, Pallavi and R. Ramakumar (2002), "Micro-credit and Rural Poverty: An Analysis of Empirical Evidence", *Economic and Political Weekly*. March 9.

EDA Rural Systems (2004): "The Maturing of Indian Micro-finance, A Longitudinal Study", *www.edorural.com*

Honohan Patrick (2005), "Measuring Micro-finance Access: Building on Cross Country Data", WPS 3606, World Bank, May.

NABARD (1997). NABARD and Microfinance. National Bank for Agriculture and Rural Development. Mumbai.

——(2003): Annual Report, Mumbai.

——(2005): Annual Report, Mumbai.

Nair Tara (2005): "The Transforming World of Indian Micro-finance", *Economic and Political Weekly*, Vol. XL No. 17.

Narayan. D, (2001), "'Consultations with the poor' from a health perspective", *Journal of Development Economics*, 44(1).

Satyamurti. V. and Haokip S. (2002): *Micro-finance: Concepts and Delivery Channels in India*. New Delhi, AIAMED.

Sundaram, I.S. (2001), "Self-Help Groups – Challenges and Opportunities", *Social Welfare*.

Thorat Y.S.P (2005), "Micro-finance in India: Sectoral Issues and Challenges", Theme Paper on High Level Policy Conference on Micro-Finance, New Delhi.

World Bank Project, (2000) Report No. 20089-IN, March.

Yunus, M. (1999): "Banker to the poor", *Micro-lending and the battle Against World Poverty*. New York Public Affairs.

13

Revival of Regional Rural Banks through Restructuring and Mergers

Janardhan G Naik

The Regional Rural Banks (RRBs), which are supposed to be an innovation in the Indian Banking system, have failed to achieve the objectives for which they were set up between 1976 and 1987. Nearly after three decades of their working, now the question is raised about their revival. In this article, it is argued that through restructuring and mergers of RRBs, revival is possible.

The Regional Rural Banks (RRBs) were set up under a separate enactment of parliament, the RRBs Act 1976, in tune with the recommendations of Shri M Narsimham, Chairman of Working Group, who was appointed in 1975 to explore the possibilities of evolving an alternative rural credit agency to benefit the rural poor. The RRBs were described as an innovation in Indian Banking system. The innovation relates to their institutional setup, objectives, functions, area of operation and customers. They are specialized institutions, distinct from commercial banks and cooperative credit agencies. For every RRB there is one sponsor Public Sector Bank. But the capital of RRB is jointly owned by the Union Government, concerned state government and the sponsor bank in the

Source: Icfai Reader, July 2006.

ratio of 50:15:35 respectively. The authorized capital of each RRB is Rs.5 crore (initially Rs.1 crore) and the issued capital is Rs.1 crore (initially Rs.25 lakhs). The RRBs are supposed to take banking to the doorsteps of rural masses, especially in those areas where banking facilities are not available. So, they are regionally based and rural oriented commercial banks, combining desirable qualities of cooperative banks and commercial banks. The RRBs have a local feel and familiarity with rural problems much like cooperative banks and organizations that are able to mobilize deposits; they have access to the money market and a modern outlook on par with other commercial banks. They provide credit to small farmers, artisans, small entrepreneurs and agricultural laborers. The RRBs are mainly regulated and supervised by the National Bank for Agriculture and Rural Development (NABARD) but are also required to follow the RBI directives.

Working of RRBs

Between 1976 and 1987, all 27 Public Sector Banks (i.e., 8 SBI group and 19 Nationalized Banks), established 196 RRBs. As on March 31, 2004, there were 196 RRBs, with a network of 14,446 branches covering 518 districts in 26 states and with 70,000 employees (see Appendix).

Performance of RRBs *(Rs. in crore)*

	2004-05		2003-04		2002-03	
	No. RRBs	Rs.	No. RRBs	Rs.	No. RRBs	Rs.
Profit-making	167	904	163	952	156	734
Loss-making	29	154	33	184	40	215

The profitability of RRBs has been very poor. Many of them have huge accumulated losses. "Having been saddled with the twin burdens of directed credit and a restrictive interest rate regime, however, RRBs have historically incurred substantial losses. These losses were accentuated by politically motivated decision-making, emphasis on subsidized ending and an overall welfare-orientation expected of such institutions."[1] Only in the recent years some of them are in blue. "163 RRBs earned profit at Rs.952.33 crore during the year 2003-04 compared to 156 RRBs earning profit at Rs.733.96 crore in the previous year. During

[1] *The Outreach/Viability Conundrum: Can India's Regional Rural Banks Really Serve Low-Income Clients?* By Snajay Sinha, Tanmay Chetan, Orlanda Ruthven and Nilotpal Pathak Working Paper 229, October 2003.

2003-04, other 33 RRBs incurred losses at Rs.183.65 crore as against 40 RRBs incurring losses amounting to Rs.214.67 crore in the previous year".[2]

"Data in respect of 196 RRBs indicate that the number of loss-making RRBs declined in 2004-05. During 2004-05, 167 RRBs earned net profits amounting to Rs.904 cr, while 29 RRBs incurred losses to the tune of Rs.154 crore".[3] State-wise analysis indicates that the maximum numbers of loss incurring RRBs are situated predominantly in the states of Bihar (9 out of 16), Jharkhand (3 out of 6) and Orissa (4 out of 9). Likewise, sponsor bank-wise analysis reveals that the maximum numbers of loss incurring RRBs are accounted for by SBI and Central Bank of India".[4]

Over time, RRBs have been able to garner small savings from the countryside, while being relatively less successful in enhancing the flow of credit to the targeted rural poor. The aggregate deposits of RRBs moved up from Rs.4,151 cr in 1990 to Rs.62,143 cr by March 2005, while advances rose from Rs.3,554 cr to Rs.31,803 cr over the same period. The credit-deposit ratio serves as an aggregative measure for gauging the effectiveness of credit delivery system. There has been a falling trend in the credit-deposit ratio over the years, from 87% in March 1990 to 51% in March 2005. The lower credit-deposit ratio implies lower credit orientation and also a cause for low profitability of RRBs.

RRBs experience high transaction cost and lower labor productivity in terms of business per employee. The policy parking of huge funds with sponsor banks has made them "lazy bankers". However, this policy has been changed from 2002-03. Now, RRBs are allowed to put these funds in Government Securities.

Even though there is an improvement in loan recovery from 57% as on June 30, 1997 to more than 75% as on June 30, 2003, NPAs, in absolute terms, stood at Rs.3,299 cr as on March 31, 2004.

---

[2] "Report of the Internal Working Group on RRBs", appointed by RBI, June 2005.

[3] "Report on Trend and Progress of Banking in India" 2004-05, RBI.

[4] "Report of the Internal Working Group on RRBs", appointed by RBI, June 2005.

Shortcomings of the RRBs

Today, RRBs face a number of impediments in their holistic growth and suffer from numerous weaknesses in achieving the goals. The Internal Working Group on RRBs[5] in its report has identified the following major shortcomings in the working of RRBs:

1. Limited Area of Operation;
2. Narrow Clientele Base;
3. Under Capitalized – deposits are very large as compared to their capital base;
4. Small Organizational Structure;
5. Low Recovery and Large Non-Performing Assets;
6. High Cost Structure;
7. Perceived as Specialized Rural (poor man's) bank;
8. Inadequate Financial Management;
9. Unskilled and Aging Staff Structure;
10. Heavy Dependence on Sponsor Banks;
11. Lack of Professionalism in Management; and
12. Erosion of Deposits.

Restructuring of RRBs

Several committees/working groups on RRBs have documented well the various problems and have made far-reaching recommendations to remedy the situation. Lending to non-target groups (Dantwalla Committee, 1978), recapitalization and investment in high-yielding government securities (Kelkar Committee, 1986), lack of freedom to take any commercial decisions by the board (Khusro Committee, 1989) and possible merger with rural subsidiaries of sponsor banks

[5] Internal Working Group on RRBs was set up by the Reserve Bank in February 2005, under the chairmanship of AV Sardesai to examine the various alternatives available within the existing legal framework for strengthening the RRBs and making them viable rural financial institutions. The group submitted its final report in June 2005.

(Narasimham Committee, 1995), employee related issues (Rao Committee, 2002) and restructuring of RRBs (Internal Working group of RRBs, A V Sardesai, June 2005) are a few of the recommendations.

Some of these suggestions have been implemented and other policy initiatives are taken particularly since mid-1990s to revitalize RRBs. One such initiative was the contribution of nearly Rs.2,200 cr by the stakeholders of RRBs as an additional capital for the 187 RRBs between 1994-95 and 1999-2000. There have been quantitative as well as qualitative improvements in the performance of RRBs following the banking sector reforms process. The policy measures undertaken with respect to RRBs, viz., the permission to relocate loss-making branches to better business centers and conversion of loss-making branches into satellite/mobile offices without impairing their performance in service areas has also had a salutary effect on their financial performance, especially profits, recovery and decline in their NPAs. Simultaneously, prudential norms on income recognition, asset classification and provisioning for loan losses following customary banking benchmarks were introduced. While there has been some improvement in the functioning of RRBs in the recent years, there is a significant room for improvement in their governance, transparency, human resources, and systems and procedures.

Restructuring and Mergers

For revitalizing the ailing RRBs, the following restructuring and merger options are available:

1. Mergers and Amalgamation of RRBs:
   a. State-level merger of RRBs of each sponsor bank;
   b. State-level merger of all RRBs involving different sponsor banks;
   c. National-level merger of RRBs and creation of Rural Bank of India;
   d. Merger with the sponsor bank itself; and
   e. Reverse merger.
2. Capital Restructuring.
3. Changing the Sponsor Bank.

4. Management Restructuring.
5. Other Options of Revival.
6. Liquidation.

1. Mergers and Amalgamations

Change of sponsor bank can be achieved though amalgamation and it is also possible to have operating synergies. Mergers will enlarge the area of operation and business opportunities for RRBs. However, the amalgamation will not automatically improve efficiency. The amalgamation options could be:

a. State-Level Merger of RRBs of each Sponsor Bank

This recommendation is from the Internal Working Group. Keeping in view "the recommendation," "the Government of India (Ministry of Finance), after consultation with NABARD, the concerned State Governments and the Sponsor banks, issued nine notifications on September 12, 2005 under Section 23-A of the Regional Rural Banks Act, 1976 providing for amalgamation of 28 RRBs into nine new RRBs sponsored by nine banks in six States, viz., Bihar, Gujarat, Karnataka, Maharashtra, Punjab and Uttar Pradesh. These amalgamations have become effective from September 12, 2005."[6] Similar notification was issued by West Bengal in January 2006. This type of merger process has resulted in the reduction of number in RRBs, from 196 to 162. It is expected that other states will also follow suit and there will be around 65 RRBs by March 31, 2006.

b. State-level Merger of all RRBs involving Different Sponsor Banks

There is no provision for two sponsor banks for the same RRB in the RRB Act. In the case where RRBs sponsored by two different banks are sought to be merged within the same state, the shareholding of one of the sponsor banks will have to be vested in the other bank under notification. The directors appointed by the outgoing sponsor bank will have to be withdrawn. The issue of any compensation to the outgoing sponsor bank will have to be settled in consultation with the sponsor bank and specified bank in the notification.

---

[6] "Report on Trend and Progress of Banking in India, 2004-05", RBI.

c. **National-level Merger of RRBs and Creation of Rural Bank of India**

As the RRB Act does not envisage more than one state government to be the shareholder of RRB, there will be transfer of shares held by one state government to the other. In an inter-state merger, the shares may be transferred to the state government where the RRB has its headquarter. Further, the directors appointed by the outgoing state government will also have to be excluded from the merged entity. When all RRBs in the state are merged there will be only one bank called "Rural Bank of India" or "National Rural Bank". Way back in 1998, the All India Regional Rural Bank Employees' Association demanded setting up of National Rural Bank in place of different RRBs. But nothing happened. The Employees' Association, on a nationwide strike on March 22, 2005, urged the Union Government again to form a "Rural Bank of India" and bring all 196 RRBs in the country under its jurisdiction.

d. **Merger with the Sponsor Bank itself**

Firstly, merger of RRBs with the sponsor bank is not provided for in the RRBs Act, 1976. Therefore, the Act needs to be amended. Secondly, such mergers would go against the spirit of setting up RRBs as local entities and for providing credit primarily to weaker sections.

e. **Reverse Merger**

A sponsor bank merging with its RRBs amounts to reverse merger, which is not a sound alternative. The Government is also not thinking along this line. "About nine proposals have been cleared to merge sponsor-wise, state-wise RRBs. There is no plan to merge the sponsor bank with the RRB. Once the number comes down from 196 RRBs, more consolidation will follow,"[7] said Shree Leeladhar.

2. Capital Restructuring

"To wipe out accumulated losses, provide for the NPAs and maintain 5% CRAR (capital to risk weighted asset ratio) for the RRBs in the existing scenario, capital to the extent of around Rs.3,050 cr would have to be infused with appropriate conditional ties," says the Internal Working Group.[8] If the capital adequacy ratio

---

[7] V Leeladhar, Deputy Governor, RBI "On the Progress of Merger of Regional Rural Banks (RRBs)", June 17, 2005.

[8] "Report of the Internal Working Group on RRBs", appointed by RBI, June 2005.

has to touch 8% (and not 9% as per Basel I norms), the capital infusion rises to Rs.3,430 crore, it is estimated.

Therefore, the authorized and issued capital of RRBs should be raised above Rs.5 crore and Rs.1 crore, respectively, to correct deposit-capital ratio and wipe out accumulated losses. This increased capital has to be subscribed in the same proportion as that of the existing one by central and state governments and sponsor banks, as per the RRB Act provisions. If any of the shareholders, like the state government or sponsor bank, is not inclined to subscribe to further capital, increase in subscribed capital will not be possible. Restructuring of the capital ownership of RRBs may be explored. The Union and State Governments may pass on their shareholdings to NABARD and also allow the new restructured Rural Banks to go public to raise capital like other PSBs. RRBs can also raise debt capital by way of bonds or debentures, as they are authorized to undertake any business specified under Section 6(1) of the Banking Regulation Act.

3. Changing the Sponsor Bank

"A change in sponsorship may inter alia improve competitiveness, work culture, management and efficiency of the concerned RRBs," feels the Internal Working Group.[9] For this, both the new and old PSBs could be considered, as they are uncomfortable with priority sector lending norms and could swap it with buying RRBs. But there is no provision in the RRB Act for transfer of sponsorship from one sponsor bank to another. There is no provision to transfer shares between the sponsor bank and other prospective sponsor bank. This calls for amending the RRB Act.

4. Management Restructuring

a. The chairmen of most of the RRBs are from sponsor banks which limits the freedom and decision-making capacity of the RRBs. Thirty years is a fairly long period to open up the top management slots to the staff of RRBs. The chairman could be appointed by the Board of RRB, in concurrence with RBI.

---

[9] "Private banks as RRB sponsors seems a good bet" by P Devarajan. *The Hindu-Business Line*, May 21, 2005. *http://www.thehindubusinessline.com/2005/05/21/stories/2005052101450600.htm*

b. The Boards of RRBs may be strengthened by making them broad-based through inclusion of professionals such as agricultural experts, bankers, etc.

c. One of the problems in the case of RRBs is the unskilled and aging staff structure which has adversely affected the performance of RRBs. This is the fallout of both policies (ban on recruitment) and other factors. There is, therefore, a need to change the human resources policies in RRBs and greater flexibility and freedom may be given to them to recruit competent and skilled staff from the open market, subject to some broad guidelines.

d. An appropriate incentive structure, career planning, relevant training, especially in skill upgradation and information technology, should be evolved for the employees of RRBs.

e. The Union Budget 2004-05 emphasized that the sponsor banks would be accountable for the performance of their RRBs. Sponsor banks are advised by the Reserve Bank to provide support to their sponsored RRBs in matters relating to efficient management, training of staff, computerization and networking of their activities.

5. Other Options of Revival

Multiple ownerships of RRBs have resulted in bureaucratic controls. A plethora of reporting rules and regulations have resulted in inefficient management practices. To improve their efficiency, there is a need to calibrate operational and supervisory practices.

6. Liquidation

The Internal Working Group is of the opinion to give 3 to 5 years for a turnaround. For those RRBs which may not turnaround within a specified time limit, an exit route may be considered subject to extent legal provisions. The provisions relating to winding up of companies do not apply to RRBs. Under Section 26, any RRB can be liquidated by the Central Government by an order directing liquidation and specifying the manner of such liquidation.

Conclusion

Revival of RRBs can be achieved through restructuring of capital and through mergers. For this, the RRBs Act needs suitable amendment. Moreover, there is a need for revamping the regulatory and supervisory framework to ensure high quality of management and governance. Only then, RRBs can be expected to meet the expectations of becoming vibrant rural financial institutions capable of meeting the growing requirements of rural India.

(Janardhan G Naik, is Professor and Head of the Department of Accountancy, Gogte College of Commerce, Belgaum. He can be reached at jgnaik52@yahoo.com).

APPENDIX

The State-Wise and Sponsor Bank-Wise Distribution of RRBs					
Sr. No	**State**	**No. of RRBs**	**Sr. No.**	**Bank**	**No. of RRBs**
1.	Andhra Pradesh	16	1	Allahabad Bank	7
2.	Arunachal Pradesh	1	2	Andhra Bank	3
3.	Assam	5	3	BOB	19
4.	Bihar	16	4	BOI	16
5.	Chhattisgarh	5	5	BOM	3
6.	Gujarat	9	6	BORajasthan	1
7.	Haryana	4	7	CBI	23
8.	Himachal Pradesh	2	8	Canara Bank	8
9.	Jammu & Kashmir	3	9	Corporation Bank	1
10.	Jharkhand	6	10	Dena Bank	4
11.	Karnataka	13	11	IOB	3
12.	Kerala	2	12	Indian Bank	4
13.	Madhya Pradesh	19	13	J&K Bank	2
14.	Maharashtra	10	14	P&S Bank	1
15.	Manipur	1	15	PNB	19
16.	Meghalaya	1	16	SBBJ	3
17.	Mizoram	1	17	SBH	4
18.	Nagaland	1	18	SBI	30
19.	Orissa	9	19	SBIND	1
20.	Punjab	5	20	SBM	2
21.	Rajasthan	14	21	SBP	1
22.	Tamil Nadu	3	22	SBS	3
23.	Tripura	1	23	Syndicate	10
24.	Uttar Pradesh	36	24	UBI	11
25.	Uttaranchal	4	25	UCO Bank	11
26.	West Bengal	9	26	UPSC Bank	1
27.	Union Bank of India	4			
	Total	**196**		**Total**	**196**

Source: Report of the Internal Working Group on RRBs, appointed by RBI, June 2005.

14

Indian SME Sector Financing – Some Winning Strategies with Specific Reference to Commercial Banks

K Ramakrishnan

This paper, while highlighting the need to develop SMEs, also deals with the constraints these units face like fragmented markets, use of inferior technology, lack of access to national and international markets and considerable delay in settlement of bills due to lack of bargaining power. In this context, the efforts by the government for provision of credit like venture capital funding, cluster-based approach, credit rating of SMEs etc., are explained. Further, some winning strategies are suggested which include setting up of dedicated SME branches, quicker processing of cases, continuous support, conducting training programmes etc.

Indian Small and Medium Enterprises (SME) Sector

Small and Medium Enterprises (SMEs) in India have been given a distinct identity and the Government of India has accorded high priority to this sector on account of the vital role it plays in balanced and sustainable economic growth.

It is considered a growth engine of our economy and plays a crucial role in the process of economic development by value addition, employment generation, fostering enterpreneurship and entrepreneurial skills, equitable distribution of ational Income, regional dispersal of industries and providing depth to the industrial base, mobilization of capital and contributing to export earnings of the country.

With the economic liberalization and globalisation of the economy, this vital sector has faced huge challenges and competition from domestic as well as multinational players. Within the SME Sector, Small scale industries including the Tiny Sector form part of the priority sector lending of banks. It is observed that growth in banks' credit to small scale industries has not kept pace with the growth in aggregate net bank credit, as evidenced by the fact that the number of SSI borrowal accounts fell from 20 lakhs to 16 lakhs and the amount outstanding to the SSI Sector grew at a falling rate, i.e., its share fell down from 14.2 per cent to 10.4 per cent of aggregate net bank credit between 2001 and 2004 respectively.

The importance of Small and Medium Enterprises (SME) has assumed significance after the Government has decided to introduce a Bill called "Small and Medium Enterprises Bill, 2005" in the coming monsoon session of the Parliament. The present definition of small scale and ancillary industries covers all those SSI Units engaged in the manufacture, processing or preservation of goods and whose investment in Plant and machinery (original cost) does not exceed Rs.1 crore. These would, *inter alia,* include units engaged in mining or quarrying, servicing and repairing of machinery. In the case of ancillary units, the investment in plant and machinery (original cost) should also not exceed Rs.1 crore to be classified under small scale industry. The investment limit of Rs.1 crore for classification as SSI has been enhanced to Rs.5 crore in respect of certain specified items under hosiery, hand tools, drugs, pharmaceuticals and stationery items & sports goods by the Government of India.

With regard to medium enterprises, no clear cut definition in terms of original investment in plant and machinery is available. A clear cut picture on this, will emerge after the above mentioned Bill on SME is passed in the Parliament. Pending approval of the above bill in Parliament, in terms of policy package announced by the Hon'ble Finance Minister on 10.08.2005, for the present, a unit with original investment in plant & machinery in excess of SSI limit and upto Rs.10 Crore is being treated as medium enterprise.

The recent 'Policy package for stepping up credit to Small and Medium Enterprises', tabled by the Finance Minister, Shri P Chidambaram in the Rajya Sabha indicates that:

"The Small Scale Industries (SSI) produce about 8000 Products, contribute 40% of the country's industrial output and offer the largest employment after agriculture. The sector, therefore, presents an opportunity to the country to harness its local competitive advantages for achieving global dominance. In recognition of these aspects, the National Common Minimum Programme makes the following declaration for accelerating the development of the Small Scale Sector.

"Household and artisanal manufacturing will be given greater technological, investment and marketing support. Small scale industry will be freed from Inspector raj and given full credit, technological and marketing support. Infrastructure upgradation in major industrial clusters will receive urgent attention."

Further, according to the Small Industries Development Bank of India (SIDBI), an apex financial Institution for promotion, financing and development of SME Sector in India, the SME Sector contributes significantly to the Indian economy and to the overall GDP growth rates as well as industry sector growth rates. In India, SME Sector is the second largest in terms of providing employment opportunities; after agriculture and the output from the SSI Sector alone constitutes 40 percent share of the value added in the manufacturing sector and one third of national exports. SMEs are the basic force that promote social stability and exist primarily in the traditional manufacturing industries which are also labour intensive.

From SSI to SME: Defining the New Paradigm

Government policy as well as credit policy have so far concentrated on manufacturing units in the Small Scale Sector. The lowering of trade barriers across the globe has increased the minimum viable scale of enterprises. The size of the unit and technology employed for firms to be globally competitive is now of a higher order. The definition of Small Scale Sector needs to be revisited and the Policy should consider inclusion of services and trade sectors within its ambit. In keeping with the global practice, there is also a need to broaden the current concept of the sector and include the medium enterprises in a composite sector of Small and Medium Enterprises (SME). A comprehensive legislation which would enable the paradigm shift from small scale industry to small and medium enterprises is under consideration of parliament. The Reserve Bank of India had meanwhile set up an internal group which has recommended:

"Current SSI/Tiny Industries definition may continue. Units with investment in plant and machinery in excess of SSI limit and up to Rs.10 crore may be treated as Medium Enterprises (ME). The definition may be reviewed after enactment of the Small and Medium Enterprises Development Bill. Only SSI Financing will be included in Priority Sector."

Special Characteristics of Small and Medium Enterprise (SME)

- SME units are promoted by first generation entrepreneurs or those with limited track record and resources. The main promoter raises resources from his close friends and relatives to fulfill the margin money requirement of Banks.
- The unit is often a family concern, the constitution being proprietorship or partnership or at the most private limited company.
- In case of first generation entrepreneurs, banks do not have the benefit of the past track record of the unit. Even in respect of existing units, due to their inability to obtain rating from credit rating agencies, Banks are not inclined to extend assistance without sufficient collaterals and the cost of funds was till recently none too attractive. Another related problem is the improper risk assessment by the banks, leading to high NPAs.
- Many small units are promoted by entrepreneurs following the herd mentality, after seeing the success of similar units set up by friends and relatives.
- The units do not generally engage the services of professional managers on an ongoing basis and depend upon consultants for setting up and stabilising the operations. Thus, they are poor in management.

- Another structural constraint faced by SME units relate to lack of availability of proper infrastructure facilities.
- There is no institutional arrangement for sourcing and assessing the appropriate technology, with the result they employ obsolete technology.
- The requirement of funds for completing the project is not realistically estimated, which lands the promoters with limited resources in difficulty, when they are faced with the need for infusion of additional Funds due to overrun. Thus, there is no proper cash flow management by the SMEs, whose creditors are typically paid in cash.
- The promoter virtually carries out all the important functions of the manager on day-to-day basis with no time left for planning for the future.
- Marketing is another grey area for the SME Units. They depend on one or two buyers for their products and face a lot of difficulty in realising the receivables in time.

Challenges Faced by the SME Sector

The challenges faced by the Small and Medium Enterprises may be briefly set out as follows:

Small and Medium Enterprises (SME), particularly the Tiny Segment of the small Enterprises, have inadequate access to institutional finance due to lack of financial information and non-formal business practices. SMEs also lack access to private equity and venture capital and have a very limited access to secondary market instruments.

a. SMEs face fragmented markets in respect of their inputs as well as products and are vulnerable to Market fluctuations.

b. SMEs lack easy access to inter-state and international markets.

c. The access of SMEs to technology and product innovations is also limited. There is lack of awareness of global best practices.

d. SMEs face considerable delays in the settlement of dues/payment of Bills by the large buyers, leading to inordinate delay in receivables.

With the deregulation of the financial sector, the ability of the banks to cater to the credit requirements of the SME Sector depends on the underlying Transaction costs, efficient recovery processes and available security. There is an immediate need for the Banking Sector to focus on credit and Finance requirements of SMEs.

Outreach of Formal Credit: Opening of New Accounts

The Commercial Banks (including Regional Rural Banks) with over 67,000 branches will make concerted efforts to provide credit cover on an average to at least 5 new Tiny, Small and Medium Enterprises at each of their semi-urban/ urban branches per year.

Facilitative Measures by the Reserve Bank of India

Reserve Bank had issued a detailed master circular on March 1, 2005 on the time to be taken for disposing of loan applications of SSI Units, the limit up to which banks are obliged to grant collateral free composite loans, norms for computation of Working Capital Credit Limits to SSI Units, opening of at least one Specialized SSI branch in each district, etc. Taking these guidelines as indicative minimum, banks will formulate a comprehensive and more liberal policy relating to advances to the SME Sector. Until the banks formulate such a policy, the extant instructions of Reserve Bank will be applicable to advances granted or to be granted by banks to SME units.

Monitoring and Review by RBI

The following Supervisory arrangements would be ensured by the RBI:

a) The existing institutional arrangements for review of credit to SSI Sector like the Standing Advisory Committee in the Reserve Bank of India and cells at the banks' head office level as well as at important Regional Centres will be made more rigorous and regular. They will also review the flow of credit to Small (SSI), Sick and Medium Enterprises.

b) At the regional offices, the Reserve Bank will constitute empowered committees with the regional director of the Reserve Bank as the Chairman to review the progress in SME financing and rehabilitation of Sick Small

(SSI) and Medium Units and to coordinate with other banks/financial institutions and the State Governments in removing bottlenecks, if any, to ensure smooth flow of credit to the sector. The said regional level committees may decide on the need to have similar committees at cluster/district levels.

c) Banks will ensure specialized SME branches in identified clusters/centres with preponderance of small enterprises to enable the entrepreneurs to have easy access to bank credit and to equip bank personnel to develop the requisite expertise. The existing specialized SSI branches will be redesignated as SME branches.

d) Boards of banks will be advised to review the progress in achieving the self-set targets as also rehabilitation and restructuring of SME accounts on a quarterly basis to ensure that the required emphasis is given to this sector.

e) For wider dissemination and easy accessibility, the policy guidelines formulated by Boards of Banks as well as instructions/guidelines issued by Reserve Bank will be displayed on the respective websites of the Public sector banks as well as the website of SIDBI. The banks would also be advised to prominently display all the facilities/schemes offered by them to the small entrepreneurs at each of their branches.

Instruments of SME Sector Financing

Inspite of various initiatives taken by the Government of India, banks and financial institutions, SMEs face certain challenges, which are universal in nature. These problems relate to the issue of collaterals, cost of loans, delay in realisation of receivables, obsolete technology, marketing, etc. In order to address the above problems in the Indian context, some innovative instruments of financing have been introduced and institutional set up has been created. Some of the major initiatives include:

Credit Guarantee Fund Trust for Small Industries (CGTSI)

Government of India, in association with SIDBI, has set up a Credit Guarantee Fund Trust for Small Industries (CGTSI) to implement the guarantee scheme. At present, Member Lending Institutions (MLIs), like banks, are provided guarantee cover of 75% of the amount of default by CGTSI, in respect of Term loan and/or working capital facilities up to Rs.25 lakh extended by the MLIs to new and existing SSI Units/IT/Software Units/Small Scale Service Business Enterprises (SSSBEs), without collateral security and/or third party guarantee. A one-time guarantee fee of 2.5% and annual service fee of 0.75% of the Credit facility sanctioned are currently charged by CGTSI from the MLIs. In order to reduce the cost of guarantee to the weaker segments of the borrowers, particularly Tiny Units, the CGTSI will be advised to reduce the one time guarantee fee from 2.5% to 1.5% for all (i) loans up to Rs.2 lakh; (ii) eligible women entrepreneurs; and (iii) eligible borrowers located in the north-eastern region (including Sikkim) and Jammu and Kashmir. Further, public sector banks will be encouraged to absorb the annual service fee in excess of 0.25% in respect of guarantee for all; (i) loans up to Rs.2 lakh; (ii) eligible women entrepreneurs; and (iii) eligible borrowers located in the north-eastern region (including Sikkim) and Jammu and Kashmir.

Venture Capital Funding

With regard to new sources of financing, many countries are considering liberalising the rules regarding Venture Capital Investments. In India also, various measures have been taken in this direction, SIDBI, along with some other institutions, has taken a lead in promoting Venture Capital Funding in the country. SIDBI has recently launched a new SME growth fund of Rs.100 crore corpus. This Fund would focus on units in Pharma, Biotech, Light Engineering, Software and others. The corpus has of late been enhanced to Rs.500 Crore.

Micro Credit/Finance

Realising the potential of Micro Finance in stimulating economic growth and enthused by the well known experience originating in Bangladesh, India has been moving aggressively on Micro Finance, which can be of extreme use to Micro Scale Enterprises. In this initiative, Self-Help Groups (SHGs) have been supported through Non-Government Organisations (NGOs)/Local Micro Finance Intermediaries (MFIs) or Non-Banking Finance Companies (NBFCs). Moreover, programmes to rope in more banks were evolved by refinancing institutions such as SIDBI and NABARD.

Cluster-Based Approach

Cluster-based approach for financing SME sector offers possibilities of reduction of transaction costs and mitigation of risk. A cluster is defined as a geographically bound concentration of similar, related or complementary Businesses. An United Nations Industrial Development Organisation (UNIDO) study defines clusters as 100 registered small scale units. In India, clusters have been in existence for decades and they came up naturally. Some names that occur instantaneously are: Tirupur (Knitwear), Moradabad (Brassware), Panipat (Cotton Blankets), Narsapur (Crochet Lace), Sivakasi (Matches and Fireworks), Coimbatore (Foundries), Gems (Gujarat) and there are 388 such Clusters in India. These 388 clusters have already been identified. Cluster-based financing would now be treated as a thrust area. Banks will increasingly adopt the cluster-based approach for SME Financing. To broaden the financing options for infrastructure development in clusters through Public-Private Partnership, SIDBI will formulate a scheme in consultation with the stakeholders.

SIDBI has already initiated the process of establishing Small Enterprises Financial Centres in select Clusters. Risk profile of each cluster would be studied by a professional credit rating agency and such risk profile reports would be made available to commercial banks. Each lead bank of a district will consider adoption of at least one cluster.

Nursing the Sick Units Back to Health: Debt Restructuring

Reserve Bank will issue detailed guidelines relating to Debt Restructuring Mechanism so as to ensure restructuring of debt of all eligible Small and Medium Enterprises at terms which are not less favourable than the Corporate Debt Restructuring (CDR) mechanism in the banking sector. The restructuring would follow upon a request to that effect from the Borrowing Unit. All accounts, except those classified as 'Loss Assets', will be eligible for restructuring, provided the industrial units are viable or potentially viable.

Based on the Reserve Bank's guidelines, banks may formulate, with the approval of their board of directors, more liberal policies relating to the restructuring of accounts. Until the banks formulate their own policies, Reserve Bank's guidelines will be operative.

A one-time settlement scheme to apply to Small Scale NPA accounts in the books of the banks as on March 31, 2004 will be introduced by the RBI. The Scheme will be in force up to March 31, 2006. It is observed that as at the end of March 2004, 17.6 percent of the NPAs of Public Sector Banks (PSBs) and 12.2 percent of Private Sector Banks were accounted for by the Small Scale Industries. This measure is expected to clean up the books of banks, though the effect would be reflected on their bottom lines.

Credit Rating of SMEs

Public Sector Banks were advised to follow a transparent rating system with cost of credit being linked to the credit rating of the enterprise. The Hon'ble Union Finance Minister, Sri P Chidambaram has launched the SME Rating Agency of India (SMERA) – which is a joint initiative of SIDBI, Dun and Bradstreet, Credit Information Bureau (India) Ltd., and some Banks on 05.09.2005 at Coimbatore, a dedicated rating agency for small and medium Enterprises. It is hoped that SMERA would enhance credit flow to Small and Tiny Sectors. Already, eight banks, including those in the private sector, have figured in SMERA and that more banks are expected to join the rating agency to give depth to its operations.

The National Small Industries Corporation has recently introduced a credit rating scheme for encouraging SSI Units to get themselves credit rated by reputed credit rating agencies. Public Sector Banks are being advised to consider these ratings appropriately and as per availability, and structure their rates of interest suitably.

SIDBI has developed a Credit Appraisal and Rating Tool (CART) as well as a Risk Assessment Model (RAM) and a Comprehensive Rating Model for Risk Assessment of Credit proposals for SMEs. Public Sector Banks are being advised to take advantage of these models as appropriate and reduce their transaction costs.

SME Sector and Union Budget – 2005-06

SSI/SME Sector:

1. Capital Subsidy Allocation for SSI sector up to Rs.173 Crore;
2. Small and Medium Enterprise Development bill to be introduced in Parliament soon;

3. Identified 108 Items for de-reservation for SSIs;
4. To launch Manufacturing Competitiveness Plan for SMEs;
5. To extend insurance scheme for 20 lakhs handloom weavers;
6. SIDBI launches Rs.500 Crore SME Growth Fund;

For the Industry in general:

1. Information Technology to offer 70 lakh jobs by 2009;
2. Textile job potential seen-12 million people in 5 years;
3. Sectors generating jobs will get highest priority from Government;
4. To set up Rs.150 crore corpus for R & D in Pharma;
5. Stable Policy Environment for Biotech, Pharma Sectors;
6. To invest Rs.3000 crore in textiles in FY06 vs. Rs.2000 crore in the previous year;
7. 10% Capital Subsidy Scheme for textile sector proposed.

Tenth Five Year Plan

The Tenth Five Year Plan for the Indian Economy has set a target of 8 percent growth rate per annum in GDP. The Plan has also noted that achieving and sustaining such ambitious growth target would require adequate attention to Small and Medium Enterprises (SMEs) which have great potential to offer wage employment. In order to pursue the growth with potential agenda, heavy reliance is placed by the Government of India on the SME sector. The given agenda marks a leap forward in the policy initiatives from protection to promotion and supports vertical expansion of units in accelerating the pace of growth of the SME Sector.

Measures to Increase the Quantum of Credit to SMEs at the Right Price

Public Sector Banks were advised to fix their own Targets for funding SMEs in order to achieve a minimum 20% year-on-year growth in Credit to the SME Sector. The objective of the Government of India as per the policy package announced by the Hon'ble Union Finance Minister on 10th August 2005 to step up credit to SMEs is to double the flow of credit to the SME Sector from Rs.67,600 crore in 2004-05 to Rs.1,35,000 crore by 2009-10, i.e., within a period of five years. The possible way forward as implied in the Policy Package of the Government of India would be through a System of the use of Risk Assessment Models by Banks to evaluate SME Credit Proposals, thereby reducing the likelihood of Probable NPAs (PNPAs).

Enhancement of Credit Flow to SME Sector – National and International Scenario

Several initiatives have been taken at the National and International levels to foster the development of SMEs and improve their access to finance. Notwithstanding these initiatives, impediments to SME finance remain, in different degrees, in both developed and developing economies, which constitute the single most important factor that could circumscribe their growth trajectory. Accordingly, the attention of policy-makers may need to focus on the following three broad issues, viz., creating a conducive business environment, development of clusters and enhancing credit-flow to SMEs, as these are widely debated in the contemporary discussions.

Governments need to take initiatives to ensure that the overall policy environment encourages industrial activity in general, and SME activity, in particular, given the letter's significant contribution to general economic activity in many countries. This would entail efforts to maintain Macroeconomic stability in terms of low fiscal deficits and debts (such that private savings are not pre-empted), low and stable inflation, low real rates of interest and a sustainable current account. This apart, initiatives would need to be taken, wherever necessary, to remove outdated and anomalous restrictions on domestic production, bring about a reduction in tariff and tax rates to Internationaly competitive levels, create a competitive environment through appropriate Legislation, if necessary provide public infrastructure support, reduce inflexibilities in the labour market with due cognizance to the need for appropriate social safety nets and invoke necessary reforms in bankruptcy and exit procedures.

Streamlining of procedures to disburse loans to SMEs, creating a regulatory/ legal framework that ensures timely payment of dues to SMEs, providing technical training to staff of financial institutions and organising general awareness programmes on SME financing would also be necessary. These measures would not only encourage SME activity but also have a salutary impact on their efficiency and hence on their overall requirements of finance.

Newer forms of SME financing need to be fostered, viz., venture capital and leasing. Commercial banks and local government funding agencies would need to play a major role in venture capital financing while insurance funds and pension funds could be tapped as important sources of finance. Leasing, on the other hand, requires a less rigorous legal and regulatory framework *vis-à-vis* bank lending, since the leasing company retains the ownership of assets till the end of the lease. Even so, strengthening of leasing laws, encouraging banks and financial institutions to support leasing companies and appropriate training through technical assisstance would help foster the development of this alternative important source of finance for SMEs.

Further, there is an underlying need to provide SMEs with the kind of infrastructural support that they may not independently be able to develop. For this, the recent policy package of government of India for stepping up credit to SMEs has proposed converting the Technology Bureau of Small Enterprises (TBSE), floated in 1995 jointly by the Small Industries Development Bank of India (SIDBI) and the Asian and Pacific Centre for Transfer of Technology (APCTT) – an United Nations Regional Institution under the aegis of the Economic and Social Commission for Asia and the Pacific (ESCAP), (which is engaged in assisting its member countries for the development, adaptation and transfer of relevant technologies), into an independent technology bank that could also provide project evaluation, risk assessment and mitigation services to SMEs adopting new Technologies. Such a service would improve the Credit Accessibility of the SMEs as well. The proposed independent Technology Bank would facilitate building stronger linkage between R&D Institutions and the SME Sector for enhancing their Productivity and Competitiveness. This would build and enhance the Capabilities and Creditworthiness of these SMEs and remove some of their Constraints.

Indian SME Sector Financing – Some Winning Strategies for Commercial Banks to Enhance Credit Flow to SMEs

1. Commercial Banks can announce a Comprehensive Credit Policy at the beginning of the Financial Year with the approval of their respective Boards.
2. Banks have to prepare Strategic Action Plans for improving Credit to SMEs.
3. Banks can work out the Target for SME Sector Advances (including SSI) with improved thrust on Medium Enterprise, against their projected NBCs.
4. Commercial Banks have to review and monitor Targets allocated to their respective Zonal Offices against their performance at regular intervals.
5. Credit Proposals received at Branches and Zonal Offices of Commercial Banks shall be disposed-off on priority.
6. In order to retain the existing Accounts, especially Large Borrowal Accounts under SME Segment, Banks would have to interact with them periodically and ascertain their Credit requirements well in advance, either for increasing the existing capacity or for setting up new Units.
7. Apart from Industrial Clusters identified by Government of India in their respective areas of jurisdiction, Commercial Banks can identify some more Industrial Clusters in the States which have their presence. Further, the Banks can explore the possibility of going in for Joint Financing of Projects in SMEs, Services and Infrastructure Sectors in the identified Clusters alongwith the Small Industries Development Bank of India (SIDBI). Theaim of the Synergy would be to provide adequate and timely Credit to SME and Tiny Industries and in Micro-Credit Operations.
8. Commercial banks' specialised SME branches and small enterprise financial centres of SIDBI could co-finance the term loan component, while commercial banks could take up working capital needs and letters of credit requirements at an interest rate of 10 percent and for women entrepreneurs, it can be at a concession of 0.5 percent.
9. Commercial banks can explore the possibilities of converting their specialised SSI branches into specialised SME branches, after seeking RBI approval.

10. In respect of certain places where there is concentration of particular industries, banks can undertake credit campaigns and interact with that particular cross-section of entrepreneurs and try to take them into their fold.
11. It shall be the endeavour of banks to provide both term loan and working capital to the units which have good potential for growth.
12. In case of bunching of proposals, banks would have to depute officers to supplement the efforts of field level functionaries for speedy disposal/appraisal of the Proposals.
13. Commercial banks have to advise credit officers at the branch/zonal office level to be in touch with district industries centres, so that they have latest data with regard to the new industries that are coming up in their area, which in turn will help banks identify the good units which can be brought into their fold.
14. Cluster-based approach is the thrust area for financing SMEs. Zonal offices of the banks have to be advised to be in touch with the industrial clusters in their area of operation for taking up good SME credit proposals.
15. Banks can conduct workshops for branch managers/officers, who are dealing in credit, in order to have better implementation of the schemes under SME sector.
16. Banks can identify select branches, equipped with trained personnel in important towns across country to focus special attention on SME Sector for quick disposal of credit and to have broad based exposure to varied industrial activities.
17. Banks can conduct one-day review sessions for senior managers (credit) at zonal offices and technical officers, who are directly connected with SSI advances, advising them to chalk out programme for lending to SME sector.
18. Banks can conduct Specialised Entrepreneur Development Programmes (EDPs) in technical oriented subjects for lady entrepreneurs.
19. Specialised SSI branches and other potential branches in metro and urban centres are to be given special targets and followed-up periodically.

20. Banks can organize Entrepreneurial Development Programmes at district level involving external agencies for mobilisation of new proposals.

21. Commercial banks can explore the possibility of holding interactive sessions with industry associations/district industries centres/small industries service institute and other promotional bodies.

22. Banks can organise buyer-seller meets.

23. Banks as conveners of SLBCs of different states can actively participate in development of industrial clusters.

Other Related Points in SSI Sector

- Commercial Bank can implement Credit Guarantee Fund Trust Scheme for Small Industries (CGTSI) for lending to the SSI sector without collateral security.
- Banks can implement National Equity Fund Scheme of SIDBI in their respective Banks.
- Banks could implement issuing Laghu Udyami Credit Card for SSI Units up to a limit of Rs.10 lakhs more vigorously.
- Banks can actively conduct intensive EDP Programmes in coordination with State Level Industry Associations (FAPSIA) involving industry expertise, in all the lead districts of various states, for encouraging new Entrepreneurs.
- Commercial banks can explore the possibility of conducting EDP specifically for women including skill development programmes.

The above are only illustrative and not exhaustive, and depending upon the local conditions, a suitable strategic plan could be adopted for stepping up Credit to SMEs, which will enable commercial banks to fulfill their commitments.

In conclusion, a number of winning Strategies could be initiated by commercial banks to promote financing and healthy growth of the Indian SME sector. However, to ensure the prospects of these enterprises in the coming years, they will have to gear up to face the challenges of liberalisation. It can be confidently said that given the inherent strengths, the SME Sector will have to develop a global vision, respond to more demanding standards of the customers and adopt key and winning strategies that could take them ahead in competition. Credit should not be a constraint for viable SME projects.

(K Ramakrishnan, Chairman and Managing Director, Andhra Bank, Hyderabad.)

15

Emerging Tools for Mitigation of Risks in Agro Business

Prasun Kumar Das

This paper starts with the reasons for failure of traditional means of agro-financing in India and classifies them under various heads ranging from the risks involved, high transaction costs, to lack of collateral. The various risks identified are credit risk, market and price risk, operational risk, production and yield risk and weather risk. The other risks listed are dispersed clientele, seasonality of agricultural crops, distorted credit cultures and risks from change in policies. The paper then moves onto identifying Government initiatives for risk mitigation which include minimum support price, farm income insurance schemes, revamping agro marketing, development of commodities markets and weather insurance. The paper concludes with a discussion on emerging tools for risk mitigation like rainfall index insurance and lending against warehouse receipts.

1. Introduction

Indian agriculture has, since Independence, made rapid strides in taking the annual food grains production from 51 million tonnes in early fifties to

206 million tonnes at the turn of the century; it has contributed significantly in achieving self-sufficiency in food and in avoiding food shortages. Over 200 million Indian farmers and farm workers have been the backbone of India's agriculture. Despite having achieved national food security the well being of the farming community continues to be a matter of grave concern for planners and policy makers. Under this backdrop, the Government of India prepared National Agriculture Policy document in 2000.

The National Policy on Agriculture seeks to actualise the vast untapped growth potential of Indian agriculture, strengthen rural infrastructure to support faster agricultural development, promote value addition, accelerate the growth of agro-business, create employment in rural areas, secure a fair standard of living for the farmers and agricultural workers and their families, discourage migration to urban areas and face the challenges arising out of economic liberalization and globalisation.

Bank credit has played an important role in farm activities to fulfil the vision of the Government and the Planners for last five decades. The finance supplied by banks over the years has been essential to many individual farm operators as well as the agripreneurs for adoption of new technologies and pursue agribusiness. As with all forms of lending, however, agricultural credit presents the bankers in India with a unique set of risks. Each agro climatic region of the country has unique conditions that are reflected in the variety of crop produced and marketed.

2. Unique Features of Agricultural Lending in India

Until the early 1980s, agricultural planners were primarily concerned with the need to increase food crop production. The adoption of the new green revolution technologies was relatively costly and small farmers were perceived as being too poor to save and to self-finance the required investments in additional farm inputs. As a result, vast amounts of financial resources from central and state governments as well as commercial banks were poured into agricultural development and agricultural projects. These programmes served as conduits for the provision of subsidised credit to small farmers often for specific production purposes.

The provision of subsidised and easily accessible credit constituted a central theme of the agricultural development strategies in the 1970s and 1980s. It was argued that enhanced access to credit would accelerate technological change, stimulate national agricultural production through increased farm output and improve rural income distribution. However, this approach failed to produce the desired results. The reasons for the failure of these policies were manifold and some of them may be described as under:

1.	Agri-lending activities in a politically sensitive environment.	↘ Agriculture is a politically sensitive sector. ↘ State interventions often occur in rural financial markets.
2.	Risks associated with agricultural lending.	↘ Similar economic activities of borrowers generate covariant risks due to market and price fluctuations, yield uncertainties, changes in domestic and international policies. ↘ State interventions (e.g., waiver and restructuring of loan overdue). ↘ Low loan repayment discipline.
3.	High financial transaction costs both for the banks and borrowers.	↘ Long distances to serve a dispersed rural clientele. ↘ Poorly developed transportation and communication infrastructure. ↘ Little knowledge about heterogeneous farm households. ↘ Expensive management and supervision of rural bank branch networks. ↘ High additional costs for borrowers: opportunity costs (e.g., lost working time), transport costs, legal hassles and fees.
4.	Specific credit demand.	↘ The provision of long-term credit can lead to matching problems between assets (loans) and liabilities (funding sources). ↘ Reduced turnover of agricultural loan portfolio over the year. ↘ Seasonality in agricultural credit demand.
5.	Lack of required loan collateral.	↘ Small farmers have few physical assets (e.g., land). ↘ Farmers face difficulties in clearly demonstrating their legal ownership of inherited assets. ↘ Legal contract enforcement problems arise even when collateral is available.
6.	Farm households are integrated production and consumption units.	↘ Demand for loans depends on the self-financing potential, access to savings deposit facilities and risk management ability of borrowers. ↘ Due to the fungibility of money borrowed funds can be used in the farm household for consumption, education, life insurance, production and investment purposes.

3. Paradigm Shift in Indian Agriculture – A Step Forward

It is true that liberalization did not benefit agricultural sector directly. However, there is evidence to show regarding indirect benefits. Relative tilt in protection to industrial sector *vis-à-vis* agricultural sector before 1991 got corrected now. Looked from another angle, the 'disprotection' to agricultural sector came down gradually. During nineties, we saw considerable export of various commodities like rice, fruits and flowers to countries in Middle East, South-East and neighbouring countries. Inspite of highest export of agricultural commodities during nineties, no one noticed deficit anywhere. 'Ship to mouth' image of the country during 60s was changing to that of 'Food exporting country' in 90s – A major paradigm shift indeed. The other areas where the intervention of the Government of India has made the agriculture sector more buoyant in the recent years are amendment in APMC Act, identification of Agri Export Zones and food park, encouragement to Contract Farming and setting up of Food Processing Units etc. These are the few examples to the road map of Indian agriculture which has become more business-oriented rather than a way of life.

4. WTO and Indian Agriculture

The WTO provides threats as well as opportunities in the agriculture sector. While agriculture on the whole might not be affected under WTO, certain crops and crop groups might be adversely affected, white other crops may gain. The past behaviour of Indian consumers does not approve the apprehension that the removal of Quantity Restrictions (QRs) would flood the Indian market with cheap foreign produce. This may be partly due to a combination of comparatively high import duties and low purchasing power of the consumers. The real problem lies in how the Indian producers respond to the competition with the developed countries like United States, Canada, and European Union, which still continue to receive agricultural subsidy and making the India agro-products uncompetitive in the world market. Under this situation, the Commercial Banks can play a greater role to convert the subsistence level farming to value added agro business farming.

5. Risks Associated with Lending to Agro Business

Under the current context of agricultural lending, particularly at this juncture when the banks are set to touch a new record by doubling the flow of credit to this sector within a span of 3 years, identification of the elements of risks involved has taken the center stage. After adoption of Basel-ll, it is expected that he banks would be assessing the risks relative to its impact on capital and earnings on three parameters i.e., Credit Risks, Market Risks and Operational Risks. The Basel-ll is silent in this particular sector of Banking. Till today the risk associated with agriculture lending other than incidence of NPA has not attracted the commercial banks as also the regulatory authorities. This may be due to low share of credit portfolio under this sector and also due to non-identification of risk elements. But with the diversification of agriculture and higher exposure in this sector by the commercial banks, the risk hedging and mitigation tools are gaining importance. Apart from some unique set of risk elements, all the three major risk components are playing an important role to make lending to agro business more risky in comparison to other sectors. The credit risk in agriculture lending is the fall out of the market as well as operational risks being faced by the agripreneurs.

5.1 Credit Risk

Credit risk is the most significant risk associated with agricultural lending. A farmer's production and ability to service debt can be affected seriously by the natural factors not directly under the farmer's control. Moreover, agricultural markets are sensitive to highly variable supply and demand conditions in both domestic and world markets that may directly or indirectly affect both the borrower's repayment capacity and the value of the product. Credit or loan default risk – refers to borrowers who are unable or unwilling to repay the loan principal and to service the interest charged.

5.2 Market and Price Risk

One of the major problems faced by farmers is the fluctuation of prices. Often, when the crop is good, they get low prices and thus are not able to get full benefit of the good production during the year. This hampers the repayment of the loans. The study made by ICICI Bank shows that the intermediaries take 75 percent of the Maximum Retail Price (MRP).

5.3 Operational Risk

Risks and uncertainty are pervasive in agricultural operation and are perceived to be more serious than in most non-farm activities. Production losses are also impossible to predict. They can have serious consequences for income generation and for the loan repayment capacity of the borrowing farmer. The type and the severity of risks which farmers face vary with the type of farming system, the physical and economic conditions, the prevailing policies, etc.

5.3.1 Production & Yield Risk: Agricultural risk has been synonymous with production risk. Reducing variability in expected yields has been a major focus of farm managers. Over time, improvements in technology and production practices have helped decrease agronomic risks and increase yields. Yield uncertainty due to natural hazards refers to the unpredictable impact of weather, pests and diseases, and calamities on farm production.

5.3.2 Weather Risk: The vagaries of weather cause significant uncertainty to farmers' cash flows resulting in unavailability of organised credit and inability to invest in sustainable agricultural techniques. Some of the current responses to adverse weather conditions include changes in cropping patterns (shift to less remunerative more sturdy crops) and reduced input usage and low technology adoption.

5.4 Other Risks of Lending Related to Agro Business

5.4.1 Dispersed Clientele: The Dispersed location of rural clients make the provision of formal financial services costly. From the lender's perspective, the long distances between communities and the inadequate rural transportation and communication facilities in many developing countries like India increase the costs of loan appraisal, loan monitoring and enforcement of loan repayments.

5.4.2 Seasonality and Loan Term Structure: The seasonal nature of agricultural production and the relative long gestation periods before crops can be harvested and sold have direct implications for the financial transaction costs of the lender. Agricultural loans are normally larger and are required for longer periods. Matching assets and liabilities is more difficult than for non-farm activities. Agricultural credit is also often repaid in "lumpy" installments. These are one or two loan repayments rather than regular weekly or monthly installments common in microcredit. This irregular pattern implies more difficult monitoring of repayment capacity and willingness.

5.4.3 **Risk of Loan Collateral Limitations:** Problems associated with inadequate loan collateral pose specific problems to rural lenders. Land is the most widely accepted asset for Lisa as collateral, because it is fixed and not easily destroyed. It is also often priced by owners above its market value and it has a high scarcity value in densely populated areas. Smallholder farmers with land that has limited value, or those who have only usufruct rights, are less likely to have access to bank loans.

5.4.4 **Distorted Credit Cultures Risks:** The local "credit culture" is distorted among farmers and lenders. Borrowers lack the discipline to meet their loan repayment obligations, because loan repayment commitments were not enforced in the past. Lenders, on the other hand, lack the systems, experience and incentives to enforce loan repayment. There is also an urgent need to change the mind set of the bank employees and the poor public image of financial institutions in rural areas.

5.4.5 **Risks from Changes in Domestic and International Policies:** Policy changes and state interventions can have a damaging impact on both borrowers and the commercial banks exposed to agro business lending.

6. Government Initiative to Mitigate Risk in Agriculture

To deal with the above-mentioned common risks, Government of India has attempted to mitigate those risks by adopting various suitable measures as per the suitability.

6.1 Minimum Support Price

The Government of India announces commodity prices before the harvesting seasons of selected crops by way of Minimum Support Price mechanism and this is being reviewed every year.

6.2 National Agriculture Insurance Scheme

Despite technological and economic advancements, the condition of farmers continues to be unstable due to natural calamities and price fluctuations. National Agriculture Insurance Scheme (NAIS) covering all farmers and all crops throughout the country with built in provisions for insulating farmers from financial distress caused by natural disasters and making agriculture financially viable and are being made more farmer specific and effective. Efforts are also being made to provide a package insurance policy for the farmers, right from sowing of the crops to post-harvest operations, including market fluctuations in the prices of agricultural produce.

6.3 Farm Income Insurance

In order to mitigate both the yield and price risks, a Farm Income Insurance Scheme (FIIS) was launched on a pilot basis during the rabi season (2003-04) in 19 districts across 12 States for wheat and rice, which was subsequently extended to 100 districts during kharif 2004. The Agricultural Insurance Company of India Limited (AICL) is implementing the above scheme.

6.4 Revamping of Agro Marketing

In order to develop integrated agricultural markets nationwide, facilitate emergence of competitive agricultural markets in the private and the co-operative sectors and to create an environment conducive to massive investments in marketing-related infrastructure, a Draft Model Act, viz., the State Agricultural Produce Marketing (Development and Regulation) Act, 2003 was framed in September 2003. It provides for establishment of private markets/yards, direct purchase centres, consumer/farmers' markets for direct sale and promotion of Public-Private Partnership in the management and development of agricultural markets.

6.5 Development of Commodities Market

Development of commodities future market in India is a recent phenomenon which has got immense potentialities to hedge the farmers from price risk and distress sale.

6.6 Weather Insurance

The annual Budget speech presented on July 8, 2004 by the finance minister highlighted risk mitigation as a tool for rural development and welfare. The Government has identified weather insurance as one of three possible tools of risk mitigation, the others being crop insurance and farm income insurance. Weather insurance as perceived by the Finance Minister appears to be the most promising at least in its design. The Government proposes to introduce the weather insurance scheme on a trial basis through Agricultural Insurance Corporation (AIC) in 20 stations in the Kharif crop season of 2004.

7. Initiatives taken by the Commercial Banks

Commercial banks are looking for a variety of ways to expand their portfolio into agriculture but due to the perception of high risks associated with lending to farmers who lack traditional forms of collateral and face price falls and yield risk, these inroads have been limited. Many traditional arrangements that commercial banks and other financial institutions use to extend lending to the agriculture sector are not well suited to the host of risks the farmers are facing. It is an empirical question to determine to what extent price yield and weather related risks impede or constrain lending to agriculture, and it is expected that this determination is done on a case-by-case basis. Nevertheless, some empirical evidence indicates that these are important risks that the commercial banks are facing while lending to agriculture sector.

8. Risk of Incidence of NPA in Agriculture Lending

8.1 Dr. Rakesh Mohan, Dy Governor, Reserve Bank of India identified the issue of perception of greater risk in Agricultural lending shows a lower ratio of 12.8 percent of NPAs, compared to 20.6 percent for small-scale industries, but higher agricultural lending compared to non-priority sectors, than 9.4 percent for non-priority areas as per the available data as on 31.03.2004.The data do suggest that agricultural lending is riskier than non-priority lending and lending to other priority sectors. The difference is not large enough to warrant excessive caution in bank lending to agriculture. But at the same time it is important that policy-makers in the banks should look into the systemic causes for risk being greater in agricultural lending than non-priority lending, which are also subject to market risks and competition from abroad. The point is to mitigate these risks-at least those that are known through means such as crop insurance and the like. Further, the culture of repayment should be encouraged through early changes in the legal structure, which should enable banks to repossess assets owned by borrowers without going through complicated legal process and access to courts. It has also been argued that unless the process of recovery gets easier, ease of lending which may result from the current growth, can lead to a bottomless pit of Non-Performing Assets and a mass of indebted farmers.

8.2 In a study on increasing the credit flow to agriculture by the commercial banks (P K Das, 2005), it revealed that there are different perceptions of risk in agriculture lending in different banks and their approach for mitigation of these risks are also different. The following are the major observation of the study:

- Out of the 16 Public Sector Bank and 2 RRBs, all 34 branch managers are of the view that incidence of NPA in agriculture is more and therefore, it is a risky proposition but they have no other alternative but to increase the farm lending.
- The top officials at the policy level in all the commercial banks are of the view that the incidence of NPA in small agriculture accounts are one of the major impediments to increase the flow of credit to agriculture and identification and mitigation are the major challenges being faced by them which requires to be addressed immediately.
- The common risk hedging and mitigation techniques being followed by the Public Sector Banks and the RRBs are: (a) extending short-term credit (repayable within one crop season); (b) dispersal of risk by allowing advances to large number of borrowers in a geographically spread area; and (c) crop insurance in case of KCC holders.

8.3 The problem of bad debts in farm lending stems primarily from crop destruction on natural calamities such as floods and drought. Very few farmers would willfully default, as they need to keep coming back to the same banks for loans in future crop seasons. Several bankers have clearly stated that it is much easier to 'work out' agricultural NPLs than industrial or retail NPLs, because willful default is low. Bank branches in rural areas are socially important entities for farmers.

8.4 Rescheduling of agriculture loans to avoid incidence of NPLs is also an important tools in practice by the commercial banks. As a solution to the impairment of the repaying capacity of the cultivators affected by crop failures due to natural calamities like recurring droughts and/or floods and the resultant dislocation of the credit system as such, the All India Rural Credit Survey Committee (1954) had recommended stabilization arrangements envisaging conversion/rescheduling of agricultural dues of the affected borrowers to the credit agencies.

9. Existing Tools of Risk Mitigation in Farm Lending

9.1 Crop Insurance

Crop production in India has been subjected to the vagaries of the climate. Some of the other problems that the Indian agriculture is constantly tackling with are the large scale damages that are caused as a result of the attack of pests and diseases. It is in a scenario such as this in India that the issue of crop insurance assumes a vital role in the stable growth of the agricultural sector. In order to provide a boost to the agriculture in India, a number of experimental crop insurance schemes have been introduced in the country.

- The Government of India introduced the Comprehensive Crop Insurance Scheme with effect from 1st April, 1985 to cover the short-term crop loans that extended to the farmers and was implemented using the Homogeneous Area approach. The coverage under this scheme was restricted to 100% of crop loan subject to a maximum of Rs.10,000 per farmer. The premium rates for the cereals were low at 2 percent and for pulses it is 5 percent. The premium and risk claims were shared in a ratio of 2:1 by the Central and State Government. The Scheme was optional to State Governments.

9.2 Farm Income Insurance (FII)

The Farm Income Insurance Scheme was launched by Government of India to provide "Comprehensive Risk Insurance" against Loss in Farm Income (Short fall in Actual Income (AI) over Guaranteed Income (GI)) in a Notified Area arising out of adverse fluctuations in yield due to occurrence of any one or combination of non-preventable natural perils such as flood, inundation, storm, cyclone, hailstorm, landslide, drought, dry spells, large-scale outbreak of pests/diseases; and adverse fluctuation of market prices, as measured against MSP:

- To provide financial support to farmers, in the event of loss in income from adverse incidence of Crop Yield (on account of natural calamities, pests and diseases) and market price fluctuations.
- To encourage the farmers to adopt prudent and progressive farming practices, both in terms of agricultural technology, and market economics.
- To enhance food and livelihood security of the farming community.
- To help stabilize farm incomes, particularly in disaster years.

10. Emerging Tools for Risk Mitigation

10.1 Rainfall Index Insurance – A New tool to Risk Mitigation in Agriculture

Water is one of the essential and most critical inputs for all plant life and, therefore, for agriculture. The Indian subcontinent is dependent on monsoons. By their very character, monsoons are irregular, both in their timing and the quantum of rainfall. That makes Indian agriculture a gamble on monsoons. In some years the rainfall is timely and adequate and in other years, the monsoons may be tardy and short and in some other years, they may be long and overabundant. Accordingly, there are good years and bad years for agriculture culminating into depressed markets and prices for the agro-products. The 'weather insurance' is a comprehensive product to protect the farmers from the problems arising due to the vagaries of weather. Adopting the weather insurance instrument now made available in our country and for giving smallholders greater access to finance could mitigate the yield risk. The weather risk management instruments designed by ICICI Lombard, A general Insurance Company are now being used by the Private sector Banks like ICICI Bank etc. as an alternative to traditional crop insurance scheme and as per the information made available to us has changed the matrix of risk mitigation in agriculture lending. The weather insurance products of Agriculture Insurance Company (AIC) have also become a popular product for small farmers.

10.2 Development of Commodities Market – A Risk Mitigation Tool for Future

The development of commodities future market in India has emerged as another risk mitigation tool for the farming community. The market risk and the price risk could be mitigated by participating in the commodities market by the farmers as individual or may be as a group activity. The market-based price risk management tools such as futures and options to manage the risk in agriculture has also attracted some of the Public Sector Banks like Canara Bank, Bank of Baroda and Union Bank of India, who have opted their stakes in NCDEX, the leading commodity exchange in India. The commercial banks could now foray into this area of financing by extending loans to individual farmers or they could act as an aggregator and the commodity desk to be established by them at their head office in line with Treasury desk. The Banking Regulation Act, which at present does not allow the banks in India to operate as an aggregator may be amended as per the requirement.

10.3 Lending against Warehouse Receipts to Mitigate the Price Risk

The commercial banks are reluctant to extend loan to the farmers against the warehouse receipt as they experienced serious problems during 1980s due to loss of the commodities stored in these warehouses due to non-compliance of risk management practices in the ware houses both under Public and Private sector. Effective and safe warehouse management was not always a reality. The commercial banks may allow the transfer of production credit to post harvest credit provided the commodities deposited with the ware house are free from price risk and storage risk. National Collateral Management Services Ltd. (NCMSL), a Mumbai-based company floated by the National Commodities and Derivatives Exchange of India (NCDEX) and the Geneva-based collateral management company, ACE (Audit Control and Expertise) Ltd., and seven other banks both in public and private sector expected to pave the way for significant strides in the banking industry, particularly given the increasing emphasis on price and storage risk management of the commodities.

11. Conclusion

The Commercial Banks in order to increase the flow of credit to farm sector are in search of comprehensive techniques to mitigate the risk of lending as well as maintaining a high standard of the quality of assets. In view of this the following risk management/hedging/mitigation techniques may be recommended for adoption by them. It may be noted that proper combination of these techniques may improve the confidence level of the field functionaries for increasing the flow of credit to this sector:

- Risk Preventive Techniques;
- Shifting of Agriculture product mix– More reliance on cash crop and livestock;
- Adequate Credit to cover the consumption need of the farming community;
- Well-distributed and timely delivery of credit;
- Risk mitigation/hedging techniques;
- Contract farming for sharing of risk;
- Crop Insurance for comprehensive coverage;
- Farm Income Insurance (FII);
- Insurance against rainfall index/weather insurance;
- Hedging market risks by taking forward trading positions to the extent of the perceived risks, and by taking advantage of the commodity exchanges in operation now, could cover price risk exposure also;
- Allow advances against well managed warehouse receipts;
- Creation of Agriculture risk funds at Bank level/Central level; and
- Specially designed life insurance products for the farmers.

(Prasun Kumar Das, Senior Manager, Allahabad Bank.)

References

1. Mohan, R. (2004), "Agricultural Credit in India: Status, Issues and Future Agenda", Inaugural Address at the Annual Conference of Indian Society of Agricultural Marketing, Hyderabad.
2. Das, P. K. (2005), "Increasing the flow of credit to agriculture by the commercial banks – the task ahead", Project report submitted to IBA under C H Bhaba Research Fellowship, 2005, Mumbai.

16

SPEECH

Inclusive Growth: Role of Financial Education*

Shyamala Gopinath

Empirical evidence suggests that access to formal financial services leads to economic development. For this, it is necessary to have financial education, which includes knowledge regarding markets, players and instruments. Financial education makes a microfinance entity plan better and optimize on the use of financial resources. Financial education is particularly relevant for people who are resource poor and who operate at the margin and are vulnerable to persistent downward financial pressures. The paper suggests various themes for conducting educational programmes for the poor.

I thank the Indian Banks Association and host Andhra Bank for inviting me for this Conference.

I am aware you have had illustrious speakers and expert sessions on various issues reverberating in policy conundrums of 'financial inclusion' and financially inclusive growth. Why I term these as conundrums is for the reason that on the

* Special Address by Ms. Shyamala Gopinath at BANCON – 2006, Hyderabad on November 4, 2006.

one hand, everyone accepts that a broad based access to formal financial services is a *sine qua non* for the aspiration of growth in GDP and economic development at large to be fulfilled, while on the other, the initiatives emerging in this direction have at best been confined to small pockets. The problem is not specific to India and many countries have been groping for the inflexion point in finding solutions to this problem. At the macro level, it is perhaps only in the recent past that this area is witnessing the academic rigour of the scale seen in the mainstream finance. It could be due to inherent nature of the issues we are grappling with. Most of the initiatives have been 'within the framework' solutions, which have inherent limitations. This point comes out all the more starkly in the context of the explosion in financial innovations and products witnessed in mainstream finance.

To elaborate this point, it would be interesting to look at the evolution of the discipline of finance in general and banking in particular. Till a few decades back, the field of finance itself was, in a sense, second cousin to the domain of 'economics' and it was only the revolutionary ideas and theories relating to asset pricing, particularly traded stocks to begin with, that changed the landscape. The subsequent academic contributions in the area of option pricin triggered the revolution in derivatives which has, in effect, commoditised the financing needs as well as options available to a certain segment of the corporate and retail sector. The above advances in the field of finance have evolved in response to a given set of circumstances in the industrial economies and the applications designed around these were aimed at a particular target group. Most of the principles have gradually found wide acceptance and have been imbibed across the globe, including India. We now need a similar revolution in fostering financially inclusive growth. However, the needs of a complex country like India are very different and finding universal solutions to these could be really challenging, particularly in fostering a 'financially inclusive growth'.

Financially inclusive growth straddles a lot of issues which have been deliberated upon at length during the previous sessions. I intend to confine my address to one of the important facets of this challenge – the challenge of financial education.

Financial Education – The Concept

Financial education can be comprehensively defined as "the process by which financial consumers/investors improve their understanding of financial products, concepts and risks and, through information, instruction and/or objective advice, develop the skills and confidence to become more aware of financial risks and opportunities, to make informed choices, to know where to go for help, and to take other effective actions to improve their financial well-being". Financial education thus, goes beyond the provision of financial information and advice. The focus of any discussion on financial education is primarily on the individual, who usually has limited resources and skills to appreciate the complexities of financial dealings with financial intermediaries on matters relating to personal finance on a day-to-day basis.

Role of Financial Education *vis-à-vis* Financial Inclusion

In the context of 'financial inclusion', the scope of financial education is relatively broader and it acquires greater significance since it could be an important factor in the very access of such excluded groups to finance. Further, the process of educating may invariably involve addressing deep entrenched behavioural and psychological factors that could be major barriers. However, the complementary relationship between microfinance and financial education is obvious and financial literacy can increase the decision-making power and prepare them to cope with the financial demands of daily life.

In countries with diverse social and economic profile like India, financial education is particularly relevant for people who are resource poor and who operate at the margin and are vulnerable to persistent downward financial pressures. With no established banking relationship, the un-banked poor are pushed towards expensive alternatives. The challenges of household cash management under difficult circumstances with few resources to fall back on could be accentuated by the lack of skills or knowledge to make well informed financial decisions. Financial education can help them prepare ahead of time for life cycle needs and deal with unexpected emergencies without assuming unnecessary debt.

As per an OECD study[1], the provision of education programmes for the un/underbanked groups can play important roles:

- They can encourage un/underbanked consumers to enter into or make better use of the financial mainstream;
- They can help to retain them as successful account holders in the short term;
- They can contribute to keeping them as savers for the long-term; and
- They can contribute to asset building among households.

Challenges in Devising a Financial Education Program

Devising financial education initiatives for the un/underbanked has to take into account the existing financial landscape, the social economic realities of this class and the fact that invariably, such groups are beset with low literacy levels.

The main difference in the financial planning for the poor families is that they have fewer resources and opportunities. When people are struggling to make ends meet on a day-to-day basis, good money management becomes a daily challenge. While they use many creative ingenuous strategies to manage their money, these often develop through trial and error rather than by design. Financial education has a role in "building the capacity of the poor to gain control, become proactive, use information and resources to enhance their economic security and more effectively use financial services". When better-informed clients become better consumers of financial services, financial institutions benefit.

Further, as already mentioned, the process of educating may invariably involve addressing deep entrenched behavioural and psychological factors that could be major barriers. For example, in case of many of the microfinance initiatives operating on the 'group liability' concept, it could be a great challenge to drive home the very basic rationale for such an arrangement, starting from inculcating the habit of small savings to appreciation of the concept of 'collective responsibility'.

---

1 "Improving Financial Literacy: Analysis of Issues and Policies", OECD, 2005.

A study[2] regarding Mexican experience has highlighted that the social and cultural factors embedded in the financial landscape greatly influence the ability of individuals to use financial services effectively. Results indicate that in addition to material resources, the inherent nature of social relations and community links played a crucial role in improving access to and use of financial services. The transformation of financial information, knowledge, experience, attitudes and social relationships into financial education and sophistication constituted a cognitive resource to reducing vulnerability. This leads us to suggest that a culture of finance is an important catalyst for individuals' change and development.

It is also important to note that financial education may contribute to behavior modification, but many factors lend to influence a person's financial behavior. Contrary to common belief, motivation is cultivated internally and rarely can be cultivated – sustainably, at least – by an external factor. The biggest obstacle to financial education is motivating individuals to pursue it. In other words, financial education does not necessarily motivate individuals; motivation brings individuals to financial education. Here the role of banks assumes importance as financial counselors of the clients.

Possible Themes

Inspite of the above challenges, it should be possible to arrive at a set of basic themes/issues that could be addressed effectively through a financial education program. As per a study conducted by the under the project "Financial Education for the Poor" by Microfinance Opportunities[3], a microenterprise resource center, a consistent demand was found for the following broad themes of financial education:

- *Money Management:* How to proactively manage money;
- *Debt Management:* How to control debt and avoid over-indebtedness;
- *Managing Savings:* How to save regularly and in a safe location.

---

2 *Financial Services as a means to Reduce Vulnerability*, Max Nino-Zarazua, University of Bath.

3 *Financial Education: A Win-Win for Clients and MFIs*, Cohen, M, Stack, K & McGuinness, E *http://www.microfinanceopportunities.org/docs/Financial_Education_A_Win_Win_for_Clients_and_MFIs.pdf*

- *Financial Negotiations:* How to strengthen clients' bargaining position *vis-à-vis* input suppliers, other household members, and financial institutions; and
- *Use of Bank Services:* How banks work and impose charges; How clients can maximize bank services, interact with banks, and effectively use ATMs.

An analysis of such programs in the OECD countries reveals that many educational programmes are integrated into the provision of specific financial services, such as first or basic bank accounts, checking and savings accounts and matched-savings plans while others adopt a broad stand-alone approach, teaching budgeting, savings and credit management, etc., with no connection to any product of service. Aims tend to vary according to the majority target population.

- For the generic unbanked, aims are to explain the benefits and use of bank account ownership and services or to build up fundamental financial literacy skills.
- For low/moderate-income underserved consumers, most programmes offer advice on general money and credit management; whereas others have a specific goal or are embedded in schemes to encourage savings, asset-building and homeownership.

These initiatives aim to build economic empowerment and increase long-term self-sufficiency in order to revitalize and stabilize disadvantaged communities.

Indian Context

Financial education has an ever more critical role to play in the changed financial landscape of the country which, while on one hand has presented with newer opportunities for future collective growth, on the other, it has also heightened fears of uncertainty in certain quarters mainly because of increasing multi-faceted choices and options in the management of personal finances and exposure to a gamut of risks. The issue of inclusive growth has been given top priority and in this direction, the banking sector is expected to play its part. The initiatives on financial inclusion so far, have been a small step in this direction. Financial education could ideally supplement these initiatives for long term efficacy.

...Some Issues

One of the major hindrances in the way of delivery of financial services is the lack of basic knowledge and lack of awareness of the products and services available from the banks. It is important to note that the Financial Inclusion Task Force of the United Kingdom, one of the pioneers to talk of financial inclusion, has identified 'access to free face-to-face money advice' as an important component of financial inclusion, apart from 'access to banking' and 'access to affordable credit'. People need information and advice when they either save their money or get into debt. Such information and guidance can best be delivered by appropriate mechanisms and if such effective mechanisms are put in place through the banks, they in turn would reinforce the demand for financial services.

Another impediment is the difficulty or the lack of ease of addressing issues that affect a common man. Despite concerted efforts, the current state of transparency coupled with the difficulty of consumers in identifying and understanding fine print information leads to an information asymmetry between the financial intermediary and the customer. It is important to understand that the lack of such awareness in itself amounts to risk and the challenge is to make customers aware of the various risk. In terms of promoting financial inclusion, much of the work is simply in providing easily understood information in a safe and engaging environment.

...Scope for Financial Education

Undoubtedly, there is a role for promoting financial education in the context of development policies and programs to reduce vulnerability and expand opportunities for the poor. To this end, there is a need to explore the potential for integrating financial literacy into various types of development programs: microfinance, vocational education, skills training, business development, health, nutrition, agriculture, and food security programs. In the late 1990s a move in the UK and US to have all Government payments made electronically contributed to heightening the importance of financial exclusion as a policy concern. Electronic government payments have made having a bank account essential in order to receive payments and benefits. This has made it all the more important for unbanked consumers to access information on basic bank accounts savings accounts and other financial services. Financial education programs would be required to access information on financial services.

In India too, improved technology will enable, for example, Governments to make all payments, including under various schemes electronically. I understand that in Andhra Pradesh, the State Government has taken initiative to make payments thorough e-seva. Other states have also launched such initiatives. Governments should now explore the possibility of direct credit to bank accounts. Eventually, part of the funds received by the beneficiary under various government schemes and deposited with the banks can form part of the seed capital for forming Self Help Groups (SHGs) for such beneficiaries.

While some banks have on their own taken steps to provide such education, any large scale delivery of financial education needs to leverage on the experience and expertise of other agencies, such as private entities, non-governmental organizations, civil society organizations, outlets of the corporate sector etc., apart from Government initiatives, wherever available.

The use of information technology offers a lot of promise in providing financial literacy and education and experience in several parts of the country through the use of rural information kiosks, mobile vans, etc., which have shown to what extent IT can be leveraged to provide information on various products and services. Information kiosks can be run by the Business Correspondents or installed in PCOs, etc., to disseminate information about not only banking products, but also other useful information like input/output prices, insurance products, health services, weather information, etc. Such variety of knowledge would help in better risk mitigation, lesser documentation hassles while sanctioning loans, etc. The kiosks need not even have any connectivity and the service personnel can perform most of the updating through electronic media like CDs. Banks can provide funds for setting-up such kiosks and meeting the running costs or the cost can be shared among banks, and the other organizations involved in the process.

Some non-banking initiatives are also being experimented in various parts of the country. In this context, the project on financial counseling service for poor self-employed women in India started by SEWA is well known. "Project Tomorrow", as it is called, was started in 2001 with a purpose to develop and test a financial counseling curriculum to help participants manage money productively, plan ways to increase assets, address life cycle events, manage risks.

Through this project, SEWA has set up a training unit and training delivery system and is developing tools and procedures to monitor the counseling work. The project began with market research to assess the needs and demand among SEWA clients for financial education, followed by a 'training of trainers' course. SEWA is now providing financial counseling to its clients through a weekly course. The initial experience suggests that participants grasp the concepts presented and welcome new perspectives stemming from such training.

...Extending the Scope

- While talking about financial education, it is important that the focus also extends to the urban populace, including the literate masses, which may not be having the financial acumen, technology suaveness and may not be 'financially literate'. It is not that the urban masses are well versed in the Internet Banking and other newer methods of banking; there continues to remain a segment, which either avoids using the services due to lack of confidence or remains unaware of the options available. Financial education to such target group would be mutually beneficial.
- There is also need for greater awareness of various products and services offered by banks. A specific case that comes to mind pertains to the housing finance sector. RBI had also raised the issue of transparency and fairness in housing loans in the recent mid-term review of monetary policy. It has been reported that some banks, while lending for housing, are not fully transparent in indicating the factors governing the benchmark in respect of floating rates as well as in regard to reset clauses. As part of consumer awareness, many initiatives have been taken to increase the disclosure levels on part of lenders, but effectiveness of all this would be predicated on the financial understanding of the person taking the loan. The short point is – Does the consumer understand the underlying principle of a floating rate or can he even ensure that the bank has been fair and transparent in its dealing with him? Clearly, there is need for financial education to prevent vulnerable consumers from falling prey to "financially disquieting credit arrangements".

  Even with regard to remittance facilities and foreign exchange encashment, the lack of awareness about the various facilities could adversely impact a population segment at the 'bottom of the pyramid' which is the beneficiary of smaller remittances from migrant workers. Recently, a

Working Group on Cost of NRI Remittances has stressed in its report the need for an ongoing 'awareness program' for imparting basic awareness on facilities existing for making remittances, particularly for migrant workers. Apart from other things, this could also help in reducing the cost of effecting remittances.

- Though the term 'financial education' has come to be associated with individual/personal finance, a very important segment that must be brought under the ambit of such initiatives relates to small entrepreneurs and small businesses. Particularly when the effort is towards 'inclusive growth', it is these segments in smaller cities and towns that could really showcase the benefits of economic growth. The focus in such cases, would obviously be different, with greater stress on awareness and timeliness of financial advice, instead of just education. Such timely advice could be the deciding factor in the success or failure of their ventures. In all probability, the promoters of these small ventures would be educated and already have a business sense and a business idea that needs to be actualized. It is here that awareness about new financial products and an understanding of their pricing could enable them to ensure that they understand the downsides of the product, present and future, and be in a better bargaining position vis-à-vis the lender.
- Finally, the concept of financial education could ideally be stretched to cover economic education as well. At a broader societal level, given the path of economic reforms India has embraced since the early nineties, and the ensuing debates, it is imperative that the society and general populace be objectively informed about the fundamental economic issues and the rationale for, at-times difficult, choices to be made in this regard. This could go a long way in creating an informed and harmonious democracy.

Conclusion

There is a need for banks and other agencies striving to extend financial education to the masses to appreciate that financial inclusion is a continuous process. Efforts to extend literacy to make the common man enabled by being aware of the evolving functional, legal and technical issues cannot be a one-time effort.

A common effort of the educational programmes typically focusses on the 'supply' side that stresses on attracting customers in the financial fold. However, what is needed is to have is an "auto pilot" concept, where the prospective customer is empowered to make/demand the desired services. This could create a qualitative 'demand' situation of the financial services.

The objective of financial education is also customer protection. It helps customers to better understand and manage financial risk and deal with complexities of the market place place and take advantage of increased competition and choice in the financial sector. The RBI, on its part, intends to advance the cause of financial education in the country as part of an overall strategy. Currently, a process of credit counseling is being encouraged to help all borrowers, particularly those in distress, to overcome current financial problems and gain access to the structured financial system.

However, in the ultimate analysis financial education is only one pillar of an adequate financial policy to improve financial literacy and expand access to financial services. It can complement, but not replace other pillars such as greater transparency, policies on consumer protection and regulation of financial institutions. I do hope that in our collective interest the issues raised in this Conference are operationalised and translated into grass root level initiatives.

INDEX

N

O

P

Q

R

S

T